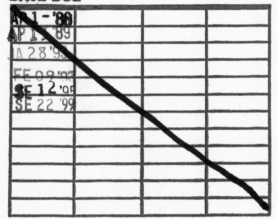

# PUBLIC POLICY-MAKING

## THIRD EDITION

## James E. Anderson

UNIVERSITY OF HOUSTON

HOLT, RINEHART AND WINSTON

New York   Chicago   San Francisco   Philadelphia
Montreal   Toronto   London   Sydney
Tokyo   Mexico City   Rio de Janeiro   Madrid

**Library of Congress Cataloging in Publication Data**

Anderson, James E.
  Public policy-making.

  Bibliography: p.
  Includes index.
  1. United States—Politics and government—
1945–      2. Policy sciences.   I. Title.
JK271.A65   1984            320.2            83-12666

ISBN 0-03-062394-4

CBS COLLEGE PUBLISHING
Holt, Rinehart and Winston
The Dryden Press
Saunders College Publishing

# Preface

In recent years the study of public policy has gained substantial currency and popularity among political scientists. Many now indicate an interest or involvement in such areas as policy studies, policy analysis, and comparative public policy. Schools and programs in public policy have been established. A Policy Studies Organization is thriving and new journals, such as *Policy Science, Policy Studies Journal, Policy Studies Review,* and the *Journal of Policy Analysis and Management,* are available to those interested in policy study.

In spite of all this interest in public policy, there is still no agreement on what policy is, how it should be studied, or even whether it is a legitimate concern for political scientists. Some still cling to the notion that process rather than policy is the proper province of political scientists. Most students—and it is for them that this book is intended—are not overly concerned with such controversies. I see no good reason why political scientists can not be concerned with both process and policy.

A policy approach to the study of politics is concerned with both. One starts with a policy problem, for example, inflation, equal employment opportunity, or relations with the Soviet Union, and is then concerned with determining what was done, how it was done, and to what effect. The roles of institutions, processes, and political elements (for example, public opinion) are all considered, as they help shape and determine what government does or does not do concerning some problem.

The focus of *Public Policy-Making* is on the processes of policy formation, implementation, and evaluation. It sets forth an approach to the analysis of the policy process which I have found useful in organizing my thinking and inquiry and in seeking to untangle its complexities. No final answers are provided, no ultimate truths are proclaimed, no techniques for making "good" policy decisions are set forth. Nor is much said about the substance of public policies, although some aspects of them are considered in Chapter 5. The third edition has been generally updated to take account of recent developments in policy analysis and political practice. New material has been added on agenda formation, the Economic Recovery Tax Act, the budgeting process, cost-benefit analysis, and policy evaluation. If, after reading this book, the student has a better understanding of the complexities of public policy formation and can attempt analysis of future public policy, then the book has served its purpose.

I would like to acknowledge the assistance of Bruce Oppenheimer, University of Houston; Richard Hardy, University of Missouri; Lawrence Gerston, San Jose State University; and Marie Schappert, Holt, Rinehart and Winston, in the preparation of this edition.

J.E.A.

# Contents

# 1

# The Study of Public Policy

The social security program is a well-known, very popular public policy. Many millions of older Americans currently depend upon it for all or part of their incomes. Many millions more expect to draw pensions from the program within this decade. The program, however, is in "trouble." In early 1983 it was estimated that, as the social security program then stood, benefits would exceed program income by $150 to $200 billion through the rest of the decade. How should this policy problem be resolved? By increasing social security taxes? By financing the program partly from general revenues? By raising the retirement age? By restricting future benefit increases? These are only some of the alternatives that policy-makers confronted. How the problem is resolved will directly affect a large portion of the population.*

The urban American who sits and frets in a motor vehicle on a congested freeway during rush hour is currently feeling the effects of various government policies, which have emphasized highway construction, helped in the past to keep gasoline prices low, neglected the maintenance and development of mass transit systems, and generally encouraged urban sprawl. The question of whether other, different public policies would have produced a more satisfactory transportation system than the nation now has can be debated. The point is, however, that the current traffic congestion which

---

*In April, 1983, legislation was approved to deal with this problem. The statute increased social security taxes, delayed a scheduled benefit increase, extended coverage to include new federal employees, imposed a tax on some of the benefits of well-to-do retirees, and provided for eventually (by the year 2027) raising the retirement age to 67.

plagues many parts of urban America is not a "natural" outcome: It did not develop simply because events followed their natural course. Rather, public policies, intentionally and unintentionally, have done much to bring about our current urban condition.

These examples should help indicate that in our daily lives we are much affected by myriad public policies. In our references to public policy the term may be used quite broadly, as in "American foreign policy," "Soviet military policy," or the "Common Market's trade policy." Or we may use a more specific reference, as when we speak of the national government's policy on sugar prices, the policy of the state of Texas on bilingual education, or the rent-control policy of New York City. Although public policy may sometimes seem rather abstract, and we often think of it as something that "happens" to someone else, this is clearly not the case.

In general usage, the term "policy" often designates the behavior of some actor or set of actors (e.g., an official, a group, a government agency) in a given area of activity, such as public transportation or school desegregation. Or, public policy may be viewed as what governments choose to do or not to do. Such usages may be adequate for ordinary discourse. However, because the concern of this book is with the formation and systematic analysis of public policy, we need a more precise definition or concept of public policy in order to structure our thinking and permit more effective communication with one another.

## WHAT IS PUBLIC POLICY?

The literature of political science is full of definitions of public policy. Sooner or later, it seems, almost everyone gives in to the urge to define public policy and does so with greater or lesser success in the eyes of critics. A few such definitions will be noted and their utility for analysis remarked upon. To be really useful and to facilitate communication, an operational definition (or concept, as I am using the two words somewhat interchangeably) should indicate the essential characteristics of the concept under discussion.

One definition of public policy holds that, "broadly defined," it is "the relationship of a government unit to its environment."[1] Such a definition is so broad as to leave most students uncertain of its meaning; it could encompass almost anything. As stated earlier, another definition states that "public policy is whatever governments choose to do or not to do."[2] There is a rough accuracy to this definition, but it does not adequately recognize that there may be a divergence between what governments decide to do and what they actually do. Moreover, it could be taken to include such actions as personnel appointments or grants of licenses, which are usually not thought of as policy matters. Richard Rose has suggested that policy be considered "a long series of more-or-less related activities" and their consequences for those concerned rather than as a discrete decision.[3] Though somewhat ambiguous, Rose's definition nonetheless embodies the useful notion that policy is a course or pattern of activity and not simply a decision to do something. Finally, let us note Carl Friedrich's definition. He regards policy as:

> ... a proposed course of action of a person, group, or government within a given environment providing obstacles and opportunities which the policy was pro-

posed to utilize and overcome in an effort to reach a goal or realize an objective or a purpose.[4]

To the notion of policy as a course of action, Friedrich adds the requirement that policy is directed toward the accomplishment of some purpose or goal. Although the purpose or goal of government actions may not always be easy to discern, the idea that policy involves purposive behavior seems a necessary part of a policy definition. Policy, however, should designate what is actually done rather than what is proposed in the way of action on some matter.

Taking into account the problems raised by these definitions, we offer the following as a useful concept of policy: A *purposive course of action followed by an actor or set of actors in dealing with a problem or matter of concern.* This concept of policy focuses attention on what is actually done as against what is proposed or intended, and it differentiates a policy from a decision, which is a choice among competing alternatives.

*Public policies* are those policies developed by governmental bodies and officials. (Nongovernmental actors and factors may, of course, influence policy development.) The special characteristics of public policies stem from the fact that they are formulated by what David Easton has called the "authorities" in a political system, namely, "elders, paramount chiefs, executives, legislators, judges, administrators, councilors, monarchs, and the like." These are, he says, the persons who "engage in the daily affairs of a political system," are "recognized by most members of the system as having responsibility for these matters," and take actions that are "accepted as binding most of the time by most of the members so long as they act within the limits of their roles."[5]

At this point it would be helpful to spell out some of the implications of our concept of public policy. First of all, purposive or goal-oriented action, rather than random behavior or accidental occurrences, is our concern. Public policies in modern political systems are not, by and large, things that just happen. They are intended to produce certain results (although it must be said that these are not always achieved). Proposed policies may be usefully thought of as hypotheses where it is suggested that to achieve particular goals certain specified actions will be undertaken. Thus, for example, to increase farms income, various production controls and income subsidies may be proposed.

Second, policies consist of courses or patterns of actions by government officials rather than their separate, discrete decisions. It is difficult to think of such matters as a decision to honor John Wayne or President Jimmy Carter's on-and-off-again position regarding what to do about the American hostages in Iran as public policies. A policy includes not only the decision to enact a law on some topic, for example, but also the subsequent decisions relating to its implementation and enforcement. Policies emerge in response to *policy demands,* those claims or demands made upon public officials by other actors, official or private, in a political system for action or inaction on some public issue. Such demands may range from a general insistence that government ought to "do something" to a proposal for specific action on the matter.

In response to such demands, public officials make *policy decisions* that authorize or give direction and content to public policy actions. Included are decisions to enact statutes, issue executive orders, or edicts, promulgate administrative rules, or make important judicial interpretations of laws. Thus, the decision by Congress to enact the Sherman Antitrust Act in 1890 was a policy decision; so was the ruling of the Supreme Court in 1911 that the Act prohibited only unreasonable restraints of trade rather than all restraints of trade. Each was of major importance in shaping that course of action called antitrust policy. Such decisions may be contrasted with the large numbers of relatively routine decisions made by officials in the day-to-day application of public policy. The Veterans Administration makes hundreds of thousands of decisions every year on veteran's benefits; most, however, fall within the bounds of settled policy and can be categorized as routine decisions.

Policy statements in turn are the formal expressions or articulations of public policy. Included are legislative statutes, executive orders and decrees, administrative rules and regulations, and court opinions, as well as statements and speeches by public officials indicating the intentions and goals of government and what will be done to realize them. Policy statements are sometimes ambiguous. Witness the conflicts that arise over the meaning of statutory provisions or judicial holdings, or the time and effort expended analyzing and trying to divine the meaning of policy statements made by national political leaders, such as the President of the United States or the rulers of the Soviet Union. Also, different levels, branches, or units of government may issue conflicting policy statements, as on environmental pollution controls or energy usage.

Third, policy involves what governments actually do, not what they intend to do or what they say they are going to do. If a legislature enacts a law requiring employers to pay no less than a state minimum wage but nothing is done to enforce the law, and consequently little, if any, change occurs in economic behavior, then it seems reasonable to contend that public policy in this instance is really one of nonregulation of wages.

It is useful here to mention the concept of *policy outputs,* the things actually done in pursuance of policy decisions and statements. The concept of outputs focuses attention on such matters as taxes collected, highways built, welfare benefits paid, restraints of trade eliminated, traffic fines collected, or foreign aid projects undertaken. An examination of policy outputs may indicate that a policy is actually somewhat or even greatly different from what policy statements indicate it should be.

Fourth, public policy may be either positive or negative in form: It may involve some form of overt government action to deal with a problem on which action was demanded (positive); or it may involve a decision by government officials *not* to take action, to do nothing, on some matter on which government involvement was sought (negative). In other words, governments can follow a policy of *laissez-faire,* or hands off, either generally or on some aspects of economic activity. Such inaction may have major consequences for a society or some of its groups.

It should be stressed that inaction becomes a public policy when it follows from officials declining to act on some problem or, to put it another way, when they decide an issue negatively. This should be differentiated from nonaction on some matter which has not become a public issue, which has not been brought to official attention. Thus, to use a slightly ludicrous example, there is no government action on the taking of earthworms—no seasons, no bag limits, etc. Is this a public policy? The answer is no, because no issue existed, no decisions were made.

Lastly, public policy, at least in its positive form, is based on law and is authoritative. Members of a society usually accept as legitimate that taxes must be paid, import controls must be obeyed, and highway speed limits must be complied with, unless one wants to run the risk of fines, jail sentences, or other legally imposed sanctions or disabilities. Thus public policy has an authoritative, legally coercive quality that the policies of private organizations do not have. Indeed, a monopoly of the legitimate use of coercion is a major characteristic distinguishing government from private organizations.

Even though authoritative, some public policies may be widely violated, as with national prohibition in the 1920s and the 55-mile-per-hour speed limit existing today in some states. Moreover, enforcement may be limited or piecemeal. Are these still public policies? The answer is yes, they either were or are currently on the statute books and enforcement existed. Whether such policies are effective or wise is another matter. Authoritativeness is a necessary but not a sufficient condition for effective public policy.

## WHY STUDY PUBLIC POLICY?

Political scientists, in their teaching and research, have customarily been most concerned with political processes, such as the legislative or electoral process, or with elements of the political system, such as interest groups or public opinion. This is not to say, however, that political scientists have been unconcerned with policy. Foreign policy and policy relating to civil rights and liberties have attracted much attention. So has what Robert Salisbury calls constitutional policy, that is, "decisional rules by which subsequent policy actions are to be determined."[6] Illustrative of the procedural and structural "givens" that make up constitutional policy are legislative apportionment, the use of the city-manager form of government, and federalism. Each helps to shape decisions or substantive policy. Also, some political scientists with a normative bent manifest concern with what governments *should* do, with "proper" or "correct" public policy. Their value-oriented approach, however, has placed them outside the mainstream of political science in recent decades because political science as a "science" is supposed to be value-free. We will return to this particular matter a little later on.

In the last decade or so, political scientists have given increased attention to the study of public policy—to the description, analysis, and explanation of the causes and effects of governmental activity. Thomas Dye has aptly summarized the concerns of policy study:

This involves a description of the content of public policy; an assessment of the impact of environmental forces on the content of public policy; an analysis of the effect of various institutional arrangements and political processes on public policy; an inquiry into the consequences of various public policies for the political system; and an evaluation of the impact of public policies on society, both in terms of expected and unexpected consequences.[7]

One is thus directed to seek answers to such questions as: What is the actual content of antitrust policy? What effects do urbanization and industrialization have on welfare policies? How does the organization of Congress help shape agricultural policy? Do elections affect the direction of public policies? Do welfare programs contribute to political quiescence or stability? Who is benefited and who is not by current tax policies or urban renewal programs?

This leads us to the question posed in the heading of this section: Why study public policy? Or to put it another way: Why engage in policy analysis? It has been suggested that policy can be studied for scientific, professional, or political reasons.[8]

*Scientific Reasons*  Public policy can be studied in order to gain greater knowledge about its origins, the processes by which it is developed, and its consequences for society. This, in turn, will increase our understanding of the political system and society generally. Policy may be regarded as either a dependent or an independent variable for purposes of this kind of analysis. When it is viewed as a *dependent variable,* our attention is placed on the political and environmental factors that help determine the content of policy. For example, how is policy affected by the distribution of power among pressure groups and governmental agencies? How do urbanization and national income help shape the content of policy? If public policy is viewed as an *independent variable,* our focus shifts to the impact of policy on the political system and environment. How does policy affect support for the political system or future policy choices? What effect does policy have on social well-being?

*Professional Reasons*  Don K. Price makes a distinction between the "scientific estate," which seeks only to discover knowledge, and the "professional estate," which strives to apply scientific knowledge to the solution of practical social problems.[9] We will not concern ourselves here with the issue of whether political scientists should help prescribe the goals of public policy. Although by no means all political scientists would agree, many argue that political scientists as political scientists have no particular skills beyond those of laymen for this endeavor. Whatever the answer here may be, it is quite correct to contend that if we know something about the factors that help shape public policy, or the consequences of given policies, then we are in a position to say something useful concerning how individuals, groups, or governments can act to attain their policy goals. Such advice can be directed toward indicating either what policies can be used to achieve particular goals or what political and environmental factors are conducive to the development of a given policy. It puts us in the position of saying, for example, *if* you want to prevent traffic congestion, *then* you should do such and such. Questions of this sort are factual in nature and are open to, indeed require, scientific study. Certainly factual knowledge is a prerequisite for prescribing for, and dealing with, the problems of society.

*Political Reasons*  As was noted above, at least some political scientists do not believe that political scientists should refrain from helping to prescribe policy goals. Rather, they say that the study of public policy should be directed toward ensuring that governments adopt appropriate policies to attain the "right" goals. They reject the notion that policy analysts should strive to be value-free, contending that political science cannot be silent or impotent on current political and social problems. They want to improve the quality of public policy in ways they deem desirable, notwithstanding that substantial disagreement exists in society over what constitute "correct" policies or the "right" goals of policy. The efforts of these political scientists usually generate both heat and light in some proportion.

We should now explicitly distinguish between *policy analysis* and *policy advocacy*. Policy analysis is concerned with the examination and description of the causes and consequences of public policy. We can analyze the formation, content, and impact of particular policies, such as on civil rights or international trade, without either approving or disapproving of them. *Policy advocacy,* on the other hand, is concerned especially with what governments *should* do, with the promotion of particular policies through discussion, persuasion, and political activism. The candidate for public office serves as a good prototype of the policy advocate. Jimmy Carter and Ronald Reagan as Presidential candidates in 1980 each had his notions of what the government should do in foreign and domestic policy. In this book the focus will be on policy analysis.

To conclude this discussion, we should note that policy analysis has three basic concerns. First, its primary focus is on the explanation of policy rather than on the prescription of "proper" policy. Second, the causes and consequences of public policies are rigorously searched for through the use of social scientific methodology. Third, an effort is made to develop reliable, general theories concerning public policies and their formation which are applicable to different agencies and policy areas.[10] So conceived, policy analysis can be both scientific and relevant to current political and social problems. Analysts with normative and "practical" orientations do not have a corner on relevance.

## THEORIES OF DECISION-MAKING

Political and social scientists have developed many models, theories, approaches, concepts, and schemes for the analysis of policy-making and its component, decision-making. Indeed, political scientists have often shown much more facility and verve for theorizing about public policy than for actually studying policy. Nonetheless, concepts and models are necessary and useful to guide policy analysis, as they help clarify and direct our inquiry on policy-making, facilitate communication, and suggest possible explanations for policy actions. Clearly, when we set out to study policy we need some guidelines, some criteria of relevance, to focus our efforts and to prevent aimless meandering through the fields of political data. What we find depends partly upon what we are looking for; policy concepts and theories give direction to our inquiry.

In this and the subsequent section, we will examine a number of concepts and models for the study of public policy, without trying to determine which is "best." Before doing this we need to distinguish between decision-making and policy-making, something that is not always done with clarity, if at all, by students of public policy. Decision-making involves the choice of an alternative from among a series of competing alternatives. Theories of decision-making are concerned with how such choices are made. A policy, to recall our earlier definition, is "a purposive course of action followed by an actor or set of actors in dealing with a problem or matter of concern." Policy-making typically involves a pattern of action, extending over time and involving many decisions, some routine and some not so routine. Rarely will a policy be synonymous with a single decision. To use a mundane example: A person is not accurate in saying it is his policy to bathe on Saturday night when, in fact, he bathes only with great infrequency, however elegant the decision-making process that results in his doing so on a particular Saturday. It is the course of action that defines policy, not the isolated event, and in this example the policy involved is essentially one of not bathing.

Three theories of decision-making that focus on the steps or intellectual activities involved in making a decision will be discussed here. To the extent that they describe how decisions are made by individuals and groups, they are empirical. Viewed as statements of how decisions should be made, they are normative. It is not always easy to separate these two qualities in decision theories, as one will discover.

## The Rational-Comprehensive Theory

Perhaps the best-known theory of decision-making, and also perhaps the most widely accepted, is the rational-comprehensive theory. It usually includes the following elements:

1. The decision-maker is confronted with a given problem that can be separated from other problems or at least considered meaningfully in comparison with them.

2. The goals, values, or objectives that guide the decision-maker are clarified and ranked according to their importance.

3. The various alternatives for dealing with the problem are examined.

4. The consequences (costs and benefits, advantages and disadvantages) that would follow from the selection of each alternative are investigated.

5. Each alternative, and its attendant consequences, can be compared with the other alternatives.

6. The decision-maker will choose that alternative, and its consequences, that maximizes the attainment of his or her goals, values, or objectives.

The result of this process is a rational decision, that is, one that most effectively achieves a given end.

The rational-comprehensive theory has had substantial criticism directed at it. Charles Lindblom contends that decision-makers are not faced with concrete, clearly defined problems. Rather, they have first of all to identify and formulate the problems on which they make decisions. For example, when prices are rising rapidly and people are saying "we must do something about the problem of inflation," what is the problem? Excessive demand? Inadequate production of goods and services? Administered prices by powerful corporations and unions? Inflationary psychology? Some combination of these? One does not, willy-nilly, attack inflation but the causes of inflation, and these may be difficult to determine. Defining the problem is, in short, often a major problem for the decision-maker.

A second criticism holds that rational-comprehensive theory is unrealistic in the demands it makes on the decision-maker. It assumes that he will have enough information on the alternatives for dealing with a problem, that he will be able to predict their consequences with some accuracy, and that he will be capable of making correct cost-benefit comparisons of the alternatives. A moment's reflection on the informational and intellectual resources needed for acting rationally on the problem of inflation posed above should indicate the barriers to rational action implied in these assumptions—lack of time, difficulty in collecting information and predicting the future, complexity of calculations. Even use of that modern miracle, the computer, cannot fully alleviate these problems. There is no need to overload the arguments, as some do, by talking of the need to consider all possible alternatives. Even a rational-comprehensive decision-maker should be permitted to ignore the absurd and far-fetched.

The value aspect of the rational theory also receives some knocks. Thus, it is contended that the public decision-maker is usually confronted with a situation of value conflict rather than value agreement, and the conflicting values do not permit easy comparison or weighting. Moreover, the decision-maker might confuse personal values with those of the public. And, finally, the rationalistic assumption that facts and values can be readily separated does not hold up in practice. Some may support a dam on a stream as demonstrably necessary to control flooding while others oppose it, preferring a free flowing stream for esthetic and ecological reasons. Recourse to the "facts" will not resolve such controversies.

Finally, there is the problem of "sunk costs." Previous decisions and commitments, investments in existing policies and programs, may foreclose many alternatives from consideration on either a short-run or a long-run basis. A decision to institute a system of socialized medicine represents a commitment to a particular mode of medical care that is not easily reversed or significantly altered in the future. An airport, once constructed, cannot be easily moved to the other side of town.

## The Incremental Theory

The incremental theory of decision-making, or, more simply, incrementalism, is presented as a decision theory that avoids many of the problems of the rational-comprehensive theory and, at the same time, is said to be more descriptive of the way in which public officials actually make decisions.[12] Incrementalism can be summarized in the following manner:

1. The selection of goals or objectives and the empirical analysis of the action needed to attain them are closely intertwined with, rather than distinct from, one another.

2. The decision-maker considers only some of the alternatives for dealing with a problem, and these will differ only incrementally (i.e., marginally) from existing policies.

3. For each alternative only a limited number of "important" consequences are evaluated.

4. The problem confronting the decision-maker is continually redefined. Incrementalism allows for countless ends-means and means-ends adjustments that have the effect of making the problem more manageable.

5. There is no single decision or "right" solution for a problem. The test

of a good decision is that various analysts find themselves directly agreeing on it, without agreeing that the decision is the most appropriate means to an agreed objective.

6. Incremental decision-making is essentially remedial and is geared more to the amelioration of present, concrete social imperfections than to the promotion of future social goals.[12]

Lindblom contends that incrementalism represents the typical decision-making process in pluralist societies such as the United States. Decisions and policies are the product of "give and take" and mutual consent among numerous participants ("partisans") in the decision process. Incrementalism is politically expedient because it is easier to reach agreement when the matters in dispute among various groups are only modifications of existing programs rather than policy issues of great magnitude or an "all or nothing" character. Since decision-makers operate under conditions of uncertainty with regard to the future consequences of their actions, incremental decisions reduce the risks and costs of uncertainty. Incrementalism is also realistic because it recognizes that decision-makers lack the time, intelligence, and other resources needed to engage in comprehensive analysis of all alternative solutions to existing problems. Moreover, people are essentially pragmatic, seeking not always the single best way to deal with a problem but, more modestly, "something that will work." Incrementalism, in short, yields limited, practicable, acceptable decisions.

Various criticisms have been directed at incrementalism. One is that it is too conservative, too focused on the existing order; hence, it is a barrier to innovation, which is often necessary for effective public policies. Another is that in crisis situations (the Cuban missile crisis, the 1981 air controllers' strike), incrementalism provides no guidelines for handling the tasks of decision. Third, geared as it is to past actions and existing programs, and to limited changes in them, incrementalism may discourage search for or use of other readily available alternatives. Fourth, incrementalism does *not* eliminate the need for theory in decision-making, as some of its more enthusiastic advocates contend. For, unless changes in policy (increments) are to be made simply on a random or arbitrary basis, some theory (of causation, relationships, etc.) is needed to guide action, to indicate what the likely effect of given changes will be.

Notwithstanding reservations of these sorts, incrementalism has become a form of conventional wisdom, especially in the budgetary process. (For further discussions of incrementalism, see chapters 3 and 4).

## Mixed-Scanning

Sociologist Amitai Etzioni agrees with the criticism of the rational theory but also suggests there are some shortcomings in the incremental theory of decision-making.[13] For instance, he says that decisions made by incrementalists would reflect the interests of the most powerful and organized interests in society, while the interests of the underprivileged and politically unorganized would be neglected. Great or fundamental decisions, such as declaration of war, do not come within the ambit of incrementalism. Although limited in number, fundamental decisions are highly significant and often provide the context for numerous incremental decisions.

Etzioni presents mixed-scanning as an approach to decision-making, which takes into account both fundamental and incremental decisions and provides for "high-order, fundamental policy-making processes which set basic directions and ... incremental processes which prepare for fundamental decisions and work them out after they have been reached." He provides the following illustration of mixed-scanning:

> Assume we are about to set up a worldwide weather observation system using weather satellites. The rationalistic approach would seek an exhaustive survey of weather conditions by using cameras capable of detailed observations and by scheduling reviews of the entire sky as often as possible. This would yield an avalanche of details, costly to analyze and likely to overwhelm our action capacities (e.g., "seeding" cloud formations that could develop into hurricanes or bring rain to arid areas). Incrementalism would focus on those areas in which similar patterns developed in the recent past and, perhaps, on a few nearby regions; it would thus ignore all formations which might deserve attention if they arose in unexpected areas.
>
> A mixed-scanning strategy would include elements of both approaches by employing two cameras: a broad-angle camera that would cover all parts of the sky but not in great detail, and a second one which would zero in on those areas revealed by the first camera to require a more in-depth examination. While mixed-scanning might miss areas in which only a detailed camera could reveal trouble, it is less likely than incrementalism to miss obvious trouble spots in unfamiliar areas.[14]

Mixed-scanning permits decision-makers to utilize both the rational-comprehensive and incremental theories in different situations. In some instances, incrementalism will be adequate; in others, a more thorough approach along rational-comprehensive lines will be needed. Mixed-scanning also takes into account differing capacities of decision-makers. Generally speaking, the greater the capacity of decision-makers to mobilize power to implement their decisions, the more scanning they can realistically engage in; and the more encompassing is scanning, the more effective is decision-making.

Mixed-scanning is thus a kind of "compromise" approach that combines use of incrementalism and rationalism. It is not really clear from Etzioni's discussion, however, just how it would operate in practice. This is something on which the reader can ponder and speculate. Certainly, though, Etzioni does help alert us to the significant facts that decisions vary in their magnitude (e.g., scope, impact) and that different decision processes may be appropriate as the nature of decisions varies.

## A Note on Decision Criteria

Whether the decision process they select is rational-comprehensive, incremental, or mixed-scanning in nature, those who make choices among alternatives must have some basis for doing so. While some "decisions" may be the product of chance, inadvertence, random selection, or inaction that permits particular actions to prevail, most decisions will involve conscious choice. The question then becomes: What kinds of criteria (values or standards) influence the actions of decision-makers? Of course, many factors appear to impinge upon political decision-makers—political and social pressures, economic conditions, procedural requirements (e.g., due process), previous commitments, the pressure of time, and so on. In our concern with these, however, we should be careful not to neglect the values of the decision-maker himself, notwithstanding that they may be difficult to determine and impossible to isolate in many instances.

Most of the values that may serve to guide the behavior of decision-makers may be summarized in four categories.

*Political Values* The decision-maker may evaluate policy alternatives in terms of their import for her political party or the clientele groups of her agency. Decisions are made on the basis of political advantage, with policies being viewed as means for the advancement or achievement of political party or interest group goals. Political scientists have often studied and evaluated policy-making from this perspective. Particular decisions will be "explained" as being made for the benefit, say, of organized labor, wheat farmers, or a given political party. The decision of the Ford Administration to raise some farm-price supports just prior to the 1976 Presidential election did appear to have a partisan hue. So did the enthusiasm of many congressional Democrats for campaign finance reform, including expenditure limits, prior to the 1972 election campaigns as they expected to have more difficulty than the Republicans in raising campaign funds.

*Organization Values* Decision-makers, especially bureaucrats, may also be influenced by organizational values. Organizations, such as administrative agencies, utilize many rewards and sanctions in an effort to induce their members to accept, and act on the basis of, organizationally determined values. To the extent this occurs, the individual's decisions may be guided by such considerations as the desires to see his organization survive, to enhance or expand its programs and activities, or to maintain its power and prerogatives. Many bureaucratic struggles between rival agencies, such as the Army Corps of Engineers and the Bureau of Reclamation in the water-resource policy area, stem from their desire to protect or expand their programs and activities.

*Personal Values* The urge to protect or promote one's physical or financial well-being, reputation, or historical position may also serve as a decision criterion. The politician who accepts a bribe to make a particular decision, such as the award of a license or contract, obviously has personal benefit in mind. On a different plane, the President who says he is not going to be "the first President to lose a war," and who acts accordingly, is also being influenced by personal considerations, such as concern for his "place in history."

*Policy Values* Neither the discussion to this point nor cynicism should lead us to conclude that political decision-makers are influenced only by considerations of political, organizational, or personal benefit. Decision-makers may well act on the basis of their perceptions of the public interest or beliefs concerning what is proper or morally correct public policy. A legislator who votes in favor of civil rights legislation may well do so because she believes it is morally correct and that equality is a desirable goal of public policy, notwithstanding that her vote may cause her some political risk. Studies of the Supreme Court indicate that the justices are influenced by policy values in deciding cases.[15]

*Ideological Values*    Ideologies are sets of logically related values and beliefs which present simplified pictures of the world and serve as guides to action for people. In the Soviet Union, Marxist-Leninist ideology has served at least in part as a set of prescriptions for social and economic change. Although the Soviets have sometimes departed from Marxist-Leninist ideology, as in the use of economic incentives to increase production, it still serves as a means for rationalizing and legitimizing policy actions by the regime. In many of the developing countries in Asia, Africa, and the Middle East, nationalism—the desire of a people or nation for autonomy and deep concern with their own characteristics, needs and problems—has been an important factor shaping both foreign and domestic policies. Nationalism has become particularly important in world politics in the twentieth century, because it fueled the desire of colonial peoples for independence and created and intensified conflicts among both old and new nations.

## SOME APPROACHES TO POLICY ANALYSIS

Just as political scientists have created theories and models to help them understand and explain the decision-making process, so have they also developed a variety of theoretical approaches to assist them in the study of the political behavior of entire political systems. Although most of these approaches have not been developed specifically for the analysis of policy formation, they can readily be converted to that purpose. The theoretical approaches that will come under brief examination here include systems theory, group theory, elite theory, functional process theory, and institutionalism. Such theoretical approaches are useful in, and to the extent, that they direct our attention to important political phenomena, help clarify and simplify our thinking, and suggest possible explanations for political activity or, in our particular case, public policy.

### Political Systems Theory

Public policy may be viewed as the response of a political system to demands arising from its environment. The *political system,* as defined by Easton, is composed of those identifiable and interrelated institutions and activities in a society that make authoritative decisions (or allocations of values) that are binding on society.[16] *Inputs* into the political system from the environment consist of demands and supports. The *environment* consists of all those conditions and events external to the boundaries of the political system. *Demands* are the claims made by individuals and groups on the political system for action to satisfy their interests. *Support* is rendered when groups and individuals abide by election results, pay taxes, obey laws, and otherwise accept the decisions and actions of the authoritative political system made in response to demands. These authoritative allocations of values constitute public policy. The concept of *feedback* indicates that public policies (or outputs) may subsequently alter the environment and the demands generated therein, as well as the character of the political system itself. Policy outputs

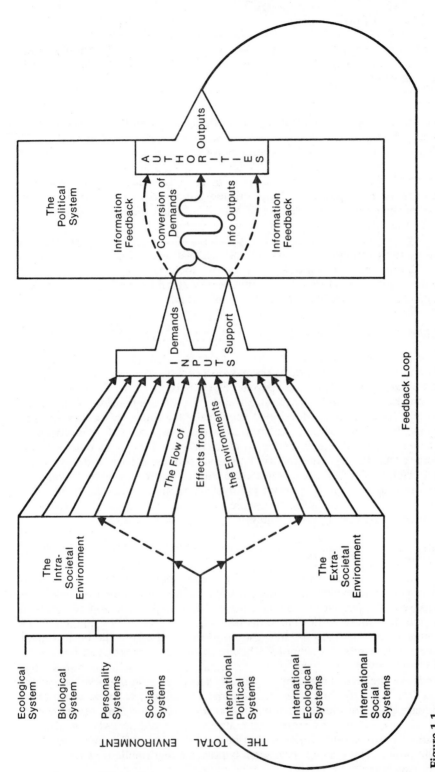

**Figure 1.1**
**Easton's "Dynamic Response" Model of a Political System.** From *A Framework for Political Analysis* (Englewood Cliffs, N.J.: Prentice-Hall, 1965), p. 110.

may produce new demands, which lead to further policy outputs, and so on in a continuing, never ending flow of public policy. (See Figure 1.1.)

The usefulness of systems theory for the study of public policy is limited by its highly general nature. It does not, moreover, say much concerning how decisions are made and policy is developed within the "black box" called the political system. Nonetheless, systems theory is a useful aid in organizing our inquiry into policy formation. It also alerts us to some significant aspects of the political process, such as: How do environmental inputs affect the content of public policy and the nature of the political system? How does public policy affect the environment and subsequent demands for action? What forces or factors in the environment act to generate demands upon the political system? How is the political system able to convert demands into public policy and preserve itself over time?

## Group Theory

According to the group theory of politics, public policy is the product of the group struggle. As one writer states: "What may be called public policy is the equilibrium reached in this [group] struggle at any given moment, and it represents a balance which the contending factions or groups constantly strive to weight in their favor."[17] Many public policies do reflect the activities of groups. Examples include the AFL-CIO and minimum wage legislation, farm groups and agricultural subsidies, shipping companies and maritime subsidies, and the National Education Association and the creation of the Department of Education.

Group theory rests on the contention that interaction and struggle among groups are the central facts of political life. A group is a collection of individuals that may, on the basis of shared attitudes or interests, make claims upon other groups in society. It becomes a political interest group "when it makes a claim through or upon any of the institutions of government."[18] And, of course, many groups do just that. The individual is significant in politics only as he is a participant in, or a representative of, groups. It is through groups that individuals seek to secure their political preferences.

Public policy, at any given time, will reflect the interests of dominant groups. As groups gain and lose power and influence, public policy will be altered in favor of the interests of those gaining influence against the interests of those losing influence.

The role of government ("official groups") in policy formation has been described in the following manner by one proponent of group theory:

> The legislature referees the group struggle, ratifies the victories of the successful coalitions, and records the terms of the surrenders, compromises, and conquests in the form of statutes. Every statute tends to represent compromises because the process of accommodating conflicts of group interests is one of deliberation and consent. The legislative vote on any issue tends to represent the composition of strength, i.e., the balance of power, among the contending groups at the moment of voting.... Administrative agencies of the regulatory kind are established to carry out the terms of the treaties that the legislators have negotiated and ratified. ... The judiciary, like the civilian bureaucracy, is one of the instrumentalities for the administration of the agreed rules.[19]

Group theory, while focusing attention on one of the major dynamic elements in policy formation, especially in pluralist societies such as the United States, seems both to overstate the importance of groups and to understate the independent and creative role that public officials play in the policy process. Indeed, many groups have been generated by public policy. The American Farm Bureau Federation, which developed around the agricultural extension program, is a notable example, as is the National Welfare Rights Organization. Public officials also may acquire a stake in particular programs and act as an interest group in support of their continuance. In the United States some welfare agency employees, including social workers, prefer current programs, with their emphasis on supervision and services (as well as benefits), to a guaranteed annual income, which would probably eliminate some of their jobs. In the Soviet Union, the bureaucracy has even been depicted as a "new class" that benefits from and supports the current system of state planning and controls.

Finally, we should note that it is rather misleading and inefficient to try to explain politics, or policy formation in terms of group struggle without giving attention to the many other factors—for example, ideas and institutions—that abound. This sort of reductionism, or unicausal explanation, should be avoided.

## Elite Theory

Approached from the perspective of elite theory, public policy can be regarded as reflecting the values and preferences of a governing elite. The essential argument of elite theory is that it is not the people or the "masses" who determine public policy through their demands and action; rather, public policy is decided by a ruling elite and carried into effect by public officials and agencies.

Thomas Dye and Harmon Zeigler, in *The Irony of Democracy,* provide a summary of elite theory:

1. Society is divided into the few who have power and the many who do not. Only a small number of persons allocate values for society; the masses do not decide public policy.

2. The few who govern are not typical of the masses who are governed. Elites are drawn disproportionately from the upper socioeconomic strata of society.

3. The movement of non-elites to elite positions must be slow and continuous to maintain stability and avoid revolution. Only non-elites who have accepted the basic elite consensus can be admitted to governing circles.

4. Elites share a consensus on the basic values of the social system and the preservation of the system. [In the United States, the elite consensus includes private enterprise, private property, limited government, and individual liberty.]

5. Public policy does not reflect demands of the masses but rather the prevailing values of the elite. Changes in public policy will be incremental rather than revolutionary. [Incremental changes permit responses to events that threaten a social system with a minimum of alteration or dislocation of the system.]

6. Active elites are subject to relatively little direct influence from apathetic masses. Elites influence masses more than masses influence elites.[20]

So stated elite theory is a rather provocative theory of policy formation. Policy is the product of elites, reflecting their values and serving their ends, one of which may be a desire to provide for the welfare of the masses. Thomas Dye has argued that development of civil rights policies in the United States during the 1960s can be suitably explained through the use of elite theory. These policies were "a response of a national elite to conditions affecting a small minority of Americans rather than a response of national leaders to majority sentiments." Thus, for example, the "elimination of legal discrimination and the guarantee of equality of opportunity in the Civil Rights Act of 1964 was achieved largely through the dramatic appeals of middle-class black leaders to the conscience of white elites."[21]

Elite theory does focus our attention on the role of leadership in policy formation and on the fact that, in any political system, a few govern the many. Whether the elites rule, and determine policy, with little influence by the masses is a difficult proposition to handle. It cannot be proved merely by assertions that the "establishment runs things," which has been a familiar plaint in recent years. Political scientist Robert Dahl argues that to defend the proposition successfully one must identify "a controlling group, less than a majority in size, that is not a pure artifact of democratic rules; . . . a minority of individuals whose preferences regularly prevail in cases of differences of preferences on key political issues."[22] It may be that elite theory has more utility for the analysis and explanation of policy formation in some political systems, such as developing or Communist-bloc countries, than in others, such as the pluralist democracies of the United States and Canada.

## Institutionalism

The study of government institutions is one of the oldest concerns of political science. Political life generally revolves around governmental institutions such as legislatures, executives, courts, and political parties; public policy, moreover, is initially authoritatively determined and implemented by governmental institutions. It is not surprising, then, that political scientists would devote much attention to them.

Traditionally, the institutional approach concentrated on describing the more formal and legal aspects of governmental institutions—their formal organization, legal powers, procedural rules, and functions or activities. Formal relationships with other institutions might also be considered. Usually little was done to explain how institutions actually operated, as apart from how they were supposed to operate, to analyze public policies produced by institutions, or to try to discover the relationships between institutional structure and public politics.

Subsequently, we should note, political scientists turned their attention in teaching and research to the political processes within governmental or political institutions, concentrating on the behavior of participants in the process and on political realities rather than formalism. To use the legislature as an example, concern shifted from simply describing the legislature as an institution to analyzing and explaining its operation over time, from its static to its dynamic aspects. In the curriculum the course on the "legislature" often became one on the "legislative process."

Institutionalism, with its emphasis on the formal or structural aspects of institutions, can nonetheless be usefully employed in policy analysis. An institution is a set of regularized patterns of human behavior that persist over time. (Some people, unsophisticated of course, seem to equate institutions with the physical structures in which they exist.) It is their differing sets of behavior patterns that really distinguish courts from legislatures, from administrative agencies, and so on. These regularized patterns of behavior, which we often call rules, structures, and the like, can affect decision-making and the content of public policy. Rules and structural arrangements are usually not neutral in their impact; rather, they tend to favor some interests in society over others, some policy results rather than others. For example, it is contended that some of the rules (and traditions, which often have the effect of rules) of the Senate, such as those relating to unlimited debate and action by unanimous consent, favor the interests of minorities over majorities. In a federal system, which disperses power among different levels of government, some groups may have more influence if policy is made at the national level; other groups may benefit more if policy is made at the state or provincial level. Civil rights groups in the United States during the 1960s received a better response in Washington, D.C., than they did in Montgomery, Alabama, or Columbia, South Carolina, for example.

In summary, institutional structures, arrangements, and procedures can have a significant impact on public policy and should not be ignored in policy analysis. Neither should analysis of them, without concern for the dynamic aspects of politics, be considered adequate.

Although individual political scientists often manifest a preference for one or another of these or other theoretical approaches, it is not really possible to say which is the "best" or most satisfactory. Each focuses attention on different aspects of politics and policy-making and seems more useful for some purposes or some situations than others. Generally, one should not permit oneself to be bound too rigidly or dogmatically to a particular model or theoretical approach. A good rule is to be eclectic and flexible and use those theories as organizing concepts that seem most useful for the satisfactory analysis and explanation of a particular public policy or political action. It is my belief that the explanation of political behavior, rather than the validation of a given theoretical approach, should be the main purpose of political inquiry and analysis. Each of the theoretical approaches discussed in this section can contribute to our understanding of policy-making.

## THE PLAN OF THIS BOOK

At this point it seems fair to give the reader some idea of what to expect in the remainder of the book. Our central concern will be with the policy process, which is a shorthand way of designating the various processes by which public policy is actually formed.[23] There is, it should be stressed, no one single process by which policy is made. Variations in the subject of policy will produce variations in the nature and techniques of policy-making. Foreign policy, taxation, railroad regulation, aid to private schools, professional licensing, and reform of local government are each characterized by distinguishable policy process. Furthermore, it makes a difference whether the primary institutional location of policy-making is the legislature, executive, judiciary, or administrative agencies. And certainly the process of forming, for instance, tax policy differs in the United States, the Soviet Union, and, say, Ethiopia.

All of this should not be taken to mean that each policy-making situation is unique and that it is impossible to develop generalizations on policy formation. Given the complexity and diversity in policy processes, it is not now possible to develop a "grand theory" of policy formation. But a useful start can be made toward what political scientists call "theory building" by seeking to generalize on such matters as who is involved in policy formation, on what kinds of issues, under what conditions, in what ways, and to what effect. Nor should we neglect the question of how policy problems develop. Such questions are really not as simple as they may first appear.

To provide a conceptual framework to guide our discussion, the policy process will be viewed as a sequential pattern of action involving a number of functional categories of activity that can be analytically distinguished, although in various instances this distinction may be difficult to make empirically. The categories are presented briefly here. (Also see Table 1.1.)

1. *Problem identification and agenda formation:* What is a policy problem? What makes it a public problem? How does it get on the agenda of government?

2. *Formulation:* How are alternatives for dealing with the problem developed? Who participates in policy formulation?

3. *Adoption:* How is a policy alternative adopted or enacted? What requirements must be met? Who adopts policy? What processes are used? What is the content of the adopted policy?

4. *Implementation:* Who is involved? What is done, if anything, to carry a policy into effect? What impact does this have on policy content?

5. *Evaluation:* How is the effectiveness or impact of a policy measured? Who evaluates policy? What are the consequences of policy evaluation? Are there demands for change or repeal?

Within this framework policy formation and implementation are perceived as political in that they involve conflict and struggle among individuals and groups having conflicting desires on issues of public policy. Policy-making is "political," it involves "politics," and there is no reason either to resist or to denigrate this conclusion, or to imitate those who dismiss policies they do not like with such phrases as "It's just a matter of politics."

This framework has a number of advantages. In actuality, policy-making often does chronologically follow the sequence of activities listed above. The sequential approach thus helps capture the flow of action in the policy process. Second, the sequential approach is open to change.[25] Additional steps can be introduced if experience indicates they are needed. Various forms of data collection and analysis—whether quantitative, legal, normative, or whatever—are compatible with it. Third, it yields a dynamic and developmental rather than cross-sectional or static view of the policy process. Moreover, it empha-

**Table 1.1  The Policy Process**

| Policy Terminology | First-Stage Policy Agenda | Second-Stage Policy Formulation | Third-Stage Policy Adoption | Fourth-Stage Policy Implementation | Fifth-Stage Policy Evaluation |
|---|---|---|---|---|---|
| Definition | Those problems, among many, which receive the serious attention of public officials. | The development of pertinent and acceptable proposed courses of action for dealing with a public problem. | Development of support for a specific proposal so that a policy can be legitimized or authorized. | Application of the policy by the government's administrative machinery to the problem. | Efforts by the government to determine whether the policy was effective and why or why not. |
| Common Sense | Getting the government to consider action on the problem. | What is proposed to be done about the problem. | Getting the government to accept a particular solution to the problem. | Applying the government's policy to the problem. | Did the policy work! |

Source: Adapted from James E. Anderson, David W. Brady, and Charles Bullock, III, *Public Policy and Politics in the United States* (North Scituate, Mass.: Duxbury, 1978).

sizes the relationships among political phenomena rather than simply listing factors or developing classification schemes. Fourth, the sequential approach is not "culture-bound," and it can be readily utilized to study policy-making in foreign policy-making systems. Also, it lends itself to manageable comparisons, as of how problems get on the policy agenda in various countries or of the ways in which policies are adopted.

In presenting this framework for the analysis of policy-making, I will concentrate upon national domestic policies in the United States, though not to the total exclusion of foreign policy or other political systems. The discussion that follows is intended to provide readers both with an understanding of the policy process and with some tools for their own analysis of policy-making.

## NOTES

1. Robert Eyestone, *The Threads of Public Policy: A Study in Policy Leadership* (Indianapolis: Bobbs-Merrill, 1971), p. 18.
2. Thomas R. Dye, *Understanding Public Policy* (Englewood Cliffs, N.J.: Prentice-Hall, 2d ed., 1975), p.1.
3. Richard Rose (ed.), *Policy Making in Great Britain* (London: Macmillan, 1969), p. x.
4. Carl J. Friedrich, *Man and His Government* (New York: McGraw-Hill, 1963), p. 79.
5. David Easton, *A Systems Analysis of Political Life* (New York: Wiley, 1965), p. 212.
6. Robert H. Salisbury, "The Analysis of Public Policy: A Search for Theories and Roles," in Austin Ranney (ed.), *Political Science and Public Policy* (Chicago: Markham, 1968), p. 159.
7. Dye, *op. cit.,* pp. 5–7.
8. The following discussion is based on Austin Ranney, "The Study of Policy Content: A Framework for Choice," in Ranney (ed.), *Political Science and Public Policy* (Chicago: Markham, 1968), pp. 13–18.
9. Don K. Price, *The Scientific Estate* (Cambridge, Mass.: Harvard University Press, 1965), pp. 122–35.
10. Dye, *op. cit.,* p. 6. Italics in original have been deleted.
11. The leading proponent of incrementalism undoubtedly is Charles Lindblom. See his "The Science of 'Muddling Through,'" *Public Administration Review,* XIX (1959), pp. 79–88; *The Intelligence of Democracy* (New York: Macmillan, 1964); *The Policy-Making Process* (Englewood Cliffs, N.J.: Prentice-Hall, 1968); and, with David Braybrooke, *The Strategy of Decision* (New York: Free Press, 1963).
12. This summary draws primarily on Lindblom's "The Science of 'Muddling Through,'" *op. cit.,* and *The Intelligence of Democracy, op. cit,* pp. 144–48.
13. Amitai Etzioni, "Mixed-Scanning: A 'Third' Approach to Decision-Making," *Public Administration Review,* XXVII (December, 1967), pp. 385–92.
14. *Ibid., p.* 389.
15. Glendon Schubert, *Judicial Policy-Making* (Chicago: Scott Foresman, 1965).
16. David Easton, "An Approach to the Analysis of Political Systems," *World Politics,* IX (April, 1957), pp. 383–400. Cf. Easton, *A Framework for Political Analysis.*

(Englewood Cliffs, N.J.: Prentice-Hall, 1965), and *A Systems Analysis of Political Life* (New York: Wiley, 1965). Those wishing to explore systems theory in depth should consult these works.

17. Earl Latham, *The Group Basis of Politics* (New York: Octagon Books, 1965), p. 36.
18. David Truman, *The Governmental Process* (New York: Knopf, 1951), p. 37.
19. Latham, *op. cit.,* pp. 35–36, 38–39.
20. Thomas R. Dye and L. Harmon Zeigler, *The Irony of Democracy* (Belmont, Calif.: Wadsworth, 1970), p. 6. This book examines American politics from the perspective of elite theory.
21. Dye, *op. cit.,* pp. 39, 66.
22. Robert A. Dahl, "Critique of the Ruling Elite Model," *American Political Science Review,* LII (June, 1958), p. 464.
23. Here it is useful to distinguish an *Institutional Process,* such as the legislative process, from the policy process. Cf. Charles O. Jones, *An Introduction to the Study of Public Policy* (Belmont, Calif.: Wadsworth, 1970), pp. 4–5.
24. This framework draws upon Harold D. Lasswell, *The Decision Process* (College Park, Md.: Bureau of Governmental Research, University of Maryland, 1956). It also benefits from Jones, *op. cit.*
25. See, generally, Richard Rose, "Concepts for Comparison," *Policy Studies Journal,* I (Spring, 1973), pp. 122–27.

# 2

# The Policy-Makers
# and Their
# Environment

This chapter will survey the environment within which policy-making occurs and some of the official and unofficial participants in policy formation and implementation. This discussion is not intended to be exhaustive; rather, the purpose is to give the reader some notion of who participates in the policy process and in what ways, as well as of what factors usually influence policy behavior.

## THE POLICY ENVIRONMENT

Systems theory suggests that policy-making cannot be adequately considered apart from the environment in which it takes place. Demands for policy actions are generated in the environment and transmitted to the political system; at the same time, the environment places limits and constraints upon what can be done by policy-makers. Included in the environment are such geographical characteristics as natural resources, climate, and topography; demographical variables like population size, age distribution, and spatial location; political culture; social structure; and the economic system. Other nations become a significant part of the environment for foreign and defense policy. The discussion here will focus on a pair of these environmental factors to which political scientists have given much attention (though not always from a policy analysis perspective), namely, political culture and socioeconomic variables.

## Political Culture

Every society has a culture that differentiates the values and lifestyles of its members from those of other societies. The anthropologist Clyde Kluckhohn has defined culture as "the total life way of a people, the social legacy the individual acquires from his group. Or culture can be regarded as that part of the environment that is the creation of man."[1] Most social scientists seem agreed that culture shapes or influences social action, but that it does not fully determine it. It is only one of many factors that may affect human behavior.

What is of interest to us here is that portion of the general culture of a society that can be designated as political culture—widely held values, beliefs, and attitudes concerning what governments should try to do and how they should operate, and the relationship between the citizen and government.[2] Political culture is transmitted from one generation to another by a socialization process in which the individual, through many experiences with parents, friends, teachers, political leaders, and others, learns politically relevant values, beliefs, and attitudes. Political culture, then, is acquired by the individual, becomes a part of his psychological make-up, and is manifested in his behavior. Within a given society, variations among regions and groups may result in distinctive subcultures. In the United States there are noticeable variations in political culture between North and South, black and white, young and old.

One political scientist contends there are three identifiable political cultures—moralistic, individualistic, and traditionalistic—and mutations thereof scattered throughout the United States.[3] The individualistic political culture emphasizes private concerns and views government as a utilitarian device to do what the people want. Politicians are interested in office as a means of controlling the favors or rewards of government. The moralistic political culture views government as a mechanism for advancing the public interest. Government service is considered public service. More government intervention in the economy is accepted and there is much concern about policy issues. Moralistic political culture is strong in states like Minnesota and Wisconsin, while individualistic political culture is dominant in Illinois and New York. The traditionalistic political culture takes a paternalistic and elitist view of government and favors its use to maintain the existing social order. Real political power centers in a small segment of the population while most citizens are expected to be relatively inactive in politics. This political culture has been strong in some of the southern states. Where such variations exist, they clearly compound the tasks of description and analysis.

No attempt will be made here to provide a full statement of the political culture of the United States or any other society. Rather, discussion will be confined to indicating and illustrating some of the implications and significance of political culture for policy formation.

A well-known sociologist, Robin M. Williams, has identified a number of "major-value orientations" in American society. These include individual freedom, equality, progress, efficiency, and practicality.[4] Values such as these—and others, such as democracy, individualism, and humanitarianism—clearly have significance for policy-making. For example, the general approach of Americans to regulation of economic activity has been practical or pragmatic, emphasizing particular solutions to present problems rather than long-range planning or ideological consistency. Moreover, concern with individual freedom has created a general presumption against restriction of private activity in favor of the broadest scope possible for private action. Stress on individualism and private property finds expression in the notion that a person should generally be free to use his property as he sees fit.

Differences in public policy and policy-making in various countries can be explained at least partially in terms of political cultural variations. Public medical care programs are of longer standing and more numerous and extensive in Western European countries than in the United States because there have been greater public expectation and acceptance of such programs in Western Europe. Again, few people in Great Britain disapprove of government ownership, whereas few in the United States approve of it.[5] This being so, it is not surprising to find considerably more government ownership of business and industry in Great Britain. Americans much prefer government regulation to ownership when control seems necessary.

Karl Deutsch suggests that the time orientation of people—their view of the relative importance of the past, the present, and the future—has implications for policy formation. A political culture oriented more to the past than to the present or future may better encourage preservation of monuments than the making of innovations. It may enact legislation on old-age pensions years before expanding public higher education. Thus, Great Britain passed an old-age pension law in 1908, but it did not significantly expand public higher education until after 1960. In contrast, Deutsch notes that the United States, with a more future-oriented culture, adopted legislation in 1862 providing for land-grant colleges and in 1935 for Social Security.[6]

Almond and Verba have differentiated between parochial, subject, and participant political cultures.[7] In a *parochial* political culture, citizens have little awareness of, or orientation toward, either the political system as a whole, the input process, the output process, or the citizen as a political participant. The parochials expect nothing from the system. It is suggested that some African chiefdoms and kingdoms and tribal societies, and modern-day Italy, are illustrative of parochial political cultures. In a *subject* political culture, like that of Germany, the citizen is oriented toward the political system and the output process; yet, he has little awareness of input processes or himself as a participant. He is aware of governmental authority, he may like or dislike it, but he is essentially passive. He is, as the term implies, a subject. In the *participant* political culture, which Almond and Verba found the United States to be, citizens have a high level of political awareness and information and have explicit orientations toward the political system as a whole, its input and output processes, and meaningful citizen participation in politics. Included in this orientation is an understanding of how individuals and groups can influence decision-making. Some of the implications of these differences in political culture for policy formation seem readily apparent. Obviously, citizen participation in policy formation in a parochial political culture is going to be essentially nonexistent, and government will be of little concern to most citizens. The individual in a subject political culture may believe that she can do little to influence public policy, whether she likes it or not. This may lead to passive acceptance of governmental action that may be rather authoritarian in style. In some instances, frustration and resentment may build until redress or change is sought through violence. In the participant political culture, individuals may organize into groups and otherwise seek to influence government action to rectify their grievances. Government, and public policy, is viewed as controllable by citizens. Also, one can assume that more demands will be made on government in a participant political culture than in either a parochial or a subject culture.

To return to an earlier point, political culture helps shape political behavior; it "is related to the *frequency* and *probability* of various kinds of behavior and not their rigid determination."[8] Common values, beliefs, and attitudes inform, guide, and constrain the actions of both decision-makers and citizens. Political culture differences help ensure that public policy is more likely to favor economic competition in the United States because individual opportunity is a widely held value, while it is more likely to tolerate industrial cartels in West Germany, because economic competition has not been highly valued there. Some political scientists shy away from using political culture as an analytic tool because they see it as too imprecise and conjectural. Notwithstanding some truth to this view, political culture still has utility for the analysis and explanation of policy.

## Socioeconomic Conditions

The term socioeconomic conditions is used here because it is often impossible to separate social and economic factors as they impinge on or influence political activity. This will become quite apparent as the discussion proceeds.

Public policies can be usefully viewed as arising out of conflicts between different groups of people, private and official, possessing differing interests and desires.[9] One of the prime sources of conflict, especially in modern societies, is economic activity. Conflicts may develop between the interests of big business and small business, employers and employees, debtors and creditors, wholesalers and retailers, chain stores and independents, consumers and sellers, farmers and the purchasers of farm commodities, and so on. Groups that are underprivileged or dissatisfied with their current relationships with other groups in the economy may seek governmental assistance to improve their situation. Customarily, it is the weaker or disadvantaged party (at least in a comparative sense) in a private conflict that seeks government involvement in the matter. The dominant group, the one that is able to achieve its goals satisfactorily by private action, has no incentive to bring government into the fray and usually will oppose government action as unnecessary or improper. Thus, it has been labor groups, dissatisfied with the wages resulting from private bargaining with employers, that have sought minimum-wage legislation, or consumer groups, who feel disadvantaged in the marketplace, who have sought consumer protection laws.

Satisfactory relationships between groups may be disrupted or altered by economic change or development, and those that feel adversely affected or threatened may demand government action to protect their interests or establish a new equilibrium. Rapid industrialization and the growth of big business in the United States in the latter part of the nineteenth century produced new economic conditions. Farmers, small businessmen, reformist elements, and aggrieved others called for government action to control big business. The eventual result was the enactment of the Sherman Antitrust Act by Congress in 1890.

It is a truism to state that a society's level of economic development will impose limits on what government can do in providing public goods and services to the community. Nonetheless, it is something that is sometimes overlooked by those who assume that the failure of governments to act on problems is invariably due to recalcitrance or unresponsiveness rather than limited resources. Clearly, one factor that affects what governments can do in the way of welfare programs is available economic resources. The scarcity of economic resources will, of course, be more limiting in many of the less developed (or "underdeveloped") countries of the world than in an affluent society such as the United States. Still, government in the United States does not have available economic resources to do everything that everyone wants done. National health insurance legislation, which seemed highly likely of enactment in the early 1970s, lost its saliency because of its estimated high cost in an era of large national budget deficits. Moreover, resources are very unequally distributed among state and local governments, which affects their ability to deal with such problems as public education, poverty, and traffic congestion.

Social conflict and change also provoke demands for government action. Recently in the United States, growing concern about women's rights and the increased use (and acceptance) of marijuana, especially by middle-class people, has produced demands for alteration in public policies to provide greater protection for women's rights (including the right to have abortions) and lesser penalties for the use of marijuana. Those with conflicting interests and values have opposed such demands, with the consequences that public officials often find themselves hard-pressed to devise acceptable policy solutions.

The ways in which socioeconomic conditions influence or constrain public policies in the American states have recently been subjected to considerable analysis by political scientists. Controversy has developed over the relative influence of political variables and of socioeconomic variables on policy. This matter clearly merits some discussion here.

One of the most prominent efforts on this question has been Dye's study of policy outputs in the fifty states.[10] He contended that the level of economic development (as measured by such variables as per capita personal income, percent urban population, median level of education, and industrial employment) had a dominant influence on state policies on such matters as education, welfare, highways, taxation, and public regulation. The impact of economic development was compared with the impact of the political system. He found that political variables (voter participation, interparty competition, political party strength, and legislative apportionment) had only a weak relationship to public policy. Dye summed up the findings of his involved statistical analysis in the following manner:

> Much of the literature in state politics implies that the division of the two-party vote, the level of interparty competition, the level of voter participation, and the degree of malapportionment in legislative bodies all influence public policy. Moreover, at first glance the fact that there are obvious policy differences between states with different degrees of party competition, Democratic dominance, and voter participation lends some support to the notion that these system characteristics influence public policy....

However, partial correlation analysis reveals that these system characteristics have relatively little *independent* effect on policy outcomes in the states. Economic development shapes both political systems and policy outcomes, and most of the association that occurs between system characteristics and policy outcomes can be attributed to the influence of economic development. Differences in the policy choices of states with different types of political systems turn out to be largely a product of differing socioeconomic levels rather than a direct product of political variables. Levels of urbanization, industrialization, income, and education appear to be more influential in shaping policy outcomes than political system characteristics.[11]

It should be noted that Dye argued not that political variables do not have *any* impact on state policy, but rather that they are clearly subordinated to socioeconomic factors.

Another study attempting to demonstrate the stronger impact of socioeconomic than political factors on policy was done by Dawson and Robinson.[12] They analyzed the effect of interparty competition and some economic variables on public welfare policy to determine whether party competition had a significant influence on welfare policy (especially expenditures). They concluded that environmental factors had a greater impact than party competition. "The level of public social welfare programs in the American states seems to be more a function of socioeconomic factors, especially per capita income."[13]

The conclusions of these and similar studies were quickly accepted by some political scientists. One declared that such research provides "a devastating set of findings and cannot be dismissed as not meaning what it plainly says—that analysis of political systems will not explain policy decisions made by those systems."[14] Is public policy really an outcome, primarily, of some kind of socioeconomic determinism? Are studies such as those just cited really conclusive on this issue? Two scholars have recently cautioned against a "simple acceptance" of such a conclusion.[15] While not discounting the importance of socioeconomic factors in influencing policy outputs, they indicate there are a number of problems and limitations in these studies.

First, there is a tendency to exaggerate the strength of the economy-policy relationship. Thus, "Dye reports 456 coefficients of simple correlations between policy measures and his four economic measures of income, urbanism, industrialization and education, but only 16 of them (4 percent) are strong enough to indicate that an economic measure explains at least one-half the interstate variation in policy."[16] This leaves quite a bit unexplained statistically. Second, the political variables used in such studies have been of limited scope, focusing only on a few aspects of the political process. Third, there is a tendency to overlook variations in the influence of economic factors on policy-making. Officials of local governments appear more strongly influenced than state officials by economic factors. Further, local officials are not equally influenced by the character of the local economy:

Where the locality has adopted reformed government structures there is less of an economy-policy linkage than where local government has an unreformed structure. The principal features of a reformed local government structure are a professional city manager, nonpartisan elections for local offices, and a council

selected at-large rather than by wards. These features seem to depoliticize the social and economic cleavages within a community, permitting local officials to
make their policy decisions with less concern for economics.[17]

Another limitation is that most of these studies are concerned with the
statistical relationships between various political and socioeconomic variables and public policy. If, when condition A exists, policy B usually occurs
with it, and the relationship is not caused by some third factor, then we can
predict that, when A exists, B will occur. Such a prediction, however, is not
an explanation, and we are still left with the task of explaining *how* political
decisions are actually made. If per capita income is directly related to the
level of welfare spending, then we must try to explain the relationship. This
is neither an insignificant task nor an easy one. Glib answers should be
avoided but, obviously, decisions are made by individuals and not socioeconomic variables.

Two conclusions can be fairly drawn from this discussion. One is that to
understand how policy decisions are made and why some decisions are made
rather than others, we must consider social and economic as well as political
factors. The second is that whether socioeconomic factors are more important than political factors in shaping public policy is still an open question.
Most of the research along this line has been focused on the American states,
and it is less than conclusive.

## THE OFFICIAL POLICY-MAKERS

Official policy-makers are those who possess legal authority to engage in the
formation of public policy. (I recognize, of course, that some who have the
legal authority to act may, in fact, be controlled by others, such as political
party bosses or pressure groups.) These include legislators, executives, administrators, and judges. Each performs policy-making tasks at least somewhat different from the others.

It is useful to differentiate between primary and supplementary policy-
makers. Primary policy-makers have direct constitutional authority to act; for
example, Congress does not have to depend upon other governmental units
for authorization to act. Supplementary policy-makers, such as national administrative agencies, must gain their authority to act from others (primary
policy-makers) and hence are at least potentially dependent upon or controllable by them. Administrative agencies who derive their operating authority from congressional legislation will typically feel a need to be responsive to congressional interests and requests. Congress, in turn, has less need
to be responsive to the agencies. This distinction between primary and supplementary policy-makers probably will not hold in countries without a coherent constitution (e.g., some African nations), or where there is little respect for the constitution (e.g., some Latin American countries).

The conflict between the President and Congress during the second
Nixon Administration over whether the President could refuse to spend appropriated funds and act on his own to terminate previously authorized programs illustrates the importance of the distinction between primary and supplementary policy-makers. If the President lacked constitutional authority for
impounding funds, as many in Congress contended, then Congress could ul-

timately control spending. This conflict over constitutional authority was essentially a conflict over whether the President could act as a primary policy-maker, which would increase the independence and power of the executive vis-à-vis Congress. The conflict was resolved in favor of Congress by several federal court decisions. Also, the Budget and Impoundment Control Act of 1974 provided that presidential decisions to impound (not spend) appropriated funds were subject to control by Congress. (See Chapter 4.) Given the different interests and constituencies of the two branches, who prevails on such matters can have profound policy implications.

The following survey of official policy-makers is intended only to be suggestive, that is, to convey a notion of their general role in policy formation, not to catalogue all of their powers and activities.

## Legislatures

The easy response to the question "What do legislatures do?" is to say that they legislate, that is, that they are concerned with the central political tasks of lawmaking and policy formation in a political system. It cannot be assumed, however, that a legislature, merely because it bears that formal designation, really has independent decision-making functions. This is a matter to be determined by empirical investigation rather than by definition.

Investigation would indicate that legislatures in American government do indeed often legislate in an independent decisional sense. In Congress, for example, the standing committees and subcommittees possess substantial authority over proposed legislation and may even act in opposition to a majority of the members of the house in which they exist. Policies on such matters as taxation, civil rights, welfare, and labor relations tend to be shaped in substantial part by Congress. In contrast, in the area of foreign policy Congress is more likely to defer to presidential leadership. In the instance of the famous Tonkin Gulf Resolution of 1964, which served as the legal justification for the subsequent expansion of the Vietnam war by the Johnson Administration, Congress hastily approved what was recommended by the President without alteration and with little deliberation. More recently, however, Congress has sought to strengthen its role in the foreign policy area, as by the War Powers Resolution of 1973, which was intended to restrict presidential use of the armed forces.

Within the American states, the role of the legislature often varies with the nature of the issue involved. Many state legislatures, because of their limited sessions, rather "amateur" membership, and inadequate staff assistance, are often unable to act independently on complex, technical legislative matters. They may simply enact bills agreed upon elsewhere. For example, the Texas legislature passed a law in the 1960s dealing with pooling (or unitization) for the common development of oil fields almost in the identical form in which it was introduced after having been agreed to and drafted by representatives of the major and independent petroleum producers organizations. The legislature did not really have the capacity to do otherwise. On other matters, such as criminal legislation, the legislature clearly does "legislate." It does not require any special skills to determine, for example, what the penalty should be for embezzlement. Such questions do not admit of scientific or technical determination. The Texas legislature is not atypical among state legislatures.

The British Parliament has been said to consent merely to laws that are originated by political parties and interest groups, drafted by civil servants, and steered through the House of Commons by the government (the Prime Minister and Cabinet). This oversimplifies the situation. The government usually gets what it wants from Commons partly because it knows what Commons will accept and requests only measures that are acceptable. In the course of approving legislation, Commons performs a vital function of deliberation, scrutinizing, criticizing, and publicizing government policies and activities and their implications for the public.

In comparison, the Russian national legislature, the Supreme Soviet, often merely ratifies or confirms decisions made by high officials within the Communist Party. So too, many Latin American legislatures are dominated by the executive and do little, if anything, in the way of independent decision-making. (The Chilean legislature was one of a few exceptions.) For such political systems, the student of policy formation may be wasting his time if he gives much attention to legislative organization and processes.

To conclude with a global generalization, legislatures are more important in policy formation in democratic than in authoritarian countries; within the democratic category, legislatures generally tend to have a larger role in presidential systems (like the United States) than in parliamentary systems (like Great Britain). In some countries such as Oman, there is no legislature in existence.

## The Executive

We live in what has been called an "executive-centered era," in which the effectiveness of government depends substantially upon executive leadership, both in policy formation and in policy execution. Consider the case of the President of the United States.

The President's authority to exercise legislative leadership is both clearly established and accepted as a necessity. The fragmentation of leadership in Congress resulting from the committee system and lack of strong party leadership renders that body incapable of developing a legislative program. Consequently, Congress in the twentieth century has come to expect the President to present it with proposals for legislation. This does not mean, however, that Congress does whatever the President recommends; such is by no means the case, and many presidential proposals are either rejected or modified in important respects before enactment. Less than 40 percent of President Nixon's policy proposals were passed by Congress. President Jimmy Carter also had much difficulty in getting what he wanted from Congress, even though it was controlled by his own party.

Legislation often delegates significant policy-making authority to the President. Foreign-trade legislation, for example, gives the President discretionary authority to raise or lower tariff rates on imported goods. The Economic Stabilization Act of 1970 essentially gave the President a free hand, if he so chose, to institute price and wage controls to combat inflation. The result was the price-wage freeze announced in August, 1971, the subsequent Phases

II, III, and IV control programs, and then the end of price and wage controls in 1974.

In the areas of foreign and military policy, which are often difficult to differentiate, the President possesses greater constitutional power and operating freedom than in domestic policy. U.S. foreign policy is largely a creation of presidential leadership and action. American policy concerning Vietnam, as we well know, has been shaped by the Presidents in office during the past two decades. Again, the decision to seek more open and friendly relations with Communist China in the early 1970s was President Nixon's. Foreign policy is to a great extent the domain of the executive. This is true not only for the United States but for all national political systems. Can anyone think of a country in which foreign policy is dominated by the legislature?

In the developing countries (e.g., Ghana, Iraq, Thailand), the executive probably has even more influence in policy-making than in modern countries. Yehezkel Dror explains:

> Because there are few policy issues, a larger proportion of them can reach the cabinet level in developing countries; because there is often no professional civil service, the executive plays a larger role in forming public policies about most issues; because power is more highly concentrated, the political executive is free to establish policies on many more issues without worrying as much about having to build coalitions.[18]

The policy-making structure, in short, is rather simple in many developing countries; executive policy-making prevails. In such countries, too, interest groups have little impact on policy-making because of their limited independence from existent political institutions.

Reflective of the important policy-making role of the executive is that in evaluating an executive—whether the President, a state governor, or some other chief executive—our focus is on his policy-making rather than his administrative activities. Presidents, for their part, are more interested in policy initiation than administration.

## Administrative Agencies

Administrative systems throughout the world differ with respect to such characteristics as size and complexity, hierarchical organization, and degree of autonomy. Although it was once common doctrine in political science that administrative agencies only carried into effect, more or less automatically, policies determined by the "political" branches of government, it has now become axiomatic that politics and administration are blended, and that administrative agencies are often significantly involved in the development of public policy. This is particularly so given the concept of policy as what government actually does concerning particular matters. Administration can make or break a law or policy made elsewhere. For example, in the eighteenth century, Catherine II of Russia decreed the abolition of a large part of the institution of serfdom. The landowning aristocracy, which really controlled the administration of the government, was largely able to prevent the implementation of the decision. In the United States, the effectiveness of state pollution-control laws has often been blunted by heel-dragging and nonenforcement in many instances by the administering agencies.

In complex industrial societies especially, the technicality and complexity of many policy matters, the need for continuing control, and the legislators' lack of time and information, have led to the delegation of much discretionary authority, often formally recognized as rule-making power, to administrative agencies. Consequently, agencies make many decisions that have far-reaching political and policy consequences. Illustrations include the choice of weapons systems by the Department of Defense, the development of air-safety regulations by the Federal Aviation Agency, the location of highways by state highway departments, and the regulation of the volume of petroleum production until the early 1970s by such agencies as the Texas Railroad Commission. As Professor Norman Thomas comments: "It is doubtful that any modern industrial society could manage the daily operation of its public affairs without bureaucratic organizations in which officials play a major policy-making role."[19]

Agencies are also a major source of proposals for legislation in such political systems as the United States and Great Britain. Moreover, American agencies typically not only suggest needed legislation but actively lobby and otherwise seek to exert pressure for its adoption. Thus the Department of Agriculture has been known to round up pressure-group support for its price-support proposals, thereby in effect lobbying the lobbyists.

In all, there is much accuracy in the view that "policy is at the mercy of administrators."

## The Courts

Nowhere do the courts play a greater role in policy formation than in the United States. The courts, notably national and state appellate courts, have often greatly affected the nature and content of public policy through exercise of the powers of judicial review and statutory interpretation in cases brought before them.

Basically, judicial review is the power of courts to determine the constitutionality of actions of the legislative and executive branches and declare them null and void if such actions are found to be in conflict with the Constitution. Clearly, the Supreme Court was making policy when, in various cases up to 1937, it held that no legislature, state or national, had constitutional authority to regulate minimum wages. After 1937, the Constitution was found (i.e., interpreted) to permit such legislation. Clearly, too, in recent years the Court has helped shape public policy by holding that segregated school systems, prayers in public schools, and malapportionment of state legislatures were unconstitutional. The thrust of policy is importantly affected by such decisions. Although the Court has used its power of judicial review somewhat sparingly, the very fact it has such power may affect the policy-making activities of the other branches. Congress may hesitate to act on some matter if there is some expectation that its action would be found unconstitutional. State supreme courts also have the power of judicial review but frequently have less discretion in its exercise because of the detailed and specific nature of most state constitutions.

Courts are also called upon to interpret and decide the meaning of statutory provisions that often are generally stated and permit conflicting interpretations. When a court accepts one interpretation rather than another, the consequence of its action is to give effect to the policy preference of the winning party. In 1954, the Supreme Court held, counter to the wishes of the Federal Power Commission and others, that the Natural Gas Act of 1938 not only authorized but required the agency to regulate the wellhead (or field) price of natural gas. This was a policy decision with far-reaching consequences that are still being felt.

The judiciary has played a major role in the formation of economic policy in the United States. Much of the law relating to such matters as property ownership, contracts, corporations, and employer-employee relationships has been developed and applied by the courts in the form of common law and equity. These are systems of judge-made law fashioned over the years on a case-to-case basis. They originated in England but have been adapted to American needs and conditions by American judges. Much of this law was developed by the state courts, and much of it is still applied by them.[20]

Judicial activism is nothing new, although in the past it was confined mostly to the areas of economic regulation and law enforcement. In the last two decades, and especially in the last few years, the courts have ventured into many areas of social and political activity that previously had been considered pretty much off-limits. Legislative apportionment, the rights of welfare recipients, the operation of public institutions such as prisons and hospitals, and the location of public facilities are primary examples. Not only are the courts getting involved but they are playing a more positive role in policy formation, specifying not only what government cannot do but also what it must do to meet legal or constitutional obligations. For instance, the Supreme Court, in a 1973 case, declared several states' abortion-control laws at issue unconstitutional as a violation of the privacy protected by the First Amendment. It then went on to specify the standards future laws would have to meet if they are to be constitutional. The growing impact of government on people's lives, the refusal or failure of the legislative and executive branches to act on many problems, the willingness of the courts to become involved, and the increasing litigiousness of at least some segments of the population probably guarantee a continuation of extended judicial involvement in policy formation in the future.

Although courts in such other countries as Canada, Australia, and West Germany have some power of judicial review, their impact on policy has been much less than that of the American courts. In the developing countries, the courts appear to have no meaningful policy-making role. The American practice of settling many important policy issues in the courts remains unique.

## UNOFFICIAL PARTICIPANTS

In-addition to the official policy-makers, many others may participate in the policy process, including interest groups, political parties, and individual citizens. They are designated as unofficial participants because, however important or dominant they may be in various situations, they themselves do not usually possess legal authority to make binding policy decisions.

## Interest Groups

Interest groups appear to play an important role in policy-making in practically all countries. Depending upon whether they are democratic or dictatorial, modern or developing, countries may differ with respect to how groups are constituted and how legitimate they are. Thus, groups appear to be more numerous and to operate much more openly and freely in the United States or Great Britain than they do in the Soviet Union. In all systems, however, groups perform an interest articulation function; that is, they express demands and present alternatives for policy action. They may also supply public officials with much information, often of a technical sort, concerning the nature and possible consequences of policy proposals. In doing so, they contribute to the rationality of policy-making.

Interest groups, such as those representing organized labor, business, and agriculture, are a major source of demands for policy action by public officials in the United States. Given the pluralist nature of American society, it is not surprising that pressure groups are many in number and quite diverse in their interests, size, organization, and style of operation. This does not mean, however, that some societal interests may not be poorly represented, if at all, by groups. Migrant workers are a case in point. Typically, the concern of an interest group is to influence policy in a specific subject area. Because several groups often have conflicting desires on a particular policy issue, public officials are confronted with the necessity of having to choose from among, or reconcile, conflicting demands. Groups that are well organized and active are likely to fare better than groups whose potential membership is poorly organized and inarticulate. The group struggle is not a contest among equals.

The influence of interest groups upon decisions depends on a number of factors. These may include (subject to the rule of *ceteris paribus*—other things being equal) the size of the group's membership, its monetary and other resources, its cohesiveness, the skill of its leadership, its social status, the presence or absence of competing organizations, the attitudes of public officials, and the site of decision-making in the political system. (On this last item, recall the discussion of institutionalism in Chapter 1.) Again other things being equal, a large, well-regarded group (e.g., the American Legion) will have more influence than a smaller, less well-regarded group (e.g., the League for Soviet-American Friendship). Or, a union with a large membership will have more influence than one with few members. Also, as a consequence of the factors enumerated here, a group may have a strong or controlling influence on decisions in one policy area and little, if any, influence in another. Whereas, the National Association of Manufacturers has much influence on some economic issues, it has little impact in the area of civil rights.

In recent years, there has been an expansion in the number of "single issue" interest groups, groups who focus their attention on a single issue or set of related issues such as gun control, milk prices, and abortion legislation. The proliferation of subcommittees in Congress with narrow jurisdictions has both stimulated the development of such groups and contributed to their importance by permitting concentration of their efforts. Some single issue groups of the past that had substantial effects on public policy were those advocating the abolition of slavery, women's suffrage, and nationwide prohibition.

In a study of the strength of pressure groups generally in the American states, Zeigler and van Dalen focused on the impact of three variables: strength of party competition, legislative cohesion (strength of parties in the legislature), and the socioeconomic variables of urban population per capita income and industrial employment.[21] Two patterns emerged from his analysis. Strong pressure groups (their particular purposes aside) seemed to be associated with weak parties, both electorally and legislatively, low urban population, low per capita income, and a higher rate of nonindustrial employment (agriculture, fishing, and forestry). Moderate or weak pressure groups seemed associated with strong, competitive parties and higher rates of urban population, per capita income, and industrial employment. Their study represents a systematic attempt to discover what affects group strength, although the findings should be viewed as suggestive rather than conclusive. Moreover, it should be kept in mind that they were not concerned with the strength of particular groups.

## Political Parties

In the United States, political parties are concerned primarily with contesting elections in order to control the personnel of government. They are, in short, concerned more with power than with policy. This situation has often led to the complaint that the Republican and Democratic parties represent a choice between Tweedledee and Tweedledum, and that, so far as public policy is concerned, it makes little difference which party is in office. Although the parties are not highly policy-oriented, such complaints ignore the meaningful impact that the parties have on policy.

Clearly, the parties appeal to different segments of society. Thus, the Democratic Party draws disproportionately from big city, labor, and minority and ethnic voters; the Republican Party draws disproportionately from rural, small town, and suburban areas, Protestants, and businessmen and professionals. The parties often come into conflict on such issues as welfare programs, labor legislation, business regulation, public power projects, public housing, and agricultural price-support legislation. The reader should not have much difficulty in differentiating between the parties on these issues. Given such policy inclinations, and the fact that party members in Congress often vote in accordance with party policy positions, which party controls Congress or the Presidency has important policy implications.

In the American state legislatures, the importance of political parties varies significantly. In one-party states, it is obvious that parties do not exercise much discipline over legislative voting, and the party has little, if any, effect on policy-making, as in the Texas and Louisiana legislatures. In contrast, in such states as Connecticut and Michigan both parties are active and cohesive and have considerable impact on legislative decision-making. When conflict over policy occurs in such states, the function of parties is to provide alternatives. In many cities, an effort has been made to eliminate party influence on policy through the use of nonpartisan elections for city officials. Policy is supposed to be made "objectively." An unintended consequence of nonpartisanship, it might be noted, is a reduction of interest and participation in politics.

In modern societies generally, political parties often perform a function of "interest aggregation"—that is, they seek to convert the particular demands of interest groups into general policy alternatives. The way in which parties "aggregate" interests is affected by the number of parties. In predominantly two-party systems, such as the United States and Great Britain, the desire of the parties to gain widespread electoral support "will require both parties to include in their policy 'package' those demands which have very broad popular support and to attempt to avoid alienating the most prominent groups."[22] In multiparty systems, on the other hand, parties may do less aggregating and act as the representatives of fairly narrow sets of interests, as appears to be the case in France. Generally, though, parties have a broader range of policy concerns than do interest groups; hence, they will act more as brokers than as advocates of particular interests in policy formation. In some one-party systems, such as the Soviet Union, they are the predominant force in policy-making.

## The Individual Citizen

In discussions of policy-making, the individual citizen is often neglected in the concern with legislatures, interest groups, and more prominent participants. This is unfortunate, as the individual often does seem to make a difference. Although the task of policy-making is generally assigned to public officials, in various instances citizens still participate directly in decision-making. In some of the American states (notably California) and some countries (such as Switzerland), citizens can and do still vote directly on legislation. Moreover, in most of the states, constitutional amendments are submitted to the voters for approval. In many local jurisdictions, bond issues and increases in tax rates must be authorized directly by the voters. In Texas the approval of voters in local governmental units is required for local sales taxes, the sale of liquor by the drink, and the operation of bingo games. A great many citizens, of course, do not avail themselves of these opportunities to shape policy directly because of inertia or indifference.

This leads to a frequently made point, namely, that citizen participation in policy-making, even in democratic politics, is thin. Many people do not vote, engage in party activity, join pressure groups, or even display much interest in politics. Survey research indicates, moreover, that voters are influenced comparatively little by policy considerations when voting for candidates for public office. Granting this, it still does not hold that citizens have no impact on policy except in the limited situations mentioned in the preceding paragraphs. Let us note some possibilities.

Even in authoritarian regimes, the interests or desires of common citizens are consequential for public policies.[23] The old-style dictator will pay some attention to what his people want in order to keep down unrest. As a Latin American dictator supposedly once said, "You can't shoot everyone." Modern totalitarian regimes, such as the Soviet Union, also seem concerned to meet many citizen wants even as they exclude citizens from more direct participation in policy formation. Thus, in recent years the Soviet regime has increased production of consumer goods and has even indicated a desire to surpass the United States in the level of consumer benefits.

Elections in democratic countries may serve indirectly to reinforce official responsiveness to citizen interests. As Charles Lindblom summarizes the argument:

> The most conspicuous difference between authoritarianism and democratic regimes is that in democratic regimes citizens choose their top policy makers in genuine elections. Some political scientists speculate that voting in genuine elections may be an important method of citizen influence on policy not so much because it actually permits citizens to choose their officials and to some degree instruct these officials on policy, but because the existence of genuine elections put[s] a stamp of approval on citizen participation. Indirectly, therefore, the fact of elections enforces on proximate policy makers a rule that citizens' wishes count in policy making.[24]

The "rule" Lindblom refers to is sometimes expressed in the aphorism that citizens have a right to be heard and officials have a duty to listen. The effect of such considerations on policy-makers is worth thinking about, although they are not amenable to rigorous measurement, given the present state of political science.

Some presidential elections in the United States have been classified as "critical" because they produce major realignments in voter coalitions and shifts in public policy. The presidential election of 1932 is a prime example. The Republican and Democratic candidates differed substantially on how they proposed to deal with the crisis of the Great Depression. The voters gave Franklin D. Roosevelt and the Democrats an overwhelming victory. The flood of New Deal legislation which followed produced major changes in government-economy relationships and in the role of government in American society generally. In such instances, large numbers of newly elected officials, chosen because of their stand on the critical question, enact legislation consistent with their party's stand. The voters, through the electoral process, help to produce basic changes in public policy. Other critical elections were those of 1860 and 1896.[25]

Some observers initially thought that the election of 1980 might have been a critical election. That, however, turned out not to be the case. The Democratic gains in the 1982 congressional elections indicated that no basic realignment in voter's allegiances had occurred. "Landslides" do not critical elections make.

Some citizens, through their intellectual activities, contribute new ideas and directions to the policy process. Thus, Rachel Carson, with her *Silent Spring,* and Ralph Nader, with his *Unsafe at Any Speed,* had a considerable impact on policy in the areas of pesticide control and automobile safety. Others, through political activism, may substantially affect policy action. Social security legislation in the 1930s was certainly affected by the activities of Dr. Francis Townsend and civil rights legislation in the 1960s by those of the Reverend Martin Luther King, Jr.

## LEVELS OF POLITICS

Not all the participants in policy-making discussed above are involved in all policy-making or decision-making situations. Some matters arouse much attention and attract a wide range of participants. Others will be less visible or

affect only a few people and will consequently stir little attention and participation. Following Emmette Redford's categories, we can distinguish three
levels of policies, based on the scope of participation normally characteristic
of each and, to a lesser extent, the kind of issue involved: micropolitics, subsystem policies, and macropolitics.[26]

Micropolitics involves efforts by individuals, companies, and communities
to secure favorable government action for themselves. Subsystem politics is
focused on particular functional areas of activity, such as airline regulation or
river and harbor improvements, and involve interrelationships among
congressional committees, administrative agencies (or bureaus), and interest
groups. Macropolitics occurs when "the community at large and the leaders
of government as a whole are brought into the discussion and determination
of [public] policy."[27]

## Micropolitics

Micropolitics often occurs when an individual seeks a favorable ruling from
an administrative agency or a special bill exempting her from a requirement
of the immigration laws, when a company seeks a favorable change in the tax
code or a television broadcasting license, or when a community seeks a grant
for construction of an airport or opposes the location of a public housing
project in its area. What is involved in each of these instances is the specific,
differentiated, and intense interest of one or a few in a society of many individuals, companies, and communities. What is required, or sought, is a decision applicable to one or a few. Typically, only a few persons and officials
will be involved in, or even aware of, such decision-making situations, however important they may be for those seeking action, and whatever the ultimate consequences of such decisions or a cluster of them may be.

In the short run at least, micropolitical decisions appear to be distributive
and can be made without concern for limited resources. That is, such decisions appear to affect only those immediately concerned and can be made on
the basis of mutual noninterference, with each seeking benefits (or subsidies)
for himself and not opposing or interfering with the efforts of others to do
likewise. Benefits received by one individual or group do not appear to be at
the expense of other individuals or groups.

The enactment of special tax provisions by Congress is illustrative of micropolitics. Almost every year Congress enacts a number of laws that make
particular changes in the internal revenue code.[28] Their effect is to grant special treatment to particular groups or individuals and enable them not to pay
taxes they otherwise would have to pay. A notorious example is the "Louis
B. Mayer amendment," which was adopted in 1951 and saved Mayer about
$2 million in income taxes by treating income he received at retirement
from his company as capital gains. Although written in the form of general
legislation, its terms were such that it was assumed that the amendment covered only Mayer and one other person. Such legislation arouses little attention on its way through Congress and becomes law with most of the public
completely unaware of its existence. Whether these special tax bills create
"loopholes" or correct "inequities" depends upon one's perspective and
whether one benefits from them.

As government programs become more numerous and extensive, as they provide more benefits for, or impose more requirements on, individuals, groups, and communities, both the opportunity and the incentive to engage in micropolitics increases.

## Subsystem Politics

In what has become a frequently quoted passage, Ernest Griffith in 1939 called attention to the existence of political subsystems and the value of studying them.

> One cannot live in Washington for long without being conscious that it has whirlpools or centers of activity focusing on particular problems.... It is my opinion that ordinarily the relationship among these men—legislators, administrators, lobbyists, scholars—who are interested in a common problem is a much more real relationship than the relationship between congressmen generally or between administrators generally. In other words, he who would understand the prevailing pattern of our present governmental behavior, instead of studying the formal institutions or even generalizations or organs, important though all these things are, may possibly obtain a better picture of the way things really happen if he would study these "whirlpools" of special social interests and problems.[29]

Since Griffith wrote that, political scientists and others have devoted considerable attention to the examination of political subsystems (also variously called subgovernments, policy clusters, and policy coalitions).

Most commonly, a subsystem involves a pattern of stable relationships among some congressional committees (or subcommittees), an administrative agency or two, and the relevant interest groups centered around a particular policy area.[30] A well-known subsystem that focuses upon river and harbor development activity includes the congressional committees on public works, the Army Corps of Engineers, and the National Rivers and Harbors Congress. Another subsystem is concerned with the management of public grazing lands in the western states and is composed essentially of the congressional interior committees, the Bureau of Land Management, and groups representing western livestock raisers. Sometimes called "iron triangles," these subsystems are often really more complex than that phrase implies.

When new legislation is needed, subsystems must either secure the approval or avoid disapproval or veto of Congress and the executive. Moreover, events in the broader political arena may occur which bring them under scrutiny. Consider the cases of the sugar and civil aviation subsystems.

The sugar subsystem is concerned with domestic sugar prices and import quotas and involves the House Agriculture Committee, the Sugar Division of the Department of Agriculture, and representatives of the sugar industry. This subsystem fell upon hard times in 1974 when the sugar program was terminated by Congress because of strong opposition from consumer and industrial user groups who became stirred up by high sugar prices in a time of inflation. Since then, however, the sugar growers have made at least a partial comeback. After some executive action by President Carter to raise the price of sugar at the behest of growers, legislation was enacted in 1981 providing for a new sugar program. Although initially opposed to it, the Reagan Administration withdrew its opposition in order to pick up some votes for its supply-side economic program. Although the sugar subsystem lost its programmatic focus for a time, it continued to exist and to prevail again.

For civil aviation a subsystem exists composed primarily of the congressional committees on commerce and the relevant appropriations subcommittees, the Civil Aeronautics Board, and such groups as the Air Transport Association and the Airline Pilots Association. The days of this subsystem are numbered, however. On the basis of deregulation legislation enacted in 1978, most economic regulation of the airlines and the CAB itself will disappear by 1985. The subsystem, partially because of some internal support for deregulation as by the CAB chairman, was unable to control what happened when airline regulation became a macropolitical issue. Together, the sugar and civil aviation examples indicate how developments in the broader political environment may disrupt subsystems. On the whole, however, subsystems display much continuity.

## Macropolitics

Some issues will attract enough attention or become sufficiently controversial as to require action in the macropolitical arena. Some issues are "born" in the macropolitical arena, such as the famous steel price crisis of 1962, the escalation of the Vietnam war, the 1981 air controllers strike, and President Reagan's proposal for a major reduction in personal income taxes. Again, a policy issue may be moved from the subsystem to the macropolitical level by the actions of public officials or others. Thus Senator Mike Monroney converted the establishment of the Federal Aviation issue in the late 1950s in an effort to secure a stronger agency to deal with airline safety. A major airplane disaster also helped by dramatizing the issue. Some matters may start at the micropolitical level and escalate into a macropolitical issue, perhaps because of their symbolic or even "scandalous" nature. The award by the Office of Economic Opportunity of a financial grant to a Chicago youth gang called the Blackstone Rangers quickly attracted wide attention and participation. A routine if somewhat ill-advised action, it added to the problems of the agency and the War on Poverty.

The central participants in macropolitics include party and congressional leaders (who may overlap), the President, and the executive departments. The communications media and a variety of group spokesmen are also often deeply involved. The range of participants is thus broad. This level of politics often attracts the most attention in studies of policy-making because it is often both quite visible and salient, as well as spectacular.

Decisions made in the macropolitical arena may be considerably different from what they would be if made at one of the other levels. Among other things, when an issue moves, say, from the subsystem to the macropolitical arena, the conflict over it is broadened. And, as E. E. Schattschneider suggests, this often changes the nature of the settlement, that is, the policy decision.[31] Broad public interests are likely to receive fullest consideration in policy-making at the macropolitical level.

A distinctive characteristic of macropolitics is presidential involvement. Whether the President more fully represents national interests than Congress, as many contend, is at least sometimes debatable. What is true, certainly, is that those interests represented by the President enjoy an advantage in the macropolitical arena. The President, because of the centrality and visibility of his office, because of his capacity to formulate policy alternatives, and because of the resources he has to use in support of his proposals, is the policy leader here. His actions will have a substantial impact on the content and direction of public policy. Compare, for example, the effect of the Johnson Administration and the Nixon Administration on antipoverty policy.

In the next chapter we will look at the formation of policy, especially as it occurs in the macropolitical arena.

## NOTES

1. Clyde Kluckhohn, *Mirror for Man* (Greenwich, Conn.: Fawcett, 1963), p. 24.
2. For an extended discussion of political culture, see Gabriel A. Almond and Sidney Verba, *The Civic Culture* (Boston: Little, Brown, 1965), and Donald J. Levine, *The Political Culture of the United States* (Boston: Little, Brown, 1972).
3. Daniel J. Elazar, *American Federalism: A View from the States* (New York: Crowell, 1966), chap. 4.
4. Robin M. Williams, Jr., *American Society,* 2d ed. (New York: Knopf, 1960), Chap. 11.
5. Levine, *op. cit.,* pp. 210–11.
6. Karl W. Deutsch, *Politics and Government* (Boston: Houghton Mifflin, 1970), p. 207.
7. Almond and Verba, *op. cit.,* pp. 11–26.
8. Deutsch, *op. cit.,* 207.
9. Cf. E. E. Schattschneider, *The Semi-Sovereign People* (New York: Holt, Rinehart and Winston, 1960), chap. 1.
10. Thomas R. Dye, *Politics, Economics, and the Public: Policy Outcomes in the Fifty States* (Chicago: Rand-McNally, 1966). Dye uses the term "policy outcome" to designate what were described as policy outputs in chap. 1, *supra.*
11. *Ibid.,* p. 293.
12. Richard Dawson and James Robinson, "The Relation Between Public Policy and Some Structural and Environmental Variables in the American States," *Journal of Politics,* XXV (May, 1963), pp. 265–89.
13. *Ibid.,* p. 289.
14. Robert H. Salisbury, "The Analysis of Public Policy," in Austin Ranney (ed.), *Political Science and Public Policy* (Chicago: Markham, 1968), p. 164.
15. Ira Sharkansky and Richard I. Hofferbert, "Dimensions of State Policy," in Herbert Jacob and Kenneth N. Vines (eds.), *Politics in the American States,* 2d ed., (Boston: Little, Brown, 1972), esp. pp. 318–23.
16. *Ibid.,* p. 320.
17. *Ibid.,* p. 321. Cf. Robert L. Lineberry and Edmund P. Fowler, "Reformism and Public Policies in American Cities," *American Political Science Review,* LXI (September, 1967), pp. 701–16.
18. Yehezkel Dror, *Public Policymaking Reexamined* (Scranton, Pa.: Chandler, 1968), p. 118.
19. Norman C. Thomas, *Rule 9: Politics, Administration, and Civil Rights* (New York: Random House, 1966), p. 6.

20. Emmette S. Redford, *American Government and the Economy* (New York: Macmillan, 1965), pp. 53–54.
21. Harmon Zeigler and Hendrick van Dalen, "Interest Groups in the States," in Herbert Jacob and Kenneth N. Vines (eds.), *Politics in the American States,* 2d ed. (Boston: Little, Brown, 1971), pp. 126–27.
22. Gabriel A. Almond and G. Bingham Powell, Jr., *Comparative Politics: A Developmental Approach* (Boston: Little, Brown, 1966), p. 103.
23. This discussion draws on Charles E. Lindblom, *The Policy-Making Process* (Englewood Cliffs, N.J.: Prentice-Hall, 1968), p. 44.
24. *Ibid.,* p. 45.
25. For further discussion, see James R. Sundquist, *Dynamics of the Party System: Alignment and Realignment of Party Systems in the United States* (Washington: Brookings Institution, 1972); David W. Brady, "Critical Elections, Congressional Parties and Clusters of Policy Changes," *British Journal of Political Science,* VIII (January, 1978), pp. 79–99; and Warren E. Miller and J. Merrill Shanks, "Policy Directions and Presidential Leadership: Alternative Interpretations of the 1980 Presidential Election," *British Journal of Political Science,* XII (July, 1982), pp. 299–358.
26. Emette S. Redford, *Democracy in the Administrative State* (New York: Oxford University Press, 1969), p. 107.
27. *Ibid,* p. 53.
28. Stanley S. Surrey, "The Congress and the Tax Lobbyist—How Special Tax Provisions Get Enacted," *Harvard Law Review,* LXX (May, 1957), pp. 1145–1182.
29. Ernest S. Griffith, *The Impasse of Democracy* (New York: Harrison-Hilton Books, 1938), p. 182.
30. The subsystem concept is discussed in J. Leiper Freeman, *The Political Process,* rev. ed. (New York: Random House, 1965).
31. Schattschneider, *op. cit,* chap. 4.

# 3

# Policy Formation and Adoption

The nature of public problems and three aspects of policy formation will be considered in this chapter: how public problems come to the attention of policy-makers; how policy proposals are formulated to deal with particular problems; and how a specific proposal is chosen for adoption from among the competing alternatives. The legislature will be the primary institutional focus of the discussion. It should be kept in mind that the items listed are functional categories of activities. While they can be distinguished for the purpose of analysis, in actuality they are often blended. For instance, someone formulating a policy proposal will often do so with the need to win support for its adoption as one of the factors guiding her efforts.

## POLICY PROBLEMS

Studies of policy formation usually give little attention to the nature of public problems. They are taken as given, and analysis proceeds from there. Some, indeed, would contend that the substance of policy problems falls outside the concern of political science. Yet, policy analysis that does not consider the dimensions of the problems that stimulate governmental action, and to which policy is directed, is less than complete. The nature of the problem— for example, whether it is foreign or domestic—helps determine the nature of the policy process. Again, the evaluation of policy requires information on the substance of the original problem in order to assess effectiveness, among other things.

For policy purposes, a problem can be formally defined as a condition or situation that produces needs or dissatisfactions on the part of people for which relief or redress is sought. This may be done by those directly affected or by others acting on their behalf.[1] Such matters as low incomes, unclean air, unwholesome food, the actions of a foreign government, or trial court procedures may become problems if they produce sufficient anxiety, tensions, or dissatisfaction as to cause people to seek relief or redress. The point to be made here is that there are all kinds of needs and problems. Only those that move people to action become policy problems. Thus, when a group, for example, has low income but accepts this condition and neither does anything about it nor somehow elicits actions by others in its behalf, then, according to the stated definition, no problem exists. Problems do not become such if they are not articulated.

This leads to a second point. Matters can be defined as problems, and therefore relief sought, by persons other than those directly affected. Thus, in the mid-1960s, poverty was defined as a public problem, and a war on poverty was declared more because of the actions of public officials and others, such as publicists, than because of the actions of the poor themselves. Of course, there is always the possibility that problems will be defined differently by those directly affected than by others.

A third point is that the definition of a problem is a political process whose outcome will affect the solutions sought. Take the energy "crisis" (or problem) as an example. Does it essentially involve the wasteful and excessive use of energy by Americans; public policies which have discouraged adequate discovery and development of energy resources; an effort by the Organization of Petroleum Exporting Countries and the petroleum companies to drive up the price of oil; excessive dependence upon petroleum because of failure to exploit nuclear, solar, and other energy sources? some combination of these, or something else? Most or all can agree that there is an inadequate supply of energy, especially at prices people find "reasonable." This, however, is really a symptom of the basic problem; that is, the conditions or circumstances which cause the short supply. People do not agree on such matters. Whose definition prevails will help shape priorities in policy-making on the problem.

A fourth point is that while problems are persistent, how they are defined may change over time. Let us take alcoholism (drunkenness) as an illustration. In the nineteenth century, drunkenness was viewed as a personal problem, the result of one's evil, wicked, or sinful ways, and therefore as one's just deserts. Early in the twentieth century, it became more common to view drunkenness as a social problem, as the response of some individuals to the social, family, and other pressures placed upon them. More recently, alcoholism (not drunkenness) has been defined as an illness (i.e., a pathological condition) requiring medical treatment, whatever its immediate personal causes. As the definition of the problem has changed, so have the social attitudes toward it tended to change. Public policy, however, has not fully caught up with the current definition.

Our concern now is not merely with problems but with *public* problems. Thus the question: What characteristics or qualities make a problem public? Most people would agree that the fact that John Smith's car is out of gasoline is a private problem, however disturbing to Smith it might be, whereas the widespread shortage of gasoline in a community or region is a public problem. What distinguishes private from public problems? Essentially, we can say that public problems are those that have a broad effect, including consequences for persons not directly involved.[2] Problems that have a limited effect, being of concern only to one or a few persons who are directly involved, can be viewed as private. Admittedly, this is not a very sharp set of definitions. An illustration may help convey the notion. Assume that an individual is unhappy with his tax burden under the existing tax laws. Acting on his own, he may seek a favorable administrative ruling to reduce his burden, or he may try to induce his representative in Congress to sponsor an amendment to the tax laws that will lessen his tax obligation. Our imaginary citizen has a problem, but it is essentially private. As another alternative, he may seek to publicize his problem and enlist in the cause others in a similar situation. A bill may be introduced in the legislature and a campaign for it launched, which actions, in turn, draw opposition. Directly or indirectly, many people become involved or perceive themselves as being affected. A public problem exists.

Many of the problems that are acted upon by government, it should be remarked, are really private problems. To a great extent, the micropolitical level of politics discussed in Chapter 2 is focused on private problems. Moreover, much of the time of many members of Congress is devoted to "case work," which involves providing assistance to individual constituents in their personal relationships with administrative agencies.

A large number and variety of public problems exist in the United States, and they can be categorized in many ways. One distinction is between procedural and substantive problems. Procedural problems relate to how government is organized, and how it conducts its operations and activities. Substantive problems are concerned with the actual consequences of human activity, whether it involves free speech, the sale of used cars, or environmental pollution. Another distinction, which is based on their origins, can be made between foreign and domestic problems. Within the domestic area, we encounter education, taxation, crime, transportation, welfare, and other problems. These really are sets of problems; for example, what is often referred to as the "welfare problem" is really a variety of problems related to the aged, the working poor, families with dependent children, and so on.

Drawing on Theodore Lowi's work,[3] problems can also be categorized as distributive, regulatory, and redistributive. This classification depends upon the number of people affected and their relationships with one another. Distributive problems involve small numbers of people and can be treated one by one: for example, the quests of communities for flood-control projects, industries for tariff concessions, and companies for governmental contracts. Regulatory problems produce demands for the restriction or limitation of the actions of others. Those who feel aggrieved by the actions of labor unions may call for regulation of their activities to prevent undesired consequences. Redistributive problems are those that call for the transfer of resources among large groups, or classes, in society. Those who define income inequality as a public problem often demand graduated income taxes and other public policies intended to transfer resources from the haves to the have-nots. Proposed policies to deal with redistribution problems are customarily highly productive of conflict and tend to involve class conflict or something akin thereto.

Before leaving this discussion of problems, it should be stressed that whether some condition or situation is regarded as a problem depends not only on its objective dimensions but also, and more importantly, on the way in which it is perceived by people. Take as an illustration the "farm problem" in the United States during the 1950s, 1960s, and early 1980s. Essentially, the problem was that of "surplus" production, which would not move in the market at prices agreeable to farmers. (It was not surplus in the sense that no one, anywhere, would not use it at some price.) For a great many nations in the world, this abundance would have been viewed as a blessing rather than a "problem." In the United States, given the frame of reference and context in which it was viewed, it was a problem. Again, whether there is an "energy crisis," and whether this is a public problem requiring governmental action, depends upon its being defined or perceived as such. Initially, petroleum company executives were more likely to see it as a public problem requiring favorable (to them) government action than were critics of the petroleum industry. Now most people have come to accept the existence of an energy crisis. They do not agree, however, as to the nature of the problem or its causes.

This leads us to another topic for consideration—namely, why are some matters, apart from the breadth of their consequences, seen as public problems requiring action, while others are not? Some insight into this question should be provided by the following discussion of the policy agenda.

## THE POLICY AGENDA

One constantly hears or reads about demands being made by this group or that individual for action by some governmental body on some problem, whether it be rough streets or crime therein, the high price of meat, or industrial monopoly. Of the thousands and thousands of demands made upon government, only a small portion receive serious attention from public policy-makers. Those demands that policy-makers either do choose or feel compelled to act upon constitute the *policy agenda*.[4] Thus, the policy agenda is distinguishable from political demands generally. It can also be distinguished from the term "political priorities," which usually designates a ranking of agenda items, with some being considered more important or pressing than others.

To achieve agenda status, a public problem must be converted into an *issue*. As Eyestone comments: "An issue arises when a public with a problem seeks or demands governmental action, and there is public disagreement over the best solution to the problem."[5] A rising crime rate is a public problem, disagreement over what to do about it, if anything, becomes an issue. In recent years important public issues have involved such matters as school prayers, sex discrimination, inflation, oil price deregulation, the Soviet grain embargo, and campaign finance reform.

There will be a number of policy agendas in a political system. Cobb and Elder identify two basic types of agendas: the systemic agenda and the institutional, or governmental, agenda. The systemic agenda "consists of all issues that are commonly perceived by members of the political community as meriting public attention and as involving matters within the legitimate jurisdiction of existing governmental authority."[6] A systemic agenda will exist in every national, state, and local political system. Some items, such as crime in the streets, will appear on more than one systemic agenda, while others, such as whether to recognize the People's Republic of China or build a new convention center, will appear only on the national and local agenda, respectively.

The systemic agenda is essentially a discussion agenda. Action on a problem requires that it be brought before a governmental institution with authority to take appropriate action. An institutional or governmental agenda is composed of those problems to which public officials feel obliged to give serious and active attention. Since there are a variety of points at which policy decisions can be made, there are also a variety of institutional agendas. At the national level, one finds congressional, presidential, administrative, and judicial agendas. An institutional agenda is an action agenda and will be more specific and concrete than a systemic agenda. Where crime in the streets may be of systemic concern, Congress will be confronted with more specific proposals for dealing with this problem area—for example, financial aid to local law-enforcement agencies.

Institutional agenda items can be separated into old items and new items, to use a not very imaginative pair of categories. Old items are those that appear with some regularity on agendas—for example, public employee pay increases, congressional reform, social security benefit increases, or budget allocations. They are familiar to officials, and the alternatives for dealing with them are somewhat patterned. New items are generated by particular situations or events, such as a nationwide railroad strike or a foreign policy crisis, or by the development of broad support for action on such issues as gun control or air-pollution abatement. Old items, it is suggested, "tend to receive priority from decision-makers, who constantly find their time is limited and that their agenda is overloaded.... Decision-makers presume that older problems warrant more attention because of their longevity and the greater familiarity officials have with them."[7] Of course, problems that reach the agenda as new items may, over time, be converted into old items. Environmental pollution and the Vietnam war are illustrative examples.

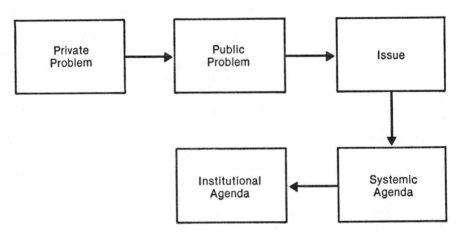

Figure 3.1
The Agenda Formation Process

It should be noted that a policy agenda is not necessarily highly structured or defined. It would probably not be possible to get complete agreement on the content of a particular agenda, whether it is that of Congress or of a city council. Yet, clues to the content of the congressional agenda are provided by presidential messages, legislation singled out by party leaders for attention, issues discussed in the communication media, and the like. Inability to enumerate all the items on a policy agenda does not destroy the usefulness of the concept for policy analysis.

Some of the ways in which issues achieve institutional agenda status were hinted at earlier. More thorough treatment of this topic, which is commonly designated as agenda-building, is now in order. At any given time many issues will be contending for the attention of public officials; however, only a few will succeed because officials lack the time, resources, interest, or will to consider all of them. Thus agenda-building is a competitive political process. What determines, then, whether an issue secures a place on an agenda? We will present a few alternatives.

One possibility is suggested by political scientist David Truman in his book on interest groups. Truman says that groups seek to maintain themselves in a state of reasonable equilibrium, and, if anything threatens this condition, they react accordingly.

> When the equilibrium of a group (and the equilibrium of its participant individuals) is seriously disturbed, various kinds of behavior may ensue. If the disturbance is not too great, the group's leaders will make an effort to restore the previous balance.... this effort may immediately necessitate recourse to the government. Other behaviors may occur if the disturbance is serious to the point of disruption.[8]

Thus American steel producers, seeing cheaper imported steel as contrary to their price and profit situation, seek limitations on steel imports. Savings and loan institutions, pinched by inflation and the competition from other lending institutions, seek and obtain government action to improve their financial situation. Moreover, when one group gets what it wants from government, this may cause a reaction by other groups, as in the case of organized labor's continued efforts after 1947 to secure repeal or modification of the Taft-Hartley Act. Interest groups thus are often able to place issues on an institutional agenda, but they by no means account for all issues achieving agenda status.[9]

Political leadership may be an important factor in agenda setting. Political leaders, whether motivated by considerations of political advantage, concern for the public interest, or both, may seize upon particular problems, publicize them, and propose solutions. Of particular importance here is the President because of his prominent role as an agenda-setter in American politics. presidential legislative recommendations almost automatically go on the congressional agenda, as did the Reagan Administration's recommendations to relax some of the pollution-control standards of the Clean Air Act and the Carter Administration's proposal to establish a Department of Energy. Members of Congress may also sometimes act as agenda setters. Area redevelopment legislation became a significant issue in the late 1950s and early 1960s largely through the efforts of Senator Paul Douglas, who first encountered the problem of depressed areas while campaigning in southern Illinois. Senator Edmund Muskie was for years a policy leader in the area of environmental pollution control. In a study of agenda setting in the U.S. Senate, Professor Jack Walker concludes that there are some "Activist legislators, motivated by a desire to promote social change and anxious to gain reputations as reformers [who] constantly search for issues that might be transformed into new items on the Senate's discretionary agenda."[10]

Items may achieve agenda status and be acted upon as a consequence of some kind of crisis or spectacular event, such as a coal mine accident or a natural disaster. This serves to dramatize an issue and attract wide attention, causing public officials to feel compelled to respond. There may be awareness, discussion, and continued advocacy of action on some matter; but, without broad interest being stirred or policy action obtained, some sort of "triggering" event seems needed to push the matter onto the policy agenda.[11] Thus the Soviet launching of the first Sputnik in 1957 helped push space exploration onto the policy agenda in the United States, notwithstanding initial professed lack of concern by some Eisenhower Administration officials. The furor touched off by the revelation that a sedative drug called thalidomide caused birth defects in babies when taken by pregnant women, and that it was not being marketed in the United States only because of the opposition of some officials in the Food and Drug Administration, made strengthening of drug licensing laws a major issue and eventuated in the Food and Drug Amendments of 1962. Indeed, until the 1960s it seemed that some kind of crisis event was required before major food or drug legislation was enacted.[12]

Protest activity, including violence, is another means by which problems may be brought to the attention of policy-makers and put on the policy agenda.[13] During the 1960s, such actions as the sit-in movement, the voters-right march in Selma, Alabama (and the brutal reaction by the Selma police), and the 1963 "March on Washington" helped keep civil rights issues at the top of the national political agenda. The riots in many Northern cities in the mid-1960s focused attention on the problems of urban blacks. A sociologist, discussing the effects of the 1965 Watts riot in Los Angeles, states: "The riot appears to have stemmed, at least in part, from frustrated efforts of the community to call attention to its plight. It seems to have been a call for help ... where other means to draw attention to the community's distress seemed socially unavailable.[14] In more recent years, groups concerned with women's rights have utilized various kinds of demonstrations in their efforts to move their concerns onto the political agenda, and with some success. The gays also have taken to the streets to call attention to their problems.

Particular problems or issues may attract the attention of the communications media and, through their reportage, either be converted into agenda items or, if already on the agenda, be given more salience. A classic example is the activities of the Pulitzer and Hearst newspapers in the 1890s, through their highly colored and often inaccurate reporting, in making Spain's treatment of its colonies, especially Cuba, a major issue and doing much to cause the United States eventually to declare war on Spain.[15] In the mid-1960s, once poverty became a major agenda item, the news media helped keep the war on poverty in the public's eye by reporting fully many of the difficulties and errors in the conduct of the antipoverty campaign. Minor events, such as a disturbance in a Job Corps camp or the misuse of a comparatively small sum of money, often were treated as major news items. Whether the news media are motivated by a desire to "create" news, report all that is newsworthy, stimulate sales, or serve the public interest is not under consideration here. Whatever their motives, as important opinion-shapers they help structure the political agenda. While both the conventions concerning how the news media are to operate and the compelling force of some events will limit somewhat the discretion the media have in selecting the events they call to the public's attention, they nonetheless do have much leeway.[16]

My purpose here has been to emphasize the variety of ways in which problems reach the policy agenda in order to illustrate this phase of the policy process.[17] I have not sought to present all the alternatives, assuming that this would be possible. It should also be apparent that all public problems do not reach the policy agenda. Policy-makers do not feel compelled to deal with some problems. To account for their inaction, the concept of *nondecision* appears as a useful analytical and explanatory tool.

Nondecision-making has been defined by Peter Bachrach and Morton Baratz as "a means by which demands for change in the existing allocation of benefits and privileges in the community can be suffocated before they are even voiced; or kept covert; or killed before they gain access to the relevant decision-making arena; or failing all these things, maimed or destroyed in the decision-implementing stage of the policy process."[18] There are various ways by which problems may be kept off a systemic or institutional agenda. At the local level, particularly, force may be utilized, as in the South during the 1950s and 1960s by various white groups to stifle black demands for equal rights. Another possibility is that prevailing values and beliefs—political culture—may operate to deny agenda status to particular problems or policy alternatives. Public acceptance of the graduated income tax has operated to deny agenda status to demands of the radical right for its repeal. Our beliefs concerning private property and capitalism have kept the issue of railroad nationalization from ever becoming a real agenda item, even in the late nineteenth and early twentieth centuries, when railroad policy was being developed, except when particular facets of railroad operations, such as passenger service (witness Amtrak), become unprofitable for private enterprise.

A third possibility has been suggested by E. E. Schattschneider. "The crucial problem in politics," he states, "is the management of conflict. No regime could endure that did not cope with this problem. All politics, all leadership, all organization involves the management of conflict. All conflict allocates space in the political universe. The consequences of conflict are so important that it is inconceivable that any regime would survive without making an attempt to shape the system." To survive, then, political leaders and organizations must prevent problems or issues that would threaten their existence from reaching the political arena (that is, achieving agenda status). The kinds of problems they are resistant to will depend upon what kinds of leaders and organizations they are, whether, for example, conservative Republicans or independent commissions. They will in any case resist considering some problems, for, as Schattschneider contends, "all forms of political organization have a bias in favor of the exploitation of some kinds of conflicts and the suppression of others because *organization is the mobilization of bias.* Some issues are organized into politics while others are organized out."[19]

In the study of the public policy-making it is important to know why some problems are dealt with and others are neglected or suppressed. Recall that public policy is determined not only by what government does do but also by what it does not do. Take the situation of migratory farm workers, whose problems usually receive short shrift from the public officials. Why is this the case? What does an answer to this question tell us about who gets what, and why, from the policy process? Is the neglect of migrant workers at least partly due to nondecision-making? Notwithstanding the somewhat imprecise nature of the concept of nondecision, it has utility for the analysis of the policy process.

## Two Cases in Agenda Setting

To illustrate the agenda concept futher, brief consideration will be given to how two recent problems, of substantially different content and scope, achieved agenda status. One is coal mine safety; the other is environmental pollution control.

Coal mining has long been a highly hazardous occupation, marked by a high rate of accidental injuries and deaths. Initially, coal mining was regulated by the states, but, because of dissatisfaction with their activities, federal regulation was sought by miners and their supporters, and obtained with the Coal Mine Safety Act of 1952. Enforcement of the Act was handled by the Bureau of Mines, which was often criticized as being too favorable toward the interests of mineowners. Frequent accidents continued, but for nearly two decades nothing was really done to strengthen mine-safety policy, even though the technology to improve safety conditions without major declines in production was available. Coal mining is concentrated in a few areas of the country, such as West Virginia and southern Illinois, and most people are both relatively unaffected by, and unaware of, the problems of miners.

Then, on November 20, 1968, an explosion occurred at the Consolidated Coal Company's No. 9 mine in West Virginia. Seventy-nine miners were trapped below the surface, and all died before they could be rescued. This tragedy focused national attention on the miners' plight, which included not only mine explosions and accidents but also black-lung disease, caused by the inhalation of coal dust. The miners staged protest meetings, engaged in wildcat strikes, and conducted other activities, including a march on the West Virginia state capitol, in demand of remedial action. Public officials felt compelled to respond. In March, 1969, the West Virginia legislature enacted a law providing for compensation of victims of black-lung disease.

The miners and their spokesmen continued to press for national legislation, with a nationwide coal strike being repeatedly threatened if action were not forthcoming. President Nixon responded by sending Congress a special message, along with a draft bill, on coal mine safety. The bill was stronger than one previously proposed by President Johnson. In October, the Senate passed a mine-safety bill by a vote of 73 to 0, and a few weeks later the House did so by a 389 to 4 vote. It was subsequently signed into law by President Nixon.

Environmental pollution is a long-standing feature of our society, but only in the past decade has it become a major public problem. Where, for example, belching factory smokestacks were once regarded as a sign of progress, now they are generally viewed as problems requiring control. Both the national and state governments have enacted a variety of pollution-control legislation, and demands for additional, and stronger, legislation continue.

Several factors have contributed to making pollution control an important item on the policy agenda.[20] The affluence of American society contributes in several ways to the problem of pollution. As Davies explains:

> The increase in production has contributed to an intensification of the degree of actual pollution; the increase in the standard of living has permitted people the comparative luxury of being able to be concerned about this; and the availability of ample public and private resources has given the society sufficient funds and skilled manpower to provide the potential for dealing with the problem.

People who are compelled to be continually concerned with securing the necessities of life will probably have little time or inclination to worry about pollution. In the developing countries, one will note little concern for the problem. Indeed, it is probably not perceived as a problem. In an affluent society, on the other hand, the conditions of life contribute to concern over pollution. More leisure time leads to greater demands for recreational resources and aesthetic pleasures, while a higher level of education enables people to understand better the nature and dangers of pollution. One can usefully regard pollution control as a "middle class issue," which helps ensure governmental attention to it.

Pollution control is an attractive public issue. It affects everyone, and a program that does something for everyone tends to be quite attractive politically. Moreover, it is difficult to oppose pollution control—except indirectly, as by contending that pollution standards increase energy use and thus contribute to the energy crisis—because one cannot win many political allies by openly favoring dirty air and water. In addition, pollution control is often tied to public health, which is another popular concern. As the old song has it, "Everybody wants to go to heaven, but nobody wants to die."

Finally, when government acts on the pollution problem, it helps create a demand for additional action. The problem is publicized and given respectability, and the public learns that something can be done to alleviate the problem. Moreover, when agencies are established to administer pollution-control programs, they develop vested interests in drawing attention to the programs. This, in turn, may lead to the development of group support for the program, an institutionalization of concern, and a continuous demand for action. The experience of the national Environmental Protection Agency is a case in point. Pollution control appears highly likely to remain on the policy agenda at all levels of government for years to come.

## THE FORMULATION OF POLICY PROPOSALS

Policy formulation involves the development of pertinent and acceptable proposed courses of action for dealing with public problems. Policy formulation does not always result in a proposed law, executive order, or administrative rule. Policy-makers may decide not to take positive action on some problem but, instead, to leave it alone, to let matters work themselves out. In other words, the fact that a public problem is on the policy agenda does not mean that positive government action will be taken. Congress wrestled with the problem of railroad regulation for two decades, and considered many policy proposals, before it finally enacted the Interstate Commerce Act of 1887. General federal aid to education was before Congress off and on for several decades before legislation was finally enacted in 1965. Awareness of a problem does not guarantee positive government action, although unawareness or nonconcern pretty much ensures inaction.

## Who Is Involved?

In this discussion of who is involved in the development of policy proposals, attention will be focused on the national level in the United States. In the twentieth century, the President and his chief aides and advisers in the Executive Office have been the major source of initiative in the development of policy proposals. The members of Congress have come to expect the President to present policy recommendations to them for consideration. Moreover, they have also come to expect the executive to provide them with draft bills embodying his recommendations. This does not mean that Congress always accepts the President's proposals; such, as you well know, is far from the case. What the members of Congress want is "some real meat to digest."

Many policy proposals are developed by officials—both career and appointed—in the administrative departments and agencies. Concerned with governmental programs in agriculture, health, law enforcement, foreign trade, and other areas, they become aware of policy problems and develop proposals to deal with them. These are transmitted to the executive and Congress for their consideration. Many such proposals will involve modification of existing laws, such as plugging up revealed loopholes. A classic case involves the soil bank legislation of 1956. It was found that the original law did not prohibit persons from leasing government grazing lands at low rates per acre while being paid much higher rates for having taken them out of "production." Corrective legislation was proposed by Department of Agriculture officials and enacted to prohibit this practice.

Special study groups or advisory commissions, composed of private citizens and officials, are sometimes created by the President to examine particular policy areas and develop policy proposals. The President's Committee on Urban Housing (1967–68) was appointed by President Johnson and charged with developing proposals to increase the production of housing for low- and moderate-income families. Many of its proposals were transmitted to Congress by the President. Such advisory commissions are employed both to develop policy proposals and to help win support for them through their usually prestigious membership. Some groups, of course, may be largely designed to give the appearance of concern and action on some problem in order to satisfy demands for action. An example is the Commission on Campus Unrest, appointed in 1970 by President Nixon. It had no discernible impact on public policy as its findings were ignored by the Nixon Administration.

It is well to note that some advisory commissions may have a substantial effect on policy in directions other than those intended by their presidential creator. An interesting glimpse into the policy process is provided by the case of the Committee to Strengthen the Security of the Free World (1962–63), which was appointed by President Kennedy to study the foreign-aid program. Unexpectedly, the Committee, in its report, while defending the program in principle, advocated a reduction in spending for foreign aid. Although this recommendation ran counter to the administration's wishes, it was decided not to reject the report so that General Lucius Clay, the Committee chairman, could testify for the program before Congress. Moreover, rejecting the report might have pushed Clay into the anti–foreign aid camp, which had seized upon the report as support for its position. Thus, President Kennedy reduced his foreign-aid request in accordance with the Committee's recommendation and got Clay to defend the program. Congress not only accepted the President's cut but made still more cuts of its own, all of which added up to the largest reduction in the history of the foreign aid program. In addition, new restrictions were added to the program.[21]

Legislators are also involved in policy formation. In the course of congressional hearings and investigations, through contacts with various administrative officials and interest-group representatives, and on the basis of their own interests and activity, legislators receive suggestions for action on problems and formulate proposed courses of actions. In some policy areas, congressmen have done much of the policy formulation. Such is the case in the area of air and water pollution, where Congress, under the leadership of such individuals as Senator Edmund Muskie and Representative Paul Rogers, has been willing to move more quickly and extensively than has the executive. Tax-reform legislation in 1969 was largely a congressional product, with the Nixon Administration getting on the bandwagon only after it was well under way.

Finally, interest groups often play a major role in policy formulation, sometimes going to the legislature with specific proposals for legislation. Or they may work with legislative and executive officials for the enactment of one officially proposed policy, perhaps with some modifications to suit their interests. Management groups were closely involved in the development of the bill that became the Labor Reform (Landrum-Griffin) Act of 1959. At the state level, interest groups often play an important role in the formulation of legislation, especially on technical and complex matters, because state legislators lack the time and staff resources needed to cope with them. Steiner and Gove report that the Illinois legislature customarily enacts legislation in the area of labor-management relations only after it has been agreed to by representatives of organized labor and industry. Thus, by custom, private groups may become the actual formulators of policy.

Competing proposals for dealing with a given problem may come from these sources. Take the example of national health insurance in the early 1970s.[22] The Nixon Administration presented to Congress a National Health Insurance Partnership Act that provided that employers make approved health-care plans available to their employees, that government-sponsored insurance be available to low-income families with children not protected by employment-based insurance, and that health services be improved through the establishment of health-maintenance organizations. Senator Edward Kennedy and Representative Martha Griffiths developed and introduced a bill providing for a comprehensive national health insurance system covering all citizens; it would be financed partly by taxes on employers and beneficiaries and partly by general revenue funds. The American Medical Association's entry was the Health Care Insurance Act ("Medicredit"), providing for income-tax credits for the purchase of private health insurance, along with federally subsidized health insurance or group insurance for low-income people. The Health Insurance Association of America, an insurance company interest group, proposed a National Health Care Act creating an insurance system in which insurance costs were met by employer and employee contributions; the poor would be covered by government subsidized, state-sponsored programs. And there were still other proposals in the arena. Policy-makers, therefore, were not confronted simply with a choice between a government health insurance program or no program at all. Rather, private and official actors had formulated a variety of proposals that compete for acceptance. (No proposal was adopted, however, because budgetary constraints developed which closed off the opportunity for policy innovation in this area.) The involvement of both public officials and private interests and compromise are basic characteristics of policy formulation in America (and in most other political systems).

## Policy Formulation as Technical Process

Policy formulation can be viewed as involving two types of activities. One is deciding generally what should be done, if anything, concerning a particular problem. Thus, in the above illustration, there is the question "What kind of national health insurance system shall we have?" In other instances, the question may be: "What kind of foreign-aid program shall we have?" or "What should be the minimum wage level and who should be covered by it?" Answers to these questions take the form of general principles. Once such questions have been resolved, the second type of activity involves the actual drafting of legislation (or the writing of administrative rules), which, when adopted, will carry these principles into effect. This is a technical and rather mundane, but nonetheless highly important, task. The way a bill is written, the specific provisions it contains, can have substantial effect on its administration and the actual content of public policy.

An interesting illustration is provided by the National Defense Education Act of 1958. A particular provision of the Act provided that students receiving graduate fellowship assistance had to sign a noncommunist affidavit, or "loyalty oath." This soon created much controversy. Liberals criticized it as unnecessary and an affront to the patriotism of students, among other things. Conservatives defended it as necessary to prevent aid from going to communists and wondered why any loyal American would object to signing such an oath. Some universities announced they would not participate in the fellowship program with the oath requirement. (Apparently few, if any, students who qualified for fellowships declined to sign the oath and take the money.) Eventually, the oath was replaced by a milder and more acceptable loyalty affirmation.

Notwithstanding the controversy sparked by the oath requirement, there was no discussion of it in either the committee hearings or the floor debates on the Act. No one advocated its inclusion in the legislation. How, then, did it get into the law? The answer to this question is not very dramatic, but such is the case with answers to many questions. The person drafting the formal language of the National Defense Education Act copied some of its fellowship provisions from a 1950 statute; one of these provisions was the loyalty oath requirement. It had caused no controversy under the earlier law. But when it was discovered in the 1958 law, the fun started. One moral that can be drawn from this is that it is often easier to get a provision into law than it is subsequently to remove it.

In practice, it is often difficult, if not impossible, to separate neatly policy formulation from policy adoption, which will be discussed in the next section. They are analytically distinct functional activities that occur in the policy process. They do not, however, "have to be performed by separate individuals at different times in different institutions."[23] Those concerned with formulating courses of action will be influenced in what they do by the need to win adoption of their proposals. Some provisions will be included, others excluded, in an effort to build support for a proposed policy. Looking further ahead, the formulators may also be influenced by what they think may happen during the administration of the policy.

## FORMULATING POLICY: THE ECONOMIC RECOVERY TAX ACT

The Economic Recovery Tax Act of 1981 was a central part of the Reagan Administration's program to control inflation and reduce the size of the national government. Other parts of the Reagan program included the reduction of domestic expenditures, a monetary policy featuring gradual growth in the money supply, and economic regulatory reform. In this account our attention will be on the Reagan Administration's 1981 tax cut, its roots, and the process by which it evolved and won adoption.

During his campaign for the Republican presidential nomination in the early months of 1980, Ronald Reagan became committed to supply-side economics. Essentially, this theory held that many of the economic problems confronting the American people were the product of high income tax rates that reduced the incentive of people to work, save, and invest. Significant tax reduction was necessary to unleash the productive capacity of the economy. Supply-side economics thus stood in contrast to traditional Keynesian economics with its focus on influencing aggregate demand for goods and services.

A prominent feature of the supply-side strategy was the Kemp-Roth tax cut proposal, which was named after two of its leading advocates, Representative Jack Kemp (R., N.Y.) and Senator William Roth (R., Del.). The Kemp-Roth proposal, which had first been introduced in Congress in 1977, called for a 30 percent reduction in marginal income tax rates (the rate a person pays on the last dollar of income taxed) spread over a three-year period. The Kemp-Roth proposals attracted support from conservatives but, until 1980, it never really came close to enactment by Congress. Support of the Kemp-Roth proposal by Reagan, however, resulted in its being written into the 1980 Republican party platform.

In February, 1981, a few weeks after taking office, President Reagan unveiled the tax reduction legislation which had been quickly put together by a few top administration officials. The administration's tax bill had two main features: (1) a 10 percent cut in income tax rates to take effect on July 1, 1981, with additional 10 percent cuts on July 1 of each of the two succeeding years; and (2) liberalized depreciation allowances for business investment, which permitted depreciation for tax purposes of vehicles over a three-year period, machinery and equipment over five years, and buildings over ten years. This was known as the "10-5-3" proposal. That the administration's tax proposal was based on supply-side economics and the Kemp-Roth proposal is quite evident.

Although there was pressure from various interest groups and congressional sources for other tax changes, these were resisted by the administration, which wanted to secure quick passage of its "clean" bill. Once that was done, the administration promised to introduce a second tax bill which might incorporate such other tax changes as tuition tax credits, the lowering of inheritance taxes, and the indexing of income tax rates to reduce the "bracket creep" caused by inflation.

The President initially barred any compromises on his tax proposal. In the Senate, where the Republicans were in the majority, there was never much doubt that the President's basic tax proposal would pass. However, the Senate has traditionally added special provisions called "sweeteners" to tax bills and there was ample interest in doing this. In the House, which had a Democratic majority, the administration needed to pick up some Democratic votes in order to put together a majority for its bill. Indeed, the Democratic leadership in the House disliked Reagan's approach to tax reduction, charging that the President's bill favored the wealthy and would result in large budget deficits.

The task of preparing a Democratic alternative to the Reagan tax proposal fell to Representative Dan Rostenkowski (D., Ill.), Chairman of the House Ways and Means Committee, and the committee's Democratic majority. They developed a proposal which included a 15 percent cut in income taxes spread over two years, with the cuts focused on low and middle income persons, increased business depreciations (but less than in the administration's proposal), and other changes in taxation. Generally, their proposal provided greater tax relief for individuals than for businesses.

In May, the administration sought to work out a compromise with Rostenkowski because it was uncertain that its "clean" bill could pass. Rostenkowski, however, was unable to get authorization to bargain from the Ways and Means Democrats. The administration, which was impatient to secure action on taxation, then turned its attention to the Conservative Democrats (the "Boll Weevils") in the House. In fact, some White House aides had been talking with the Boll Weevils at the same time other officials were dealing with Rostenkowski.

To win the support of the conservative Democrats, the administration offered to include some tax cuts in its proposal which had been targeted for the second bill. Examples included tax breaks for small oil and gas royalty holders, lower inheritance taxation, and savings incentives. Also, the income tax cut was scaled back to 25 percent and business depreciation was reduced somewhat. Business groups remained unenthusiastic about the proposal, so a few days later the administration added some more special tax advantages for business.

In the meantime, the Democratic majority on the Ways and Means Committee had continued working on its alternative, which they hoped would defeat the administration proposal when the legislation reached the House floor. In mid-July, by an 18 to 17 vote, the Democratic majority approved a provision reducing the windfall profits tax on oil, which had been adopted in 1978. This represented an effort on their part to secure the support of the conservative Democrats, many of whom were from oil-producing states. Not to be outbid, the administration hastily revised its proposal. Added to it were more sweeteners, including tax breaks for oil producers, increased charitable deductions, annual indexation of income tax rates, and relief from estate and gift taxes. Generally, these changes were intended to pick up a handful of swing votes. "Both Republicans and Democrats admitted that their bills were more products of a political bidding war than blueprints for sound economic policy."[24]

A couple of days before the House action on the tax legislation was scheduled to occur, President Reagan addressed the nation on television and urged the public to support his proposal. As a consequence, the members of Congress were inundated by a tidal wave of communications mostly supportive of the President's position. When the vote was taken in the House, the members voted 238 to 195 to adopt the Republican tax proposal rather than the Democratic alternative. One hundred ninety Republicans were joined by forty-eight conservative Democrats in support of the administration. (Only one Republican representative voted against the administration.)

The Senate completed its action on the administration's tax proposal on the same day as the House. Of the 118 amendments to the tax bill considered by the Senate, 80 were adopted. The special interest nature of some of the amendments is illustrated by one which permitted taxpayers in southern Alabama to claim a $10 tax credit for every pecan tree planted to replace one destroyed by Hurricane Frederick in 1979. (This provision was later abandoned.) There were, however, only a few major differences between the House and Senate bills, such as on the scope of tax breaks for oil producers and increases in tax credits for child care. Annual indexation of income tax rates, which appeared in both bills, was added at the insistence of Senator Robert Dole (R., Kan.), chairman of the Senate Finance Committee. According to one explanation, "Dole figured there was so much junk being put in the tax bill that there might as well be some real reform, too."[25]

The differences between the House and Senate tax bills were readily resolved by a conference committee. Signed into law by the President in mid-August, the Economic Recovery Tax Act of 1981 contained a three-year, 25 percent cut in income tax rates; indexation of income tax rates after 1984; new business depreciation allowances; and an array of tax breaks on such items as oil production, estates and gifts, interest income, charitable contributions, deposits into retirement accounts, income from new tax-exempt savings certificates, foreign earned income, child care, and the income of two-earner married couples. It was estimated that the act would reduce federal tax revenues by amounts ranging from $39 billion in 1982 to $280–290 billion in 1987.[26]

In this case study, one sees how the policy formulation and adoption processes become interwoven in actuality. Formulation must be concerned not only with developing a preferred or satisfactory policy alternative but also with winning its approval. An affirmative decision is the payoff of the policy process; its price may be concession and compromise, taking less or more than what one would really prefer. In the instance of the Economic Recovery Tax Act, the Reagan Administration's basic tax reduction proposal emerged relatively intact; however, to secure its adoption the administration had to agree to myriad amendments. To put it another way, the administration had to share the formulation function with Congress and a variety of interest groups. The result was tax legislation which reduced revenues substantially more than the administration originally intended. In 1982 Congress, concerned about large prospective budget deficits, enacted legislation increasing taxes by $98 billion over a three-year period, in part by eliminating or reducing some of the 1981 tax cuts.

## MAKING POLICY DECISIONS

A policy decision involves action by some official person or body to approve, modify, or reject a preferred policy alternative. In positive fashion it takes such forms as the enactment of legislation or the issuance of an executive order. It is well here to recall the distinction made in Chapter 1 between policy decisions, which significantly affect the content of public policy, and routine decisions, which involve the day-to-day application of policy. Furthermore, a policy decision is usually the culmination of a variety of decisions, some routine and some not so routine, made during the operation of the policy process.

What is typically involved at the policy decision stage is not selection from among a number of full-blown policy alternatives but, rather, action on what we have chosen to call a preferred policy alternative—one for which the proponents of action think they can win approval, even though it does not provide all that they might like. As the formulation process moves toward the decision state, some proposals will be rejected, others accepted, still others modified; differences will be narrowed; bargains will be struck, until ultimately, in some instances, the policy decision will be only a formality. In other instances, the question will be in doubt until the votes are counted or the decision is announced.

Although private individuals and organizations also participate in making policy decisions, the formal authority rests with public officials—legislators, executives, administrators, judges. In democracies, the task of making policy decisions is most closely identified with the legislature, which is designed to represent the interests of the populace. One frequently hears that a majority of the legislature represents a majority of the people. Whatever its accuracy as a description of reality, such a contention does accord with our notion that the people should rule in a democracy. Policy decisions made by the legislature are usually accepted as legitimate, as being made in the proper way and hence binding on all concerned. Generally, decisions made by public officials are regarded as legitimate if the officials have legal authority to act and meet accepted standards in taking action.

In the remainder of this chapter, several aspects of policy decision-making will come under examination. These include decision criteria; types of decision-making; majority-building in Congress; presidential decision-making; and incrementalism.

### Decision Criteria

Decision-making can be studied either as an individual or as a collective process. In the first instance, the focus is particularly on the criteria used by individuals in making choices. In the latter, the concern is with the processes by which majorities are built, or by which approval is otherwise gained, for specific decisions. Individual choices, of course, are usually made with some reference to what others involved in the decisional situation are likely to do.

An individual may be subject to a variety of influencing factors when deciding how to vote on or resolve a particular policy question. Which of these forces is most crucial, so far as her choice is concerned, is often hard to assess. Public officials frequently make statements explaining their decisions in the *Congressional Record*, constituency newsletters, speeches, press conferences, court opinions, memoirs, and elsewhere. The reasons they give for their decisions may be those that were really controlling; or they may be reasons that are acceptable to the public at large or to important constituents, while the actual bases for choice go unstated. Nonetheless, it is often possible, through careful observation and analysis, to determine what factors were operative in a given situation, if not necessarily to assign them specific weights. A number of criteria that may influence policy choice are discussed here.

*Values*   In Chapter 1, some of the values (preferences, standards) that a person may employ in making decisions, including political, organizational, policy, and personal values, were presented. There is no need to repeat that discussion here; rather, some aspects of individual values as decision criteria will be more fully commented upon, because the decision-maker's values are probably the most direct and pervasive criteria for deciding what to do. Officials often develop strong commitments to particular ways of handling given problems, such as public rather than private development of hydroelectric power sites, or the use of monetary rather than fiscal policies in combating inflation. On appropriations for the armed forces, a congressman who is a hawk will probably favor increased funds, while a dove will probably support a reduction in funds. Decisions may also be made on the basis of one's ideology, which may be defined as a coherent set of values and beliefs concerning government and politics. Thus, for example, a legislator, in deciding how to vote on a bill, might only have to determine whether it is a conservative or liberal measure and act accordingly. Of course, it may not always be easy to give a bill or proposal an ideological tag. Probably few officials make decisions solely on ideological grounds.

*Political Party Affiliation*   Party loyalty is a significant criterion for most members of Congress, although it is often difficult to separate from such other considerations as leadership influence and ideological commitments. Relatively few votes in Congress meet the "90 percent versus 90 percent" definition of a party vote, in which 90 percent or more of the Democrats are lined up against 90 percent or more of the Republicans. In the past century, party voting, as so defined, was at its peak during the McKinley era, when approximately 50 percent of the votes in the House were party votes.[27] Since then, party voting has declined, and in recent years only 2–8 percent of House roll-call votes have been party votes.[28] If, however, the test of a party vote is relaxed to "50 percent versus 50 percent," then about half of the House roll-call votes during the 1950s and 1960s qualify as party votes. In comparison, it may be noted that most of the votes in the British House of Commons meet the "90 percent versus 90 percent" party vote standard.

Party affiliation does remain as the best predictor of how congressmen will vote on issues. If one knows a congressman's party affiliation, and the party positions on issues, and then uses party affiliation as the basis for predicting votes, he will probably be correct more often than he will be using any other single indicator. If the political parties in Congress are not strong, disciplined parties, neither are they unimportant in their impact on legislative decision-making.

Party loyalties or attachments vary in importance among issue areas. Party conflict has developed most consistently on such matters as agricultural price supports, business regulation, labor, and social welfare legislation. In the agricultural area, for example, Democrats have tended to favor high price supports and production controls, while Republicans have preferred lower price supports and fewer controls. Again, Democrats have been more inclined to support the development of new welfare programs, such as medicare, and the expansion or increased funding of existing ones, such as public assistance, than have Republicans. In some other issue areas, such as civil rights, veterans' benefits, public works, and foreign policy, it has often been difficult or impossible to delineate distinct and persistent party differences.

*Constituency Interests*   A bit of conventional wisdom in Congress holds that, when party interests and constituency interests conflict on some issue, the congressman should "vote his constituency." It is, after all, the voters in his district who hold the ultimate power to hire and fire. In acting for the interests of his constituents, a representative may act as a delegate carrying out the instructions of his constituents, or he may act as a trustee and exercise his best judgment in their behalf when voting on policy questions.[29] Of course, he may try to combine these two styles, acting as a delegate on some issues and as a trustee on others.

In some instances, the interests of his constituents will be rather clear and strongly held, and the representative will act contrary to them at his peril. In the past, Southern congressmen were well aware of the strong opposition among their white constituents to civil rights legislation and voted accordingly. Again, a legislator from a strong labor district will probably have little doubt concerning his constituents' interests on minimum wage and right-to-work legislation. On a great many issues, however, a representative will be hard put to determine what his voters want. Large portions of the electorate have little, if any, knowledge of most issues. How, then, does the representative measure which way the wind is blowing from his district if no air currents are moving? In such situations, the legislator will have to make his decision on the basis of his own values, or on other criteria, such as recommendations from party leaders or the chief executive.

Nonelected public officials, such as administrators, may also act as representatives. Agencies often have well-developed relationships with particular interest groups and strive to represent the latter's interests in policy formation and administration. The Department of Agriculture is especially responsive to the interests of commercial farmers, while the Federal Maritime Commission has viewed itself as the representative of international shipping interests in the national administrative system. The decision and actions of the two agencies have reflected the interests of their constituents. Some commentators have contended that administrative agencies may be more representative of particular interests in society than are elected officials.[30] Whatever the validity of this contention, it is clear that legislators are not the only officials influenced by the need or desire to act representatively in making decisions.

*Public Opinion* Political scientists have devoted much time and effort to studying the formation, content, and change of public opinion on political issues. The more philosophically inclined have been concerned with what should be the role of public opinion in the governmental process. Our concern here is with the effect of public opinion on the actions of policy-makers. Are the choices of policy-makers shaped or determined by public opinion? Does public opinion serve as a decision criterion? It is well to proceed tentatively in answering such questions, bearing in mind V. O. Key's comment that "to speak with precision of public opinion is a task not unlike coming to grips with the Holy Ghost."[31]

A useful way to approach the problem of the effect of public opinion on policy-making is to distinguish between decisions that shape the broad direction, or thrust, of policy and the day-to-day, often routine, decisions on specific aspects of policy. Public opinion is probably not a significant decision criterion in the second category. To draw on Key again, "Many, if not most, policy decisions by legislatures and by other authorities exercising broad discretion are made under circumstances in which extremely small proportions of the general public have any awareness of the particular issue, much less any understanding of the consequences of the decision."[32] The legislator deciding how to vote on a particular tax amendment or public works bill will probably be unaffected in any direct sense by public opinion. Of course, he may try to anticipate the reaction of the public to such votes, but this will leave him with substantial latitude, given the lack of awareness mentioned above.

Nonetheless, the general boundaries and direction of public policy may be shaped by public opinion. Given existing public attitudes, such actions as the nationalization of the steel industry, the repeal of the Sherman Antitrust Act, or major revision of the social security program appear highly unlikely. Conversely, officials may come to believe that public opinion demands some kind of policy action, as was the case with labor-reform legislation in 1959 and tax reduction legislation in 1981. These were generalized rather than specific "demands," which left much discretion on details to Congress. In the area of foreign policy, public opinion appears to accord wide latitude to executive officials, as the conduct of American intervention in Vietnam during the 1960s clearly indicates. Ultimately, however, growing public opposition to the Vietnam war appears to have contributed to President Johnson's decision not to run for re-election in 1968 and the beginning of efforts to "wind down" the war and withdraw.[33]

In summary, policy-makers do not appear unaffected in their choices by public opinion. The relationship between public opinion and policy actions, however, is neither as simple nor as direct as was once assumed. But the elected public official who totally ignores public opinion and does not include it among his decision criteria, should there be an official so foolish, is likely to find himself out of luck at the polls.

*Deference* Officials confronted with the task of making a decision may decide how to act by deferring to the judgment of others. The "others" to whom deference is given may or may not be hierarchical superiors. Administrative officials often do make decisions in accordance with the directives of department heads or chief executives. This is how we expect them to act, especially when the directives of superiors are clear in meaning—which, it must be added, they sometimes are not. Administrators may also defer to the suggestions or judgments of members of Congress, as Department of Agriculture officials did when receiving advice from Congressman Jamie Whitten, former Chairman of the House Agricultural Appropriations Subcommittee. Because of his influence, Whitten was sometimes referred to as the "permanent Secretary of Agriculture."[34]

Members of Congress often have to vote on issues that are of little interest to them (because they do not affect their constituents), or on which they have little information, or which are highly complex in nature. On such matters, congressmen often decide how to vote by seeking the advice of other legislators whose judgment they trust, whether party leaders, committee chairmen, or policy experts. When a congressman is unable to decide how to vote on the basis of his own analysis of an issue, deference to someone whose judgment he trusts is a reasonably rational, low-information strategy for making decisions. Donald Matthews argues that, because of the widespread practice of deference to policy experts, "few institutions provide more power to the exceptionally competent member than does the House of Representatives."[35]

Judges, too, make decisions by deference. For example, when they interpret a statute, in the course of either applying it to a particular case or determining its constitutionality, they often defer to the intent of the legislature.[36] Statutory language is often ambiguous and its meaning unclear. In trying to determine what the legislature intends by particular phrases such as "restraint of trade" or "all lawful means," they may refer to such materials as committee hearings and reports and floor debates on the law in question. In the course of debate on bills, legislators often strive to build a record of legislative intent to inform both courts and administration on their intended meaning. Those who argue that legislative debates are meaningless ignore this function of debate, among other things.

*Decision Rules*   Those confronted with the task of making many decisions often develop rules of thumb, or guidelines, to focus attention on particular facts and relationships and thereby both simplify and regularize the decision-making process. There is no set of decision rules common to all decision-makers, although some may be widely utilized. What guidelines, if any, apply in a particular situation is a matter to be determined by empirical investigation. A few examples will be presented here to illustrate the concept.

The rule of *stare decisis* (in effect, "let the precedents stand") is often used by the judiciary in deciding cases. According to this decision rule, or principle, current cases should be decided in the same way as similar cases were in the past. The use of precedents to guide decision-making is by no means limited to the judiciary. Executives, administrators, and legislators also frequently make decisions on the basis of precedents. They are often urged to do so by those who would be affected by their actions, particularly if this will help maintain a desired *status quo.* Those adversely affected by existing precedents are likely to find them lacking in virtue and utility.

In the antitrust area, some *per se* rules have been developed. Certain actions, such as price fixing and market allocation, have been held to be *per se* (in effect, "as such") violations of the Sherman Antitrust Act. If the action is found to exist, that is sufficient to prove violation, and no effort is made to inquire into the reasonableness or other possible justifications of the action. *Per se* rules add simplicity and certainty to antitrust decision-making.

Richard Fenno, in his study of a number of congressional committees, has found that each commitee has some decision rules that help shape its decision-making activities. Thus, the House Appropriations Committee, seeking independence of the executive, has a "rule" to the effect that it should reduce executive budget requests, and, in fact, most requests are reduced. Again, the House Post Office and Civil Service Committee have as a decision rule, in Fenno's words, "to support maximum pay increases and improvement in benefits for employee groups and to oppose all rate increases for mail users."[37] Fenno points out that every committee has decision rules, although some rules are easier to discover than others.


## Styles of Decision-Making

Most policy decisions of any magnitude are made by coalitions, which often must take the form of numerical majorities, whether one's focus is on Congress, North Dakota State Legislature, the Omaha city council, the Danish Folketing, or the British Parliament after the 1974 elections. Even when a numerical majority is not officially required, the support of others is needed to ensure that the decision is implemented and compliance achieved. The commander can yell "Charge!" and have the bugle blown, but, if the troops all ride off to the cantina, he is apt to experience a difficult afternoon with the Indians. More to the point, perhaps, the President is often vested with final authority to make decisions, but he will need to gain the support or cooperation of other officials if his decisions are to be effective. As Richard Neustadt, an astute commentator on the Presidency, has remarked: "Underneath our images of Presidents-in-boots, astride decisions, are the half-observed realities of Presidents-in-sneakers, stirrups in hand, trying to induce particular department heads, or Congressmen or Senators, to climb aboard."[38] President Kennedy sometimes told friends who offered policy suggestions or criticisms, "Well, I agree with you, but I'm not sure the government will."[39] These comments point up the coalitional nature of much presidential decision-making, and the President's need to persuade others to go along.

Nowhere, perhaps, is the coalitional nature of decision-making better illustrated than in the Danish Folketing (Parliament), where the 179 seats are divided among nine parties. The Liberal Prime Minister governed on the basis of a coalition formed by his party and the Social Democratic, Democratic Center, and the Christian Peoples parties. In taking policy actions, the Prime Minister had always to think first about holding his coalition together, lest he lose his majority and his power to govern. In 1982 the liberals were replaced by a four-party conservative coalition, which needs the support of two other parties to remain in office.

In this section, three styles of decision-making will be examined—namely, bargaining, persuasion, and command. Our focus will turn from individuals' decisions to decision-making as a collective process.

*Bargaining*   The most common style of decision-making in the American political system is bargaining. Bargaining can be defined as a process in which two or more persons in positions of power or authority adjust their at least partially inconsistent goals in order to formulate a course of action that is acceptable but not necessarily ideal to the participants. In short, bargaining involves negotiation, give-and-take, and compromise in order to reach a mutually acceptable position. In the private realm, it is epitomized in collective bargaining over the terms of work by union leaders and management officials. For bargaining to occur, the bargainers must be willing to negotiate, they must have something to negotiate about, and each must have something (i.e., resources) that others want or need.

Two factors seem especially important in making bargaining the dominant mode of decision-making in our society. One is social pluralism; that is, the presence of a variety of partially autonomous groups—labor unions, business organizations, professional associations, farm organizations, environmental groups, sportsmen's clubs, civil rights groups, and so on. Although partially autonomous, they are also interdependent and "must bargain with one another for protection and advantage."[40] The second factor to note is the use of such constitutional practices as federalism, the separation of powers, and bicameral legislatures, which serve to fragment and disperse political power among many decision points. Major policy decisions at the national level often require the approval of all branches of government, plus acceptance by state or local governments and affected private groups. Such is the case with current federal aid to education and environmental pollution-control policies.

Bargaining may be either explicit or implicit in nature. When bargaining is explicit, the bargainers (group leaders, party officials, committee chairmen, department heads, executives, and so on) state their agreements (bargains) in clear terms in order to minimize the likelihood of misunderstanding. The U.S. Constitution is a good illustration of explicit bargaining between large and small states, North and South, and other interests. An explicit bargain was struck by Wilbur Mills, Chairman of the House Ways and Means Committee, and President Johnson in 1968 when Mills agreed to go along with the administration's income-tax increase proposal only after the President had agreed to a reduction in expenditures.[41] In international politics, treaties exemplify explicit bargains. Here we can note that bargaining in international politics is widely accepted because the idea of national interests is well accepted. In domestic politics bargaining, however necessary and prevalent, is often looked upon as incompatible with a quest for the "public interest" or, in more crude language, as a "sell out."

More frequently, however, bargaining is probably implicit in nature. In implicit bargaining, the terms of agreement among the bargainers are often vague or ambiguous and may be expressed in such phrases as "future support" or "favorable disposition." Such bargaining frequently occurs in Congress, where one member will agree to support another on a given bill in return for future cooperation. Understandings or gentlemen's agreements may be developed by administrators concerning their responsibilities for the administration of particular programs so as to eliminate conflict among themselves. In some instances, implicit bargaining may be sufficiently nebulous so that it is unclear whether an agreement actually exists. In Congress, bargaining frequently involves procedural actions intended either to slow down or to accelerate the handling of legislation.

Two common forms of bargaining are log-rolling and compromise. Log-rolling usually involves a straightforward "mutual exchange of support on two different items. This is a prevalent form of bargaining because not every item on an agenda interests every leader to the same extent."[42] A good illustration of log-rolling involves the Omnibus Rivers and Harbors Bill passed by Congress each year. The legislation includes a substantial number of separate and independent river- and harbor-improvement and flood-control projects. The congressman who wants a project for his state or district in effect agrees to support the projects for other congressmen's states or districts. Farm legislation and, in the past, tariff legislation have also involved much log-rolling.

Compromise usually involves explicit bargaining, is normally centered on a single issue, and involves questions of more or less of something. Here the bargainers regard "half a loaf as better than none" and consequently adjust their differences so as to come into agreement. A classic example is the Missouri Compromise of 1820, which temporarily settled conflict between Northern and Southern interests over the extension of slavery into the Louisiana Territory. To simplify, the North wanted slavery excluded from the Territory, while the South wanted no prohibition. It was finally agreed by Congress that slavery would be prohibited in the Territory (except Missouri) north of 36′30°. The Civil Rights Act of 1964 involved many compromises between those wanting stronger legislation and those wanting weaker or no legislation, especially on the provisions dealing with public accommodations, equal employment opportunity, and judicial enforcement. Issues involving money—for instance, budgets—are probably the most likely and easiest matters on which to compromise.

*Persuasion* Attempts to convince others of the correctness or value of one's position, and thereby cause them to adopt it as their own, involve persuasion. Unlike the bargainer, the persuader seeks to build support for what she wants without having to modify her own position. This may involve trying to convince others of the merits of one's position, or the benefits that will accrue to them or their constituents if they accept it, or some combination of the two. The persuader thus seeks to induce others "to do it her way." Attorneys who argue cases before the Supreme Court not only present their side of the issue but seek to persuade a majority of the Court of the correctness of their position. Presidential meetings with congressional leaders are often sessions in which presidential programs are explained, their benefits for congressmen and their constituents outlined, and appeals made for congressional leaders' support. Within Congress, appeals by party leaders to the rank and file to the effect that "Your party needs your support on this issue, can't you go along?" are essentially persuasive in content. Statements by officials to the public explaining and justifying particular programs, such as a price freeze, represent efforts to convince the public to comply with them.

*Command* Bargaining involves interaction among peers; command involves hierarchical relationships among superordinates and subordinates. It is the ability of those in superior positions to make decisions that are binding upon those who come within their jurisdiction. They may use sanctions in the form of either rewards or penalties—although usually sanctions are thought of as penalties—to reinforce their decisions. Thus, the subordinate who faithfully accepts and carries out a superior's decision may be rewarded with favorable recognition or a promotion, while the one who refuses to comply may be fired or demoted. President Nixon's decision to institute a price-wage freeze in August, 1971, on the basis of authority granted by the Economic Stabilization Act was essentially one of command. The Office of Management and Budget engages in command behavior when it approves, rejects, or modifies agency requests for appropriations and proposals for legislation prior to their transmittal to Congress. On the whole, however, command is more characteristic of decision processes in dictatorial rather than democratic societies and in military rather than civilian organizations because of their greater hierarchical qualities. Command is the primary style of decision-making in many Latin American and African countries.

In practice, bargaining, persuasion, and command often become blended in a given decisional situation. The President, although he has authority to make many decisions unilaterally, may nonetheless also bargain with subordinates, modifying his position somewhat and accepting some of their suggestions, in turn, for more ready and enthusiastic support of his decision.[43] Within agencies, subordinates often seek to convert command relationships into bargaining relationships. A bureau that obtains considerable congressional support may thus put itself into position to bargain with, rather than simply be commanded by, the department head. A pollution-control agency may have the authority to set emission standards and act to enforce them on the basis of its statutory authority. It may, however, bargain with those potentially affected in setting the standards in hope of gaining easier and greater compliance with the standards set. Presidential and gubernatorial efforts to win support for legislative proposals typically involve a combination of persuasion and bargaining.

In summary, bargaining is the most common form of decision-making in the American policy process. Persuasion and command are supplementary to it, being "better suited to a society marked by more universal agreements on values and a more tightly integrated system of authority."[44] Nowhere is the bargaining process better illustrated than in Congress, to which we now turn our attention.

## Majority-Building in Congress

The enactment of major legislation by Congress requires the development of a numerical majority or, what is more likely, a series of numerical majorities. These are most commonly created by bargaining. Even if a majority in Congress are agreed on the need for action on some issue, such as labor union reform, they may not agree on the form it should take, thereby making bargaining essential.

A highly important characteristic of Congress, which has much importance for policy formation, is its decentralization of political power. Three factors contribute to this condition. First, the political parties in Congress are weak, and party leaders have only limited power to control and discipline party members. In contrast with party leaders in the British House of Commons, who are strong and have a variety of means to ensure support of party policy proposals by party members, congressional leaders, such as the floor leaders, have few sanctions with which to discipline or punish recalcitrant party members. The party leadership has only "bits and fragments" of power—desired committee assignments, office space, use of the rules, the ability to persuade—with which to influence the rank and file. The member who chooses to defy his party's leadership can usually do so with impunity, and, indeed, not a few people will probably applaud his independence.

Second, the system of geographical representation and decentralized elections contributes to the decentralization of power in Congress. Members of the House and Senate are nominated and elected by the voters in their constituencies and owe little or nothing for their election to the national party organizations or congressional leaders. It is their constituencies that ultimately possess the power to hire and fire them, and it is therefore to their constituencies that congressmen must be responsive, at least minimally, if they wish to remain in Congress. From time to time, important interests in a congressman's district may be adversely affected by party programs. Conventional congressional wisdom holds that, when party and constituency interests conflict, the member should "vote his constituency," as his re-election may depend upon it.

A third factor contributing to the decentralization and dispersion of power in Congress is the committee system. There are twenty-two standing committees in the House and fifteen in the Senate with jurisdiction over legislation in such areas as agriculture, appropriations, energy and natural resources, international relations, and human resources. Traditionally, the standing committees have done most of the legislative work in Congress. Almost all bills are referred to the appropriate standing committees for consideration before being brought to the floor of the House or Senate for debate and decision. The standing committees possess vast power to kill, alter, or report unchanged bills sent to them. Most bills sent to committees are never heard from again. The committee chairs, who gained their positions on the basis of seniority, had much power over the operation of their committees. They selected the committee staff, scheduled and presided over meetings, set the agenda, scheduled hearings and chose witnesses, and decided when votes would be taken. Through long experience, they were often highly knowledgeable on the policy matters within the jurisdiction of their committees. Because of the fairly large number of interests that came within the jurisdictions of the committees, the committee chairs could act as brokers to build compromises among conflicting or differing interests.

During the last decade, various reforms to reduce the power of committee chairmen and other changes have occurred in Congress. As a consequence, much of the power of the standing committees has shifted to their subcommittees, of which there are over 200, and the subcommittee chairs. The subcommittees, whose jurisdictions are of course more specialized or narrowly focused than the parent committees, now handle most of the legislative activity and make many of the decisions on legislation. In the House, for example, almost all legislative hearings are now conducted by the subcommittees. The subcommittee chairs can act with substantial independence in the conduct of their subcommittees. As a consequence of this shift to "subcommittee government," more members of the House and Senate are now importantly involved in the policy process and have an opportunity to make policy innovations. Another consequence is that the committees have lost much of their role as arenas in which interests could be mediated and compromised. The subcommittees are more responsive to particularized interests and single interest groups, thereby further fragmenting the legislative process. The standing committees, of course, have not lost all their importance but they are no longer the "feudal baronies" they were once depicted as being.

The decentralization of power in Congress, together with the complexities of its legislative procedures, usually requires the formation of a series of majorities for the enactment of major legislation. There are a number of decision stages through which a bill must pass in the course of becoming a law.[45] Briefly, these would be, in the House: subcommittee, committee, Rules Committee, and finally floor action; similarly in the Senate: subcommittee, committee, and floor action. Assuming the bill is passed in different versions by the two houses, a conference committee must agree on a compromise version, which then must be approved by the two houses. If the President approves it, the bill becomes law; if, however, he vetoes it, the bill becomes law only if it is passed again by a two-thirds majority in each house. There are thus 10 or 12 stages at which a bill requires the approval of some kind of majority. If it fails to win majority approval at one of these stages, it is probably dead. Should it win approval, its enactment is not assured; rather, its supporters face the task of majority-building at the next stage.

Extraordinary majorities are sometimes needed to get bills through some stages of the process. Reference has already been made to the two-thirds majorities needed to overcome a presidential veto. Rarely are bills able to get these majorities. During the 1945–1980 period, of 622 bills vetoed only 33 were subsequently enacted into law. In the Senate, the debate on a bill can be effectively terminated only by unanimous consent or by cloture. The cloture rule provides that debate may be terminated upon a motion signed by sixteen senators, with the concurrence of three-fifths of the entire membership (or 60 senators). Since a single senator can block the ending of debate by unanimous consent, this leaves cloture as the only alternative for shutting off a filibuster. Because of the difficulties in winning cloture, Southern Democrats were consistently able to block the enactment of major civil rights legislation through filibusters or the threat thereof until the adoption of the Civil Rights Act of 1964. In 1965, legislation to repeal the provision of the Taft-Hartley Act authorizing state right-to-work laws passed the House but was defeated in the Senate by a conservative filibuster. Apparently, a majority of the Senate favored repeal, but they were unable to secure the two-thirds vote then necessary to close debate.

The multiplicity of stages, or decision points, in the congressional legislative process provides access for a variety of groups and interests. Those who lack access or influence at one stage may secure it at another stage. It becomes quite unlikely that a single group or interest will dominate the process. The complexity of the process, however, has a conservative effect in that it gives an advantage to those seeking to block the enactment of legislation. And it is well to remember that many groups are more concerned with preventing than with securing the enactment of legislation. All they have to do to achieve their preference is to win the support of a majority, or at least of a dominant actor, at one stage of the process. Here is support for a familiar generalization, namely, that procedure is not neutral in its impact.

Much bargaining is necessary for the enactment of legislation by Congress. Those who control each of the decision points may require the modification of a bill as a condition for their approval. Or they may exact future support for some item of interest to themselves. Bargaining is facilitated not only by the many decision points but also by the fact that legislators do not have intense interest on many of the matters on which they must decide. It is no doubt easier for them to bargain on such issues than on issues on which they have strong feelings. At this point, however, it does not seem necessary to elaborate further upon the ubiquity of bargaining in Congress.

## Presidential Decision-Making

Apart from his role in the legislative process, the President can be viewed as a policy adopter in his own right. In the area of foreign affairs, much policy is a product of presidential action, based either on his constitutional powers or broad delegations of legislative authority. The decision, in 1972, to recognize Communist China and to adopt a policy of warmer relations with the Chinese was President Nixon's alone. In the area of domestic policy, some statutory delegations of authority to the President are of a breadth and generality approaching the constitutional. A notable example is the Economic Stabilization Act of 1970, which gave the President almost a blank check to institute a system of price-and-wage controls to combat inflation: "The President is authorized to issue such orders and regulations as he may deem appropriate to stabilize prices, rents, wages, and salaries at levels not less than those prevailing on May 25, 1970." Anything really worthy of the designation of public policy done under that Act was a product of presidential action. Presidential action did more than fill in the details; for all practical purposes, it created the basic wage-price control policy. It is, of course, not always easy to draw neat lines between policy formulation, adoption, and implementation. The argument is simply that it is reasonable to consider the President as a policy adopter, among other things.

By considering some of the general factors that shape and limit presidential decision-making, we not only can gain useful insight into presidential decision-making but also can discover another perspective from which to view decision-making in general. Before proceeding further, we must remember that presidential decision-making is an institutional process. A variety of agencies, aides, and advisers (both official and unofficial) assist the President in the discharge of his responsibilities. But whether he simply approves a recommendation from below or makes his own independent choice, the President alone has the ultimate responsibility for decision.

What factors help shape and limit presidential decision-making?[46] One is permissibility, an aspect of which is legality. The President is expected to act in conformity with the Constitution, statutes, and court decisions. The lack of a clear constitutional basis certainly contributed to congressional criticism of the Nixon Administration's Cambodian bombing policy in the summer of 1973 and to an agreement by the administration to cease bombing after August 15, 1973, without congressional authorization. Another aspect of permissibility is acceptability. Foreign policy decisions often depend for their effectiveness upon acceptance by other nations, while domestic policy decisions, such as that by President Reagan to recommend elimination of the Department of Energy, may depend upon their acceptance by Congress, or executive-branch officials and agencies, or the public.

A second factor is available resources. The President does not have resources to do everything he might want to do, whether by resources one means money, manpower, patronage, time, or credibility. Funds allocated to defense are not available for education or medical research. Only a limited number of appeals to the public for support for his actions can be made without the possibility of diminishing returns. Time devoted to foreign policy problems is not available for domestic matters. While the President has considerable control over the use of his time, he does not have time to concern himself with everything that he might wish.[47] A lack of credibility may also limit the President, as the experience of Presidents Johnson and Nixon attests.

A third factor is available time, in the sense of timing and the need to act. A foreign policy crisis may require a quick response, as was the case with the Cuban Missile crisis in 1962, without all the time for deliberation and fact-gathering one might prefer. Domestic policy decisions may be "forced," as by the need to submit the annual budget to Congress in January or the constitutional requirement to act on a bill passed by Congress within ten days if the President wishes to veto it (barring the possibility of a pocket veto). And, as Sorensen states:

> There is a time to act and a time to wait. By not acting too soon, the President may find that the problem dissolves or resolves itself, that the facts are different from what he thought, or that the state of the nation has changed. By not waiting too long, he may make the most of the mood of the moment, or retain that element of surprise which is so often essential to military and other maneuvers.[48]

Previous commitments may also help shape presidential decisions. These commitments may be personal—for example, campaign commitments and previous decisions. While too much emphasis can be placed on consistency, the President must avoid the appearance of deception or vacillation if he is to retain his credibility. President Kennedy rejected a tax cut as an antirecessionary measure in the spring of 1961. The economist Paul Samuelson, one of his advisers, later commented: "Whatever the merits of the tax cut, it seemed politically out of the question. The President had run on a platform that asked sacrificing of the American people. How then could he begin by giving them what many would regard as a 'handout'?"[49] Kennedy, of course, later did propose a tax cut, but by 1963 conditions had changed. Commitments may also take the form of traditions and principles, such as that of fighting only if attacked. During the Cuban Missile crisis an air strike without warning on the missile sites was rejected as a "Pearl Harbor in reverse." A "first-strike" strategy has been excluded from American foreign policy generally.

Finally, available information can be an important factor. Many sources of information, official and unofficial, are available to the President and at times, particularly with regard to domestic policy, he may be subject to drowning in a torrent of words and paper. Still, the President may be confronted by a shortage of reliable information, especially in the area of foreign affairs. Reliable information on the possible reactions to a Berlin airlift, the resumption of nuclear testing, or the mining of Haiphong harbor may be scarce because of the need to predict the future—and predicting the future is an uncertain task, except, perhaps, for a few who claim a sixth sense. Domestic policy de-

cisions may also involve uncertainty. This is quite obvious in the area of economic-stability policy. Will a cut in income taxes restore full employment? Will a price-wage freeze destroy the inflationary psychology contributing to inflation? When all the advice is in, the President has to make a choice, which is a calculated one, that the action taken will produce the desired result.

As a leader in policy formation, the President is subject to a variety of pressures and constraints, however great his legal powers may appear to be. Legal authority, by itself, often does not convey the capacity to act effectively. Thus, the President may have to persuade because he cannot command; he may have to bargain because he cannot compel action. President Truman once remarked, "I sit here all day trying to persuade people to do the things they ought to have sense enough to do without my persuading them.... That's all the powers of the Presidency amount to."[50] An overstatement, perhaps, yet a remark worth reflecting upon.

## Incrementalism

The term incrementalism is used, as we have seen, to designate a decision-making process that is characterized by limited analysis and that yields decisions differing only marginally from previous decisions. The belief that political decision-making in the United States is essentially incremental has gained wide acceptance among political scientists. Not infrequently, incremental theory is given both a prescriptive and a descriptive quality that implies or asserts that this is the way decisions properly should be made as well as how they actually are made. One American government textbook goes so far as to contend that even the New Deal is an illustration of incrementalism, given the historical precedents and events leading up to it. If the New Deal as a whole is incremental, then just about everything since Creation can be regarded as incremental and it too may have been such as it occurred in stages (according to *Genesis*).

In actuality, if nonincremental decisions or policies are defined as being those that depart sharply from past practice or that require large increases or decreases in the commitment of resources to given policies, in recent decades there have been quite a few nonincremental, or fundamental, policy decisions.[51] Some examples include the Social Security Act, the Marshall Plan, the interstate highway program, Medicare, revenue sharing, the 1961 decision to put a man on the moon, the 1971 wage-price freeze, and the Reagan Administration's 1981 economic program. Although such decisions may be vastly outnumbered by incremental decisions, they significantly shape the content and thrust of public policy. Rather extensive policy analysis and debate usually precede such decisions.

Nowhere, probably, can incrementalism be better illustrated than in the federal budgetary process. (Budget decisions are typically policy decisions.) Congressional analysis of budget requests is usually limited to items for which increases over the previous year are sought, and total agency budgets often change only marginally from one year to another.[52] There is not, however, agreement as to what constitutes an incremental (or marginal) budget change.[53] Wildavsky regards budget increases of 30 percent or less as incremental but, it should be noted, if an agency's budget expands annually at this rate it will double in three years and increase tenfold in a decade. It would be hard to consider this marginal change. Clearly, the less restrictive the definition of increment, the more incremental action one finds.

Within the framework of an agency's total budget substantial (nonincremental) changes may be made in particular programs or policies handled by the agency. A recent study of the Atomic Energy Commission budgets for fiscal years 1958–72 found that the total budget changed only marginally from year to year.[54] Within that context, though, five AEC programs were canceled, and a few experienced either sharp continuing declines or increases, while most fluctuated widely in financial support. As this study clearly hints, policy-making through the budgetary process may not be so stable and incremental as many scholars have contended. It also suggests that "the program director, the operating-level bureaucrat, is a central figure in the determination of public policy."[55]

It is also possible that fundamental changes in public policy may be brought about by incremental means without their ever being considered on their merits. Eidenberg argues, for example, that the United States's involvement in a major land war in Vietnam was the product of an incremental decision process.[56] Step by step American participation expanded from financial and material aid to the use of military "advisers," to the commitment of combat troops, to increasing numbers of combat troops. "When in 1968 Johnson announced he would not run again, he became the victim of his earlier neglect to consider fully the implications and costs of an indeterminate and deepening American involvement in Vietnam." Another example of how a policy can be altered fundamentally by incremental means involves the federal income tax. Over the years, a plethora of particular laws have greatly reduced its progressivity by creating exemptions, opening up loopholes, providing tax credits, and so on for various individuals and groups. Upper-income persons benefit far more than lower-income persons from these added provisions.

Incrementalism is a useful descriptive and analytical decision theory. If, however, it is stretched to include all decisions, it loses its value as an analytical device. We need to recognize that policy-making involves both incremental and fundamental decisions. Further, as policy analysts, we should be careful to avoid making incrementalism a prescriptive theory or a rationalization of the existing state of things in decision-making.[57]

Similar processes and problems of public policy-making are probably encountered by executives and legislatures at every level of government and in every industrialized democratic political system. Many of these processes and problems may also occur in nondemocratic systems. There is evidence to indicate, for example, that bargaining as a decision-style sometimes occurs among elites in some communist political systems, such as the Soviet Union.

## NOTES

1. David G. Smith, Pragmatism and the Group Theory of Politics," *American Political Science Review,* LVIII (September, 1964), pp. 607–10. In this discussion of public problems, I have been much benefited by Charles O. Jones, *An Introduc-*

*tion to the Study of Public Policy* (Belmont, Calif.: Wadsworth, 1970), chaps. 2 and 3.

2. See John Dewey, *The Public and Its Problems* (Denver: Swallow, 1927), pp. 12, 15–16.

3. Theodore J. Lowi, "American Business Public Policy: Case Studies and Political Theory," *World Politics,* XVI (July, 1964), pp. 677–715.

4. Cf. Layme Hoppe, "Agenda-Setting Strategies: The Case of Pollution Problems." Unpublished paper presented at the annual meeting of the American Political Science Association (September, 1970).

5. Robert Eyestone, *From Social Issues to Public Policy* (New York: Wiley, 1978), p. 3.

6. Roger W. Cobb and Charles D. Elder, *Participation in American Politics: The Dynamics of Agenda-Building* (Boston: Allyn and Bacon, 1972), p. 85.

7. *Ibid,* p. 89.

8. David B. Truman, *The Governmental Process* (New York: Knopf, 1951), p. 30.

9. Jones, *op. cit.,* p. 29.

10. See Jack L. Walker, "Setting the Agenda in the United States Senate: A Theory of Problem Selection," *The British Journal of Political Science,* Vol. 7 (October 1977), pp. 423–446.

11. Cf. Cobb and Elder, *op. cit.,* pp. 84–85.

12. Mark V. Nadel, *The Politics of Consumer Protection* (Indianapolis: Bobbs-Merrill, 1971), p. 28 and *passim.*

13. See Michael Lipsky, "Protest as a Political Resource," *American Political Science Review* LXII (December, 1968), pp. 1144–58.

14. Lewis Coser, *Continuities in the Study of Social Conflicts* (New York: Free Press, 1967), p. 101.

15. This is discussed, in fascinating style, in W. A. Swanberg, *Citizen Hearst* (New York: Scribner's, 1961), pp. 79–169.

16. Norton E. Long, *The Polity,* ed. by Charles Press (Chicago: Rand-McNalley, 1962), pp. 152–54.

17. Those wishing to pursue this topic further should consult the highly informative study by Cobb and Elder, *op. cit.*

18. Peter Bachrach and Morton S. Baratz, *Power and Poverty* (New York: Oxford University Press, 1970), p. 44.

19. E. E. Schattschneider, *The Semi-Sovereign People* (New York: Holt, Rinehart and Winston, 1960), p. 71.

20. This discussion is based on J. Clarence Davies III, *The Politics of Pollution* (Indianapolis: Bobbs-Merrill, 1970), pp. 21–24. The quotation is from p. 21.

21. Thomas R. Wolanin, "The Impact of Presidential Advisory Commissions, 1945–1968." Unpublished paper presented at the annual meeting of the American Political Science Association (September, 1972), p. 22.

22. Various health-care proposals are analyzed in Anne R. Somers, *Health Care in Transition: Directions for the Future* (Chicago: Hospital Research and Educational Trust, 1971).

23. Jones, *op. cit.,* p. 53.

24. *Congressional Quarterly Weekly Report,* Vol. 39 (July 25, 1981), p. 1323.

25. Steven R. Weisman, "Reaganomics and the President's Men," *The New York Times Magazine* (October 24, 1982), p. 90.

26. John L. Palmer and Isabel V. Sawhill, eds., *The Reagan Experiment* (Washington:

The Urban Institute Press, 1982), pp. 111–115. For a partial summary of the 1981 act, see Joseph A. Peckman, ed., *Setting National Priorities: The 1983 Budget* (Washington: The Brookings Institution, 1982), pp. 251–262. See also *Congressional Quarterly Weekly Report,* Vol. 31 (August 8, 1981), pp. 1431–1438.

27. David W. Brady, "Congressional Leadership and Party Voting in the McKinley Era: A Comparison to the Modern House," *Midwest Journal of Political Science* XVI (August, 1972), pp. 439–41.

28. Julius Turner, *Party and Constituency: Pressures on Congress,* rev. ed. by Edward V. Schneier, Jr. (Baltimore: Johns Hopkins Press, 1970), p. 17.

29. A thorough discussion of concepts of representation can be found in John C. Wahlke *et al., The Legislative System* (New York: Wiley, 1962).

30. E.g., Peter Woll, *American Bureaucracy,* 2d ed. (New York: Norton, 1977).

31. V. O. Key, Jr., *Public Opinion and American Democracy* (New York: Knopf, 1961), p. 14.

32. *Ibid.,* pp. 81–90.

33. Cf. John E. Mueller, "Trends in Popular Support for the Wars in Korea and Vietnam," *American Political Science Review,* LXV (June, 1971), pp. 358–75.

34. Nick Kotz, *Let Them Eat Promises: The Politics of Hunger in America* (Englewood Cliffs, N.J.: Prentice-Hall, 1969).

35. Donald R. Matthews and James A. Stimson, "The Decision-Making Approach to the Study of Legislative Behavior." Unpublished paper presented at the annual meeting of the American Political Science Association (September, 1969), p. 19.

36. Robert H. Salisbury, *Governing America: Public Choice and Political Action* (New York: Appleton-Century-Crofts, 1973), p. 237. Chap. 13 contains a very useful treatment of decision-making.

37. Richard F. Fenno, Jr., *Congressmen in Committees* (Boston: Little, Brown, 1973), pp. 48, 64.

38. Richard E. Neustadt, "White House and Whitehall," *The Public Interest,* II (Winter, 1966), pp. 55–69.

39. As quoted in Roger Hilsman, *The Politics of Policy Making in Defense and Foreign Affairs* (New York: Harper & Row, 1971), p. 1.

40. Robert A. Dahl and Charles E. Lindblom, *Politics, Economics, and Welfare* (New York: Harper & Row, 1953), p. 328. Chaps. 12 and 13 present a thorough and insightful discussion of bargaining in American politics.

41. See the good discussion of this episode in Lawrence C. Pierce, *The Politics of Fiscal Policy Formation* (Pacific Palisades, Calif.: Goodyear, 1971), chap. 7.

42. Lewis A. Froman, Jr., *People and Politics* (Englewood Cliffs, N.J.: Prentice-Hall, 1962), p. 56.

43. Cf. Richard E. Neustadt, *Presidential Power* (New York: Wiley, 1980).

44. Dan Nimmo and Thomas D. Ungs, *American Political Patterns,* 2d ed. (Boston: Little, Brown, 1969), p. 367.

45. A good discussion of congressional procedures can be found in Walter J. Oleszak, *Congressional Procedures and the Policy Process* (Washington: The Brookings Institution, 1978).

46. In this discussion I will depend substantially on an insightful little book by Theodore C. Sorensen, *Decision-Making in the White House* (New York: Columbia University Press, 1963). Sorensen served as Special Counsel to President Kennedy.

47. Cf. George Reedy, *The Twilight of the Presidency* (New York: World, 1970).

48. Sorensen, *op. cit,* p. 29.
49. Paul A. Samuelson, "Economic Policy for 1962," *Review of Economics and Statistics,* XLI (February, 1962), p. 3.
50. As quoted in Neustadt, *Presidential Power, op. cit.,* pp. 9–10.
51. Cf., Charles L. Schultze, *The Politics and Economics of Public Spending* (Washington, D.C.: Brookings Institution, 1968), pp. 77–79.
52. A leading work is Aaron Wildavsky, *The Politics of the Budgetary Process,* 3d ed. (Boston: Little, Brown, 1979).
53. John J. Bailey and Robert J. O'Connor, "Operationalizing Incrementalism: Measuring the Muddles," *Public Administration Review, Public Administration Review* XXXV (January-February, 1975), pp. 60–66. Also John R. Gist, " 'Increment' and 'Base' in the Congressional Appropriations Process," *American Journal of Political Science,* XXI (May, 1977), pp. 341–352.
54. Peter B. Natchez and Irvin C. Bupp, "Policy and Priority in the Budgetary Process," *American Political Science Review,* LXVII (September, 1973), pp. 951–63.
55. *Ibid.,* p. 963.
56. Eugene Eidenberg, "The Presidency: Americanizing the War in Vietnam," in Allen P. Sindler (ed.), *American Political Institutions and Public Policy* (Boston: Little, Brown, 1969), pp. 68–126. The quotation is on pp. 119–20.
57. For a good critique of incrementalism, see Robert Goodin and Ilmar Waldner, "Thinking Big, Thinking Small, and Not Thinking at All," *Public Policy,* XXVII (Winter, 1979), pp. 1–24.

# The Implementation
# of Policy

Once the legislative adoption stage of the policy process has been completed, we can begin to refer to something called public policy. It must be kept in mind, however, that the content of policy, and its impact on those affected, may be substantially modified, elaborated, or even negated during the implementation stage. Indeed, in some instances, legislation does not do much more than authorize an agency or the executive to make policy on some matter. The Economic Stabilization Act and Consumer Product Safety Act are cases in point. (Such terms as application, administration, and effectuation can be used as synonyms for implementation and will be so employed here.) In actuality, it is often quite difficult, if not impossible, to differentiate neatly the adoption of policy from its implementation, just as earlier it was indicated that policy formation and adoption are hard to demarcate. There is, indeed, much truth in the aphorism that policy is made as it is being administered and administered as it is being made. The policy process has some of the appearance of the proverbial "seamless web" so often invoked in scholarly discussions.

Some policy decisions are essentially self-executing, such as the Nixon Administration's decision to formally recognize the government of the People's Republic of China (which, in doctrinaire days, was called Communist China) or the decision of the Canadian Parliament in 1964 to replace the Red Ensign with the Maple Leaf Flag as the official national flag. But relatively few such decisions, which entail clearcut, one-time action, are made, so that those concerned with the analysis of public policy can ill afford to neglect the implementation stage of the policy process. Much that occurs at this stage may seem at first glance to be tedious or mundane, yet its consequences for the substance of policy may be quite profound. Moreover, closer examination will reveal that highly intense political rights and environmental protection legislation should be very familiar cases in point.

This chapter will begin with an examination of the budgetary process because of its importance for policy implementation. Attention will then be given for four other aspects of implementation: participants in policy implementation, the nature of the administrative process, compliance with public policy, and the effect of implementation on policy content and impact.

## THE BUDGETARY PROCESS

Few indeed are the public policies which can be put into effect without the expenditure of money; many programs, such as social security, aid to families with dependent children, and unemployment compensation, involve primarily the expenditure of funds. The effectiveness of programs may be importantly affected by the adequacy of their funding. At an extreme, a policy without funding will become a nullity. Thus in 1973 Congress eliminated the subversive activities control program not by repealing the legislation upon which it was based but by ceasing to appropriate money for its administration. Although the agency (the Subversive Activities Control Board) administering the program had never succeeded in registering a single subversive person or organization (e.g., the Communist Party), the program was of symbolic importance to some conservatives and a source of employment to a few others for over two decades. It is also possible for a department or agency to be better funded than necessary. Thus the Reagan Administration sought and obtained increased funding for defense programs in the early 1980s. Some commentators were doubtful that the Defense Department could wisely use all of the additional funds.

The major facets of the national budgetary process will be sketched in this section. This will not be done in detail because the major purpose here is to indicate how the budgetary process helps shape the nature and implementation of public policies. The budget submitted by the President to Congress in January of each year is for a single fiscal year which extends from October 1 of one calendar year through September 30 of the following year. Preparation of the budget begins nine months or so before it is sent to Congress. (Figure 4.1 presents a detailed view of budget preparation.)

Most of the day-to-day work in developing the budget is handled by the Office of Management and Budget and the executive departments and agencies. OMB provides instructions, policy guidance, and tentative budget ceilings to help the departments and agencies develop their budget requests. The latter, who are directly and specifically affected by budget decisions, are expected to act as the advocates of increased spending (appropriations). What they request is subject to review and revision by OMB in accordance with the policies and programs of the President. Agencies sufficiently aggrieved by OMB decisions may appeal them to the President who, more often than not, will uphold OMB.

The budget sent to Congress will reflect the President's decisions and priorities on such matters as its size, its possible effects on the economy, major directions or emphases in public policy, and the allocation of funds

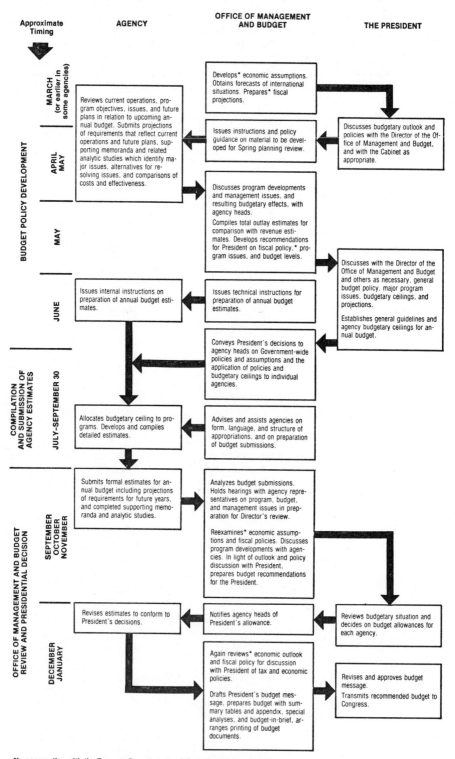

| Approximate Timing | AGENCY | OFFICE OF MANAGEMENT AND BUDGET | THE PRESIDENT |
|---|---|---|---|

**BUDGET POLICY DEVELOPMENT**

**MARCH** (or earlier in some agencies)

Develops* economic assumptions. Obtains forecasts of international situations. Prepares* fiscal projections.

Reviews current operations, program objectives, issues, and future plans in relation to upcoming annual budget. Submits projections of requirements that reflect current operations and future plans, supporting memoranda and related analytic studies which identify major issues, alternatives for resolving issues, and comparisons of costs and effectiveness.

**APRIL MAY**

Issues instructions and policy guidance on material to be developed for Spring planning review.

Discusses budgetary outlook and policies with the Director of the Office of Management and Budget, and with the Cabinet as appropriate.

Discusses program developments and management issues, and resulting budgetary effects, with agency heads.

**MAY**

Compiles total outlay estimates for comparison with revenue estimates. Develops recommendations for President on fiscal policy,* program issues, and budget levels.

Discusses with the Director of the Office of Management and Budget and others as necessary, general budget policy, major program issues, budgetary ceilings, and projections.

**COMPILATION AND SUBMISSION OF AGENCY ESTIMATES**

**JUNE**

Issues internal instructions on preparation of annual budget estimates.

Issues technical instructions for preparation of annual budget estimates.

Establishes general guidelines and agency budgetary ceilings for annual budget.

**JULY-SEPTEMBER 30**

Conveys President's decisions to agency heads on Government-wide policies and assumptions and the application of policies and budgetary ceilings to individual agencies.

Allocates budgetary ceiling to programs. Develops and compiles detailed estimates.

Advises and assists agencies on form, language, and structure of appropriations, and on preparation of budget submissions.

**OFFICE OF MANAGEMENT AND BUDGET REVIEW AND PRESIDENTIAL DECISION**

**SEPTEMBER OCTOBER NOVEMBER**

Submits formal estimates for annual budget including projections of requirements for future years, and completed supporting memoranda and analytic studies.

Analyzes budget submissions. Holds hearings with agency representatives on program, budget, and management issues in preparation for Director's review.

Reexamines* economic assumptions and fiscal policies. Discusses program developments with agencies. In light of outlook and policy discussion with President, prepares budget recommendations for the President.

**DECEMBER JANUARY**

Revises estimates to conform to President's decisions.

Notifies agency heads of President's allowance.

Reviews budgetary situation and decides on budget allowances for each agency.

Again reviews* economic outlook and fiscal policy for discussion with President of tax and economic policies.

Drafts President's budget message, prepares budget with summary tables and appendix, special analyses, and budget-in-brief, arranges printing of budget documents.

Revises and approves budget message. Transmits recommended budget to Congress.

*In cooperation with the Treasury Department and Council of Economic Advisers.

Figure 4.1

among the various agencies and programs. Lyndon Johnson in 1967 wanted both "guns and butter"—increased spending for both the Vietnam war and the social welfare programs of his Great Society. Ronald Reagan, on the other hand, in 1981 wanted less welfare spending and more spending for national defense. In 1977 Jimmy Carter sought to reduce spending on water resource projects, which are much favored in Congress, by eliminating funding for nineteen projects on a "hit list." This caused a deterioration of his relationship with Congress. Funding for most of the projects was eventually restored.

## Congressional Authorization

The Constitution provides that "no money shall be drawn from the treasury, but in consequence of appropriations made by law," which means appropriations legislation enacted by Congress. Here we should note that two steps are involved in funding public policies and programs. The first is the adoption of substantive legislation which establishes a program and authorizes expenditures in its behalf. The second is the appropriation of money, actually making it available, for the program. Authorization legislation is handled by the legislative commitees (Agriculture, Commerce, Foreign Relations, etc.) while appropriations legislation is the domain of the House and Senate appropriations committees. It is not uncommon for programs for which funding is authorized to either go unfunded or to be funded at levels lower than those authorized. Different committees and processes in Congress produce different policy results.

For purposes of legislative enactment, the President's budget, which comes to Congress as a single document, is broken up into a dozen or so appropriations bills. These are referred to the House Appropriations Committee which by custom acts first on the budget. Its subcommittees hold hearings and do most of the legislative work on the budget bills. What they recommend is usually accepted by the full committee and its recommendations in turn are usually approved with few changes by the House.

The Senate Appropriations Committee, to which appropriations bills passed by the House are sent, does not engage in as intensive an examination of budget request as does the House committee. Rather, the Senate Appropriations Committee focuses on "items in dispute," to serve as an appellate body to which agencies, who have had their budget requests cut in the House, can appeal for the restoration of at least part of the cuts. The Senate frequently responds positively to such pleas.

Conference committees are used to resolve the differences in the House and Senate versions of appropriations. Often this involves splitting the difference between the two bills. Compromises are considerably easier to reach on money matters than on "social" issues, such as abortion or gun control. These involve "moral" matters on which it is hard to compromise or divide up the difference.

Dissatisfaction with the fragmented and disjointed nature of the appropriations process, concern over the rapid growth of government spending and continued budget deficits, and a desire for greater congressional concern with the fiscal policy implications of the budget were factors contributing to the adoption of Budget Impoundment Control Act of 1974.[1] The budget reform facets of this act provided for a congressional budget process which could set overall levels of revenue and expenditures and establish priorities among functional areas in the budget (Agriculture, international relations, transportation, etc.). New budget committees in the House and Senate were created to handle these tasks.

In brief form the new budget process is to work as follows. By May 15 of each year the Congress is supposed to adopt a preliminary budget resolution reported by the budget committees. This resolution sets targets both for overall revenues and expenditures, and for spending within the various functional areas. From then until early September the regular appropriations process (as set forth above) is supposed to consider and approve the various appropriations bills. Then, by September 15, Congress is to pass a second budget resolution which either affirms or revises the targets set in the first resolution. If necessary, reconciliation legislation revising appropriations or other spending legislation, or raising or lowering taxes, to meet the budget targets is to be enacted before the fiscal year begins on October 1. The reconciliation process was first used in 1980, when it was urged by the Carter Administration to reduce spending by several billion dollars. It was used again in 1981 when it was combined into the first budget resolution to achieve a major reduction in spending by the Reagan Administration of $35 billion. This produced significant changes in several domestic and welfare programs.

Observers seem to agree that the new budgetary process has improved the quality of congressional decision-making on the budget. Budget decisions are better considered and debated, if not easier to reach. Not until 1981 was the process used to produce a major change in budget policy, and that does not seem likely to be easily repeated.

## Budget Execution

The obligation and expenditure of money, once appropriated, rests with the various departments and agencies. To begin spending, however, they must first secure an apportionment from OMB. An apportionment usually regulates the rate of spending on a quarterly basis and is intended to limit the need for supplemental appropriations during the fiscal year. OMB may also direct agencies to set aside funds for contingencies or not to spend funds when efficiencies or altered needs permit savings to be achieved without restricting the accomplishment of agency goals.

The amount of discretion that agency officials have in spending funds and achieving policy objectives is significantly affected by the language of appropriations legislation. The more detailed it is the less discretion agencies have. Specific restrictions or instructions may also be written into the legislation, as in 1976 when an amendment to an appropriations bill required the Occupational Safety and Health Administration to get rid of "nuisance standards." On the other hand Congress may sometimes provide agencies with "lump sum" or very broad appropriations which confer much discretion in the expenditure of funds, albeit within the boundaries provided by other legislation controlling agency action.

The practice of presidential impoundment of funds has been productive of much controversy in recent years.[2] Presidents have long claimed authority to prevent the expenditure of funds for purposes they disagreed with on budgetary or policy grounds. Presidents Truman and Eisenhower refused to spend funds for military programs of which they did not approve. President

Lyndon Johnson impounded funds to combat inflation, although much of what he impounded was subsequently released. Impoundment was usually done on a limited and selective basis; and, although some dissatisfaction was created in Congress, major confrontations were usually avoided.

President Richard Nixon, however, precipitated a major conflict over impoundment. Following his re-election in 1972, he engaged in the extensive impoundment of funds for programs involving water pollution, mass transit, food stamps, medical research, urban renewal, and highway construction. Various rationales were given including the need to prevent the inflationary effects of "reckless" spending. In various instances, however, it was clear that the administration was using impoundment to terminate programs. Most of the impoundments were held to be illegal by the federal courts.

A major result of the controversy created by the Nixon Administration's actions was the inclusion of some controls on impoundment in the 1974 budget act. Under the act a *deferral* of expenditures, in which the executive seeks to delay or stretch out spending until a future time when it is needed, can be done unless and until either house of Congress disapproves. In contrast, a *rescission* of funds, which cancels existing budget authority and thus stops the expenditure of funds, becomes effective only if within forty-five days of being notified both houses approve a rescission bill. It is, in actuality, not always easy to distinguish deferrals from rescissions. Overall, the effects of the new impoundment procedures are to give Congress more (and the executive less) authority over the spending of funds and to make appropriations legislation more of a mandate to spend what is appropriated.

## The Budget and Public Policy

The budget conveys a good picture of the government's total policy program for the year it covers. In the budget one will find answers to such policy issues as the balance between private and public (federal) spending, the balance between military and civilian spending, whether medical research will be accelerated or slowed, whether welfare spending generally as well as particular welfare programs will be expanded or contracted, whether there will be more or less antitrust and other regulatory enforcement, and so on. This happens because the budgetary process is a means for making choices among competing social values and allocating resources to achieve them. It is in all a highly political process involving both money and the content of public policies.

The nature and effectiveness of public policies depend considerably upon the amount of funds appropriated to implement or enforce them. Whether antitrust policy is vigorous or lax, the number of children enrolled in Headstart programs, the amount of public housing constructed, the number of illegal aliens apprehended, and effectiveness of industrial health and safety regulations are all matters affected by appropriations. The Occupational Health and Safety Administration, for example, has funding only to hire inspectors sufficient to permit inspection of covered workplaces on the average of once every ten years. On the other hand, increased funding for the Headstart program permits enrollment of more children and the provision of more services to them. Other factors affecting implementation will be treated in the next section of this chapter.

The budget process provides the President and Congress with an opportunity to review periodically the various policies and programs of the government, to assess their effectiveness, and to inquire into the manner of their administration. Every policy and program will not be considered in detail every year but over a period of a few years all or most will come under scrutiny. Thus the budgetary process provides a continuing opportunity for the exertion of presidential and congressional influence on the implementation of policies. Favored agencies and programs will likely prosper; those under attack may suffer cutbacks. Although most of the budget decisions made will be incremental, this does not much diminish their importance.

## WHO IMPLEMENTS POLICY?

In the United States, as in other modern political systems, public policy is implemented primarily by a complex system of administrative agencies. These agencies perform most of the day-to-day work of government and thus affect citizens more directly in their actions than do any other governmental units. Nonetheless, it would not be necessary for policy analysts to be much concerned with public administration (that is, all those structures and processes involved in the implementation of public policy) were it not for the fact that agencies often have much discretion (that is, the opportunity to make choices among alternatives) in carrying out the policies under their jurisdiction. They do not automatically apply whatever the legislature or other policy adopters decide, although at one time it was widely assumed they did.

A classic feature of the traditional literature of public administration was the notion that politics and administration were separate and distinct spheres of activity. Politics, Frank Goodnow wrote in 1900, was concerned with the formulation of the will of the state; it was concerned with value judgments, with determining what government should or should not do, and it was to be handled by the "political" branches of government, that is, the legislature and executive.[3] Administration, on the other hand, was concerned with the implementation of the will of the state, with carrying into effect, more or less automatically, the decisions of the political branches. Administration was concerned with questions of fact, with what *is* rather than what *should* be, and consequently could focus on the most efficient means (or "one best way") of implementing policy. Were this indeed the case, the policy analyst could end his inquiry with the adoption of policy. However, with the possible exception of a few archaic or poorly informed souls, no one today accepts this politics-administration dichotomy.

Administrative agencies often operate under broad and ambiguous statutory mandates that leave them with much discretion to decide what should or should not be done. Thus, the Interstate Commerce Commission is directed to fix "just and reasonable" railroad rates; the Federal Communications Commission, to license television broadcasters for the "public convenience and necessity"; the Forest Service, to follow a "multiple use" policy in the management of national forests that balances the interests of lumber companies, sportsmen, livestock grazers, and other users; the Consumer Product Safety Commission, to ban products which present an "unreasonable hazard"; and the Environmental Protection Agency, to ensure that the "best practicable" devices for the control of water pollutants were in use by 1977. Such statutory mandates are, in effect, directives to the agencies involved to go out and make some policy. Those who participate in the legislative process frequently are unable or unwilling to arrive at precise settlements of the conflicting interests on many issues. Only by leaving some matters somewhat nebulous and unsettled can agreement on legislation be reached. Lack of time, interest, information, expertness and the need for flexibility in implementation may also contribute to the delegation of broad authority to agencies. The product of these factors is often a statute couched in general language, such as that noted above, which shifts to agencies the tasks of filling in the details, making policy more precise and concrete, and trying to make more definitive adjustments among conflicting interests. Under these conditions, the administrative process becomes an extension of the legislative process and administrators find themselves immersed in politics.

Although legislatures have delegated much policy-making authority to administrative agencies, especially in the twentieth century, it should not be assumed that legislatures cannot act in rather precise fashion. An illustration is social security legislation, which sets forth in rather definite terms the standards of eligibility, the levels of benefits, the amount of additional earnings permitted, and other considerations for old age and survivor's benefits. Most administrative decisions on these benefits simply involve applying the legislatively set standards to the facts of the case at hand. Under such circumstances, administrative decision-making becomes largely routine and is therefore unlikely to produce controversy. In comparison, the disability standard under the social security program has produced considerable controversy. Disability is defined as the inability to engage in any substantial gainful activity by reason of a medically determinable physical or mental impairment expected to result in death or to be at least of twelve month's duration. This definition of disability leaves much scope for interpretation, conjecture, and disagreement.[4]

While administrative agencies are the primary implementors of public policy, many other actors may also be involved, and they should not be neglected in our study of policy-making. Those that will be examined here include the legislature, the courts, pressure groups, and community organizations. They may either be directly involved in policy implementation or act to influence administrative agencies, or both.

*The Legislature*  Congress may affect administration in a variety of ways. The more detailed the legislation passed by Congress, the less discretion agencies have. Specific limitations on the use of funds, for example, may be written into statutes. The committee reports that accompany bills reported from committees often contain suggestions or statements concerning how the legislation should be implemented. These do not have the force of law but will be ignored by administrators only at their peril. The legislative and appropriations committees often attempt to influence the actions of agencies that fall within their purview. Senatorial approval is required for many top-level administrative appointments, and this may be used as a lever to influence policy. A classic example was the Senate's rejection of the reappointment of Leland Olds to the Federal Power Commission in 1949 because of petroleum industry opposition to his position in favor of regulating the field price of natural gas.[5] The legislative veto arrangement, under which congressional approval must be secured before some action can be taken permits

Congress, or its committees, to control particular action. Scores of laws passed by Congress in recent years have contained such provisions. In 1982, for example, Congress used the legislative veto to kill a proposed FTC trade regulation rule intended to prevent deception in the sale of used automobiles. Finally, we can note that much of the time of many congressmen is devoted to "casework," which quite frequently involves problems that constituents are having with administrative agencies. The constituents, of course, want their congressman to secure favorable action for them.

*The Courts*  Some laws are enforced primarily through judicial action. Laws dealing with crimes are the most obvious example. Some economic regulatory statutes, such as the Sherman Antitrust Act, are enforced through law suits brought in the federal district courts, many of which are eventually appealed to the Supreme Court. Because of this and the generality of the Sherman Act, the meaning of antitrust policy depends greatly upon judicial interpretation and application of the Act. Generally, though, administrative regulation, in which primary responsibility is assigned to an agency for the enforcement of a statute, is much more commonplace than judicial regulation in the American political system. In the nineteenth century, however, it was quite common for legislatures to enact statutes requiring or prohibiting some action and then to leave it to citizens to protect their rights under the law through proceedings brought in the courts.

In some instances, the courts may be directly involved in the administration of policy. Naturalization proceedings for aliens are really administrative in form, but they are handled by the federal district courts. Bankruptcy proceedings are another illustration. A complex system of trustees, receivers, appraisers, accountants, auctioneers, and others is supervised by federal bankruptcy courts. In all, it is "a large scale example of routine administrative machinery."[6] Many divorce and domestic relations cases handled by state courts also appear essentially administrative, involving matters of guidance and management rather than disputed law or facts.

Most important, however, the courts affect administration through their interpretation of statutes and administrative rules and regulations, and their review of administrative decisions in cases brought before them. Courts can facilitate, hinder, or largely nullify the implementation of particular policies through their decisions. The story of how the Supreme Court destroyed the effectiveness of national railroad regulation under the Interstate Commerce Act of 1887 by unfavorable rulings is familiar history. Recent rulings by the federal courts that the Federal Trade Commission has authority under existing law to issue trade regulation rules should facilitate the Commission's trade regulation and consumer protection activities.

*Pressure Groups*  Because of the discretion often vested in agencies by legislation, once an act is adopted, the group struggle shifts from the legislative to the administrative arena. Given the operating discretion of many agencies, a group that can successfully influence agency action may have a substantial effect on the course and impact of public policies. Sometimes relationships between a group and an agency may become so close as to lead to allegation that the group has "captured" the agency. In the past, it was frequently stated that the Interstate Commerce Commission was the "captive" of the railroads,[7] and it is not uncommon now to hear comments to the effect that the Federal Maritime Commission is unduly influenced by the shipping companies. Also, groups may complain to Congress or the executive if they believe a statute is not being implemented in accordance with the intent of Congress.

Groups may become directly involved in administration, as when representation of particular interests is specified on the boards of plural-headed agencies. A common illustration of this is state occupational licensing boards, whose governing statutes frequently provide that some or all of the board members must come from the licensed profession. Occupational licensing (and regulatory) programs are usually controlled by the dominant elements within the licensed groups. Consequently, such programs usually do more to protect the interests of the licensed group than those of the general public.

Advisory groups are another means by which groups may become included in policy administration. Take the case of the National Industrial Pollution Control Council, which was created in April, 1970, by President Nixon. The Council, which is composed of representatives of major corporations and trade associations, provides advice to the White House and to agencies responsible for the implementation of environmental policy. Although it is difficult to judge the impact NIPCC has had on environmental policy, its existence provides big business with a regularized form of access to the policy process not afforded to most other groups concerned with the environment. It is estimated that there are between 1,100 and 1,600 advisory committees located in federal administrative agencies and departments. One observer has remarked that, "as a means for guaranteeing the institutional participation by non-government groups in the administrative process, advisory committees are a commonplace feature of American government."[8]

*Community Organizations*   At the local level, community organizations have sometimes been utilized for the administration of federal programs. Examples include local draft boards, under the now defunct selective service program; farmer committees, under the price-support and soil-conservation programs of the Department of Agriculture; and Community Action agencies providing for "maximum feasible participation" of the poor, under the Community Action program created by the Economic Opportunity Act of 1964. Participatory democracy of this sort may give those involved considerable influence over the application of programs at the grass-roots level. Thus, local draft boards, especially when only a portion of eligible males were needed to meet military needs, clearly helped shape selective service policy with regard to who got drafted and who did not.[9] Many losers went to Vietnam.

In short, a variety of participants affect the administration of a given policy. In addition to those discussed above, political party officials and executive staff agencies may also become involved. Certainly this is true for the Office of Management and Budget, whose concerns extend beyond agency funding. In 1981, for example, OMB was given authority by President Reagan to supervise the issuance of economic rules and regulations by executive branch agencies. The range of participants will vary from one policy area to another; hence, policy analysis should include whoever has an impact on the implementation of policy.

## THE ADMINISTRATIVE PROCESS

The term "administrative process" is used to designate the movement or operation of the administrative system over time. This discussion will focus on some aspects of the administrative process that seem especially to have consequences for the implementation, content, and impact of policy. These include administrative organization, administrative politics, and administrative policy-making. The matter of compliance—that is, conformity to policy directives, or objectives, by those to whom they apply—will be discussed in the next section.

### Administrative Organization

One could say that one administrative agency looks pretty much like another or, in another usage, if you have seen one agency, you have seen them all. If one were indeed to take such a position, he would be making a serious mistake. Agencies, in fact, differ greatly in such respects as their structure, operating styles, political support, expertness, and policy orientation. Those seeking to influence the nature of public policy often show much concern over the particular agency or type of agency that will administer a given policy. Conflict over questions of administrative organization can be every bit as sharp as conflict over substantive policies. The formation of administrative organizations is a political as well as a technical task.

Most public policies are not self-executing; hence, if they are to be carried into effect, responsibility for their implementation must be assigned either to an existing agency or to a new agency established for this purpose. The creation of new agencies is usually handled by the legislature. At the national level, however, some have been created by the executive under administrative reorganization authority that permits the President to propose reorganization plans; such plans go into effect automatically unless disapproved by either house of Congress. The Environmental Protection Agency was created by a Nixon Administration reorganization proposal in 1970 and now handles pollution-control enforcement activities formerly spread among a number of agencies. The effect has been to give a sharper focus to the administration of antipollution policies. A few other agencies, such as ACTION and the Social and Rehabilitation Service, have been set up on the basis of broad substantive authority given by Congress to the executive.

The discussion in this section will be focused on the policy implications of administrative organization. A number of propositions will be presented and illustrated to indicate how organizational considerations affect policy, and, thus, why they should receive the attention of policy analysts.

1. When a new program is adopted, the contending interests may seek to have its administration awarded to an agency they think will be more favorable to their interests. A major consideration during the enactment of the Occupational Safety and Health Act of 1970, the first major general industrial-safety bill passed by Congress, was who should administer it. Organized labor and most liberal Democrats favored locating all standard-setting and enforcement activity in the Department of Labor, which they regarded as sympathetic toward labor. Many Republicans, the Nixon Administration, and busi-

ness groups wanted an independent board, or boards, to make and enforce standards, to avoid Labor Department control of the program. The result was a compromise. The Department of Labor was given authority to set standards, to enforce them, and to assess penalties. Within the department these tasks are handled by the Occupational Safety and Health Administration (OSHA). An independent, three-member quasi-judicial Occupational Safety and Health Review Commission was created to hear appeals from Labor Department actions. A National Institute for Occupational Safety and Health was established within the Department of Health, Education, and Welfare to conduct research so as to create an information base for health standards. Both organized labor and business expressed satisfaction with this administration arrangement. OSHA has become a highly controversial agency because of some of its rule-making and enforcement actions. Some of the penalties it has imposed have been reduced on appeal by the review commission.

In 1953, an independent Small Business Administration was set up to handle assistance programs for smal business, following the dismantling of the Reconstruction Finance Corporation by the Eisenhower Administration. Some argued that control of such programs rested properly with the Department of Commerce. But small-business interests and their congressional supporters argued that the Department of Commerce was too oriented toward big business to administer satisfactorily, from their point of view, small-business programs. The Office of Economic Opportunity was given primary control of administering the War on Poverty partly because it was thought that old-line agencies like the Departments of Labor and Health, Education, and Welfare would not be sufficiently sympathetic and vigorous. "The best way to kill a new idea," President Johnson remarked at one point, "is to put it in an old-line agency."[11]

2. Administrative organization may be used to emphasize the need for, or facilitate action on, particular policy problems. Thus, the Kennedy Administration (unsuccessfully) and the Johnson Administration (successfully) sought creation of a Cabinet-level Department of Urban Affairs to emphasize urban problems and facilitate action thereon. Conservative and rural interests opposed its creation because they were afraid it would indeed have this result. Interestingly enough, some private housing organizations who had opposed it during the Kennedy Administration, when it was to be called the Department of Urban Affairs, supported its establishment during the Johnson Administration as the Department of Housing and Urban Development. One reason for their switch was their belief that inclusion of the word housing in the title of the department would produce stress on housing support programs economically beneficial to them.[12]

Another good example is the struggle over the formation of an Agency for Consumer Advocacy. A bill passed by the House of Representatives in 1971 but defeated by a filibuster in the Senate would have created an independent, nonregulatory agency to represent consumer interests in actions before other agencies and the courts. Other unsuccessful efforts to accomplish this were launched in 1973 and 1975. The prospects for creation of the agency appeared brighter in 1977 when it received the support of the Carter Administration. Its supporters believed that such an agency would provide more effective representation of consumer interests and, consequently, foster policy actions by agencies and courts more favorable toward consumers.

Conservatives and business groups opposed the proposal as giving too much power to the proposed agency, notwithstanding the fact that it would have no regulatory or enforcement powers. They, of course, did not openly oppose the protection of the consumer, as this is not a politically popular thing to do. They succeeded in defeating the legislation providing for the establishment of the agency in 1978. The issue dropped off the political agenda.

3. The internal structure of an agency may be fashioned to help secure desired action. Take the case of the National Institutes of Health, which were set up within the Department of Health, Education, and Welfare in the 1950s. It would have been quite logical to have named the various institutes according to the kind of research they would support, such as pathology, microbiology, biochemistry, and genetics. This is the way university research centers are usually organized. Instead, among the institutes established were the National Cancer Institute, the National Heart and Lung Institute, and the National Institute of Arthritis and Metabolic Diseases. This action was based on the reasoning that, while it might be easy for a congressman to vote against an appropriation for microbiology, he would be highly reluctant to vote against funds for cancer or heart research. This has proved effective, for Congress consistently provides more funds for the NIH than what is requested by the executive budget officials.

4. Independent agencies may, over time, become closely aligned with their clientele, that is, those directly served or regulated by an agency. With respect to independent regulatory commissions, such as the Interstate Commerce Commission and Civil Aeronautics Board, it has been stated: "Deprived of the influences on policy that flow from the give-and-take of other departments, and from the directions of the chief executive, the independent commission gravitates toward an industry point of view."[13] To gain political support needed to survive and to enlist cooperation in the performance of its tasks, the agency may incline toward the policy positions of its clientele. Moreover, since these will be the viewpoints most commonly presented to agency personnel, they may come to appear quite reasonable and acceptable. If regulatory commissions do sometimes succumb to the interests of the regulated (and there is evidence to support this contention),[14] then independence—in effect, isolation—as a feature of their organizational structure facilitates this condition, which, in turn, has clear consequences for the thrust of policy.

5. Once a group has developed a satisfactory relationship with an agency, it will oppose changes in the agency's structure or departmental location that might disrupt the relationship. Thus, the railroads have steadfastly opposed locating the Interstate Commerce Commission in an executive department, such as Transportation. Merchant shipping interests have opposed moving the Maritime Administration, which subsidizes ship construction and operations, from the Commerce Department to the Department of Transportation. Such moves might appear logical, but they *could* have the effect of opening the agencies to competing pressures and ultimately changing their operating patterns and policy. Generally speaking, groups prefer a satisfactory present situation to an unknown future one, which, from their perspective, may bring disagreeable changes.

6. Those who support an existing program may seek to have it moved to

another agency to avoid hostile or unfavorable handling of it. Conversely, opponents of a current program may seek to lessen its impact, or even kill it, by getting it reassigned to a hostile agency. A classic illustration of the first possibility involves the Forest Service, which was transferred early in this century from the Department of Interior to the Department of Agriculture at the behest of conservationists. According to Gifford Pinchot, "The national forest idea ran counter to the whole tradition of the Interior Department. Bred into its marrow, bone, and fiber, was the idea of disposing of the public lands to private owners."[15] This policy view was clearly unfavorable to forest conservation. It is, of course, no longer held by the Interior Department, but the Forest Service remains in Agriculture, notwithstanding some attempts by Interior to reacquire it. In 1971, supporters of the Volunteers in Service to America (VISTA) program, a part of the War on Poverty, maintained it was being transferred from the Office of Economic Opportunity to the new ACTION Agency in order to kill it. This, however, has not happened.

Proponents of strong mine safety policy long contended that the Bureau of Mines was too oriented to the interests of mine owners to be a really effective safety enforcement agency. Indeed the bureau had been established primarily to help promote development of the mining industry. In response to pressures for a new enforcement agency, the Secretary of the Interior established a new Mining Enforcement and Safety Administration (MESA) in the department in 1973. The Bureau of Mines was left with its promotional programs. In 1978 the proponents of stronger enforcement succeeded in getting MESA shifted to the Department of Labor, where it was given expanded duties and renamed the Mine Safety and Health Administration (MSHA).

When policy, therefore, is viewed as a "course of action," its substance is affected by how it is administered. How it is administered depends, at least partly, on what agency administers it. And, when you have seen one agency, you have *not* seen them all.

## Administrative Politics

A statute confers upon an agency only legal authority to take action on some topic. How effective the agency is, what it actually does or accomplishes, will be affected by the political context in which it operates and the amount of political support it has. To put it differently, politics affects how an agency exercises its discretion and carries out its programs.

The environment in which an agency exists may contain many "forces" that, at one time or another, may exert influence on its actions.[16] Among these forces are the following:

*Relevant Laws, Rules and Regulations, Accepted Modes of Procedures, Concepts of Fair Play*   These are the basic "rules of the game" that help inform and guide official behavior and to which officials are expected to conform. Public opinion and group pressures may focus adversely on administrators who violate the "rules of the game," as by proposing not to follow a given statutory provision or by enticing someone to violate a law so that he can be prosecuted. Officials who "snoop around" may cause trouble for themselves.

*The Chief Executive*   Agencies either are located in the presidential chain of command or are otherwise subject to presidential control and direction in such forms as personnel appointments, budget recommendations and expenditure controls, and policy directives. Agencies and officials in the Executive Office of the President are included here.

*The Congressional System of Supervision*   This includes the standing committees and subcommittees thereof, committee staffs, committee chairmen, influential congressmen. Congressional influence is fragmented and sporadic rather than monolithic and continuous. It emanates from parts of Congress, rarely from Congress as a whole.

*The Courts*   Agencies may be affected by the judiciary's use of its powers of judicial review and statutory interpretation. Thus, in 1954, the Supreme Court held that the Federal Power Commission had not only the authority but the duty to regulate the field price of natural gas, something that at the time the Commission preferred not to do.[17] While the Federal Power Commission has been significantly affected by judicial action, the Federal Reserve Board and the Bureau of the Mint are little affected thereby.

*Other Administrative Agencies*   Agencies with competing or overlapping jurisdictions may exert influence on each other, as, for example, the Department of Agriculture does on the ICC in agricultural rate cases. Water agencies such as the Corps of Engineers and the Bureau of Reclamation have been rivals for the right to control particular projects. Or one agency may aspire to take over a program of another agency. Thus, the Department of Labor and HEW eventually acquired some of the poverty programs, such as the Job Corps and Head Start, initially run by the Office of Economic Opportunity. Agencies not infrequently have imperialistic designs on one another.[18]

*Other Governments*   State governments, municipal and local governments, or associations of state and local officials may attempt to influence national agency decisions. Associations of state highway officials are much concerned about the activities of the Bureau of Public Roads. The Environmental Protection Agency encounters quite a lot of pressure, criticism, and resistance from state and local governments in the development and implementation of pollution-control standards.

*Interest Groups*   The role of groups was dealt with earlier in the chapter. Suffice it to say here that an agency that is affected by a variety of groups, such as the Forest Service, will act differently than one affected primarily by a single group, such as the Veterans Administration or one that experiences little group pressure, such as the Government Printing Office.

*Political Parties*   The role of party organization has declined in recent years, but appointments to administrative positions as well as agency decisions may be influenced by considerations of party welfare and party policy orientation. It makes a difference whether the White House is controlled by the Democrats or the Republicans. Witness the decline of OEO under the

Nixon Administration and the disappearance of its successor, the Community Services Administration during the Reagan Administration.

*Communications Media*   The mass communications media have an independent role apart from their use as forums for pressure groups and others. The media may play an important role in shaping public opinion toward an agency by revealing and publicizing its actions, favorably or unfavorably. Agencies evidence much concern with maintaining a "good press" or a favorable public image. Some of OEO's political difficulties were due to the extensive press coverage of its administrative difficulties, however minor in terms of the amount of money or number of persons involved. The Federal Bureau of Investigation, in contrast, has usually been quite well-treated by the media.

Each of these forces is multiple rather than monolithic in nature. A variety of pressure groups, state and local governments, or congressional actors may focus on a single agency. Conflicting viewpoints may be held either by members of the same category or by those in different categories. A number of forces operate on an agency pushing and pulling against each other with varying intensity and growing and ebbing over time.

The field of forces surrounding an agency will be drawn from the above categories and will form the *constituency* of the agency, that is, "any group, body, or interest to which [an administrator] looks for aid or guidance, or which seeks to establish itself as so important (in his judgment) that he 'had better' take account of its preferences even if he finds himself averse to those preferences."[19] (Note that this is a broader concept than that of clientele, referred to earlier.) The constituency of an agency is dynamic rather than static. Some "constituents" will be concerned with the agency only as particular issues arise or are settled; others will be more or less continually involved and will compose the stable core of the agency's constituency. For example, the stable core of the Civil Aeronautics Board's constituency includes the commercial airlines and the congressional commerce and appropriations committees. The chief executive, Department of Commerce, congressional small-business committees, and state aeronautics agencies are intermittently involved with the CAB. Other things being equal, those constituents that continually interact with an agency will probably have the most success in influencing agency action.

The nature of an agency's constituency will affect its power and capacity to make policy decisions and carry policy into effect. The relationship of an agency to one part of its constituency will depend on the kinds of relationships it has with other parts. For example, an agency with strong presidential support tends to be less responsive to pressure groups than an agency without such support. On the other hand, strong congressional and group support may lessen presidential influence, as in the case of the Army Corps of Engineers. An agency encountering criticism from state and local government officials may find its congressional support waning also. In general, it can be said that agency policy-making and implementation activities will reflect the interests supported by the dominant elements within its constituency, whether they are hostile or supportive.

An agency's clientele is an important part of its constituency. Some agencies benefit from having large active clienteles, such as the Veterans Administration and the Department of Agriculture. But size alone is not enough. Consumers are a vast group, but, because they are poorly organized and lack self-consciousness as a group, they provide little support to consumer agencies, such as the Food and Drug Administration. If the FDA has been unduly responsive to food and drug manufacturers, it is partly because of lack of consumer support and partly because the agency both needs the cooperation of and encounters organized pressure from food and drug companies. Some agencies have underprivileged or disadvantaged clienteles, such as OEO, most welfare agencies, and the Federal Bureau of Prisons. OEO was hindered in its efforts to administer the War on Poverty by the fact that its clientele, the poor and especially the black poor, did not constitute a good source of political support.

Agencies who provide services to their clientele, rather than regulate them, usually draw more support from their clientele. Most people prefer receiving benefits to being restricted or controlled. An agency with a foreign clientele, such as the Agency for International Development, can draw little political support from its clientele. The lack of an internal clientele has clearly been to the disadvantage of the foreign-aid program.

An examination of an agency's constituency and clientele can provide considerable insight into, and explanation of, why an agency acts as it does. It should not, however, be assumed that an agency is an inert force at the mercy of its constituency or the dominant elements therein. Agencies, because of their expertise, organizational spirit, or administrative statecraft, can exert independent control over events and help determine the scope of their power.[20]

Any bureaucratic agency has some expertise in the performance of its assigned tasks, whether those involve garbage collection or foreign policy. All bureaucratic skills, however, do not receive equal deference from society. Agencies whose expertise is derived from the natural and physical (i.e., "hard") sciences will receive more deference than those drawing from the social sciences, which are less highly regarded in society. Compare the situations of the National Aeronautics and Space Administration and the National Cancer Institute with the Office of Education and the Law Enforcement Assistance Administration. Considerable deference is shown to the military as "specialists in violence," and Congress often defers to the judgment of the Department of Defense and the Joint Chiefs of Staff in the military and defense policy areas. Professional diplomats, on the other hand, no longer receive the deference in foreign policy that they once did. Power based on expertise may vary considerably from one time to another as conditions and attitudes change.

Some agencies are more able than others to generate interest in, and enthusiasm for, their programs from both their own members and the public. This can be designated as organizational spirit. Its existence "depends to a large extent upon the development of an appropriate ideology or sense of mission on the part of an administrative agency, both as a method of binding outside supporters to the agency and as a technique for intensifying the loyalty of the organization's employees to its purposes."[21] The Marine Corps, the Peace Corps, the Forest Service, and the Office of Economic Opportunity (in its early years) are agencies served with considerable fervor and commitment by their members. Many agencies display substantial zeal in their early years, only to ease into bureaucratic routine as the years go by, as has happened in some national regulatory commissions.

Leadership, or what Francis Rourke calls administrative statecraft, can also contribute to an agency's power and effectiveness. Although agency leadership, like all organizational leadership, is situational, being shaped significantly by factors in the environment other than the leader himself, still leadership can have a significant impact on agency operation and success. Some agency leaders will be more effective than others in dealing with outside interest groups, cultivating congressional committees, opening the organization to new ideas, and communicating a sense of purpose to agency personnel. The revitalization in the 1970s of the Federal Trade Commission was aided by the leadership of Caspar Weinberger, Miles W. Kirkpatrick, and Louis Engman as successive chairmen.[22] John Connally, former governor of Texas, was a capable and vigorous Secretary of the Treasury during the first Nixon Administration and, under his leadership, the Department had a major role in economic policy development. The State Department played a diminished role in foreign policy formation during the first Nixon Administration because of the rather quiescent leadership of then Secretary of State William Rogers. Henry Kissinger (who later became Secretary of State) dominated foreign policy in his capacity as a presidential assistant.

## Administrative Policy-Making

Although administrative agencies are often deeply involved in policy formation at the legislative stage, attention here will be on how agencies shape policy through the implementation of legislation. Two facets of agency action will be examined: characteristics of agency decision-making and the ways in which agencies develop policy. It is well to keep in mind here the distinction between decisions and policy.

In agency decision-making, hierarchy is of central importance. Although in legislatures, all members have an equal vote at the voting stage, within agencies those at upper levels have more authority over final decisions than those at lower levels. To be sure, factors such as the decentralization of authority, the responsiveness of subunits to outside forces (such as pressure groups), and the participation of professionals in administrative activity work against hierarchical authority, but the importance of hierarchy should nonetheless not be underestimated. Complexity, size, and the desire for economical operation and more control over the bureaucratic apparatus all contribute to the development of hierarchical authority. As for its consequences for decision-making, it is a means by which discrete decisions can be coordinated with one another and conflicts among officials at lower levels of decision can be resolved. Hierarchy also means that those at the upper levels have a larger voice in agency decisions because of their high status, even though lower-level officials may have more substantive expertness. A separation of power and knowledge may thus threaten the rationality of administrative decisions.[23] Hierarchy can also adversely afffect the free flow of ideas and information in an organization, because subordinates, for example, may hesitate to advance proposals they think may run counter to "official" policy or antagonize their superiors.

Administrative agencies constitute "a governmental habitat in which expertise finds a wealth of opportunity to exert itself and to influence policy."[24]
Agencies in their decision-making are clearly affected by political considerations and also by the wish to protect their own power. Thus, the Department
of Commerce is unlikely to make policy decisions which sharply conflict
with important business interests. Nor is the Tennessee Valley Authority
likely to ignore important interests within its region. Agencies nonetheless
do provide a context within which experts and professionals, official and private, can work on policy problems. Technical considerations and professional advice play an important part in most administrative decision-making.
Whether it is the Federal Aviation Agency considering adoption of a rule pertaining to aircraft safety, the Environmental Protection Agency setting emission standards, or the President confronted with a major choice on military
policy, each needs good information on the technical feasibility of proposed
alternatives. Decisions that are made without adequate consideration of their
technical aspects, or which run counter to strong professional advice, may
be deemed bad on both technical and political grounds. President Nixon's
decision to institute Phase III of his price-and-wage control program, which
provided for a freeze on many prices, ran counter to much professional economic advice and proved to be both economically ineffective and politically
disadvantageous.

Secrecy also plays a role in administrative decision-making. In comparison
with that of legislatures, administrative decision-making is a relatively invisi-
ble part of government. Agencies may hold public hearings, issue press releases, and the like, but they exercise considerable control over what information becomes available on their internal deliberations and decisions, and,
consequently, much of what they do is little noticed by the public or reported by the news media. This secrecy, or invisibility, can contribute to the
effectiveness of decisions by providing an environment for presentation and
discussion of policy proposals that might otherwise be avoided as publicly
unpopular. Deliberations by Kennedy Administration officials during the 1962
Cuban missile crisis were more effective because of their private nature.[25]
Secrecy may also facilitate the bargaining and compromise often necessary to
reach decisions and take action, because officials will find it easier to move
away from privately stated than publicly stated positions. On the other hand,
the private nature of administrative deliberation may mean that some pertinent facts are not considered, and that significant interests are not consulted.
While secrecy contributed to the effectiveness of the Cuban missile-crisis decisions, it had the opposite effect with regard to the Bay of Pigs invasion the
previous year. Secrecy is, on the whole, more characteristic of administrative
deliberations in the foreign policy area than in domestic matters. In the latter
area, secrecy has been reduced in recent years by legislation intended to
open the administrative process to greater public scrutiny and participation.

Finally, administrative decision-making is very frequently characterized
by bargaining. Experts and facts are important in administrative decision-
making, as has been noted, but so also are accommodation and compromise.
Some agencies may be less involved in bargaining than others. The National
Bureau of Standards and the Patent Office come to mind as two agencies
whose decisions seem primarily expert decisions based on factual records.

Economic regulatory agencies, such as the Interstate Commerce Commission and Environmental Protection Agency, often find it necessary to bargain with those whom they regulate. In setting emission standards, EPA has had to bargain with both polluters and state and local officials in order to reach tolerable decisions and secure compliance. A notable example of bargaining involves the consent decrees used by the Antitrust Division of the Department of Justice to close most civil antitrust cases. Negotiated in privacy—it should be observed—by representatives of the Division and of the alleged offender, the consent decree provides that the Division will drop its formal proceedings in turn for the alleged offender's agreeing to stop certain practices, such as price-fixing or proposed acquisition of a competitor. Negotiations with foreign countries for tariff reductions are another good illustration of bargaining, in this instance with foreign administrators.

Turning now to the second concern of this section, administrative decisions may be productive of policy (recall how it was defined in Chapter 1) in several ways—namely, rule-making, adjudication, law enforcement, and program operations.

*Rule-Making* A rule may be defined as an agency statement of general applicability and future effect that concerns the rights of private parties and has the force and effect of law. Some rules fill in the details of general statutory provisions; others define the meaning of words such as "small business" or "discriminate" that appear in statutes; still others state how an agency will act in certain matters, as in the location of highways. Many national administrative agencies have been delegated rule-making (or legislative) authority by Congress. Thus, the Securities and Exchange Commission is authorized to make certain rules governing the stock exchanges "as it seems necessary in the public interest or for the protection of investors," and the Occupational Safety and Health Administration is empowered to make rules setting health and safety standards for working conditions that employers must meet. The initial set of rules issued by OSHA occupied several hundred pages of small print. In each of these instances, policy is to a substantial extent the product of agency rule-making. Or, to put it differently, agencies make much of the policy that they implement.

In exercising their rule-making powers, agencies have a great deal of discretion or leeway in what they do, because, as was previously noted, the legislation delegating power to agencies is often quite general or vague in nature. Customarily, though, agencies can exercise their power only in given areas. Thus, the Federal Communications Commission is restricted to the communications industry, the National Highway Traffic Safety Administration to motor vehicles, and the Comptroller of the Currency to banking. It should not be assumed, however, that only regulatory agencies have rule-making powers. Such agencies as the Departments of Health and Human Services, Agriculture, and Housing and Urban Development also possess vast power. Many of their programs involve the expenditure of large sums of money, and they make many administrative rules governing their disposition and use. Collectively, the volume of rules made in a year's time by national administrative agencies and reported in the *Federal Register* is greater than the legislation enacted by Congress and recorded in the *U.S. Statutes-at-Large.*

*Adjudication*    Agencies can make policy when they apply existing laws or rules to particular situations by case-to-case decision-making. In so doing, they act in much the same manner as courts, just as they act in legislative fashion when engaged in rule-making. In the past, the Federal Trade Commission has made policy by applying the legislative prohibition of unfair methods of competition to specific cases. Over time, these cases marked out public policy and indicated the kinds of practices banned by the general prohibition. Again, an agency may make policy when it gives a particular interpretation to a statutory provision in the course of applying it in a case. Thus, the National Labor Relations Board, which administers labor-management relations legislation, makes statutory interpretations in deciding unfair-practices cases that then serve to inform its action in future cases. In such instances NLRB opinions become policy statements of much interest to those concerned with policy in this area.

Agencies not infrequently choose to make policy through adjudication even though they have rule-making authority. (They may be authorized, but not required to make rules.) An agency may find it no easier than a legislature to agree on what form a general policy should take, especially in a novel or highly controversial situation. Those affected by agency action may be left in the dark as to what policy is supposed to be when it is made on a case-by-case basis. Agencies, indeed, have often been criticized for relying too much on adjudication and too little on rule-making in the development of policy.

Much of the adjudication engaged in by administrative agencies is rather routine, such as the hundreds of thousands of decisions made annually by the Veterans Administration and the Social Security Administration on applications for benefits. Still, within the framework of statutory language, seemingly routine decisions may shift the direction or affect the impact of policy. Noteworthy in this regard is the operation of the Internal Revenue Service, which routinely closes most cases of disputed income-tax returns by informal adjudication (and bargaining). IRS statistics for fiscal year 1972, which were obtained under a Freedom of Information Act proceeding, for example, showed that, in cases that did not end up in the courts—and most do not—the agency settled for 67 percent of the amounts owed in the $1–$999 range, while settling for an average of 34 percent when $1 million or more was allegedly owed. Moreover, settlements varied widely from district to district, ranging from 12 percent of the amount alleged by IRS in the St. Paul district to 76 percent in Pittsburgh.[26] Obviously, such actions significantly affect policy content and impact.

*Law Enforcement*    Agencies may also make policy through their general law-enforcement actions. A statute may be enforced vigorously or even rigidly, in a lax manner, or not at all; it may be applied in some situations and not in others, or to some persons or companies and not to others. Everyone is familiar with the discretion possessed by the police officer on the beat or, what is more likely, in the patrol car. A ticket may be issued to a speeder, or he may be let off with a warning. If no one is ticketed unless he exceeds posted speed limits by a certain rate, this amounts to an amendment of public policy. Even when statutory provisions are quite precise, thus seeming to eliminate discretion in their interpretation, enforcement officers still have some discretion with respect to whether they will be enforced.

The Hepburn Act of 1906, which dealt primarily with railroads, also authorized the Interstate Commerce Commission to regulate the rates charged by pipeline companies. Except for requiring the filing of rates, however, the ICC took no action by itself on the subject until 1934. It did not actually complete a pipeline rate proceeding until 1948, and then no effective action resulted. Since then, the ICC has continued to do little to carry out this authorization,[27] essentially substituting a policy of minimal regulation for the legislatively declared policy of regulation. The ICC's reluctance to carry out congressional intent illustrates an aspect of the administrative process that needs more systematic attention from policy analysts. Policy may be shaped by administrative inaction or apathy as well as by agency action and zeal. Inaction often affects only the inarticulate general public and consequently may pass unnoticed.

Agency enforcement activity depends not only on the attitudes and motives of agency officials, as well as external pressures, but also on the enforcement techniques available to the agency. Opponents unable to block the legislative enactment of a law may seek to blunt its impact by handicapping its enforcement. Take the case of the equal-employment opportunity provisions of the Civil Rights Act of 1964, which prohibit firms or unions representing 25 or more employees from discriminating against individuals because of their race, color, religion, national origin, or sex. Along with the rest of the Act, these provisions were adopted over strong opposition. The Equal Employment Opportunity Commission was established to enforce them through investigations, conferences, and conciliation, which means essentially voluntary action. If this failed, the EEOC could recommend civil action in the federal courts, which would require the cooperation of the Department of Justice. Moreover, the law provided that EEOC could not act on complaints from states in which there was an antidiscrimination law and an agency to enforce it, unless the state agency was unable to complete action within 60 days. Complaints had to be filed "in writing under oath," which is not a customary requirement for a law violation complaint. This undoubtedly had a chilling effect on many Southern blacks as well as others. Whatever the intent behind these provisions, they clearly limited the effectiveness of the law by making the successful completion of cases a slow, tedious process. After 1964, the EEOC and many supporters of stronger enforcement advocated giving the agency authority to issue "cease-and-desist orders"[28] in discrimination cases and then on its own initiative to seek their enforcement in the federal courts. Opposition to this change was particularly strong from conservatives and Southerners. In 1972, the EEOC was finally empowered to initiate court action on its own, but not to issue cease-and-desist orders when conciliation of complaints was not successful. Though perhaps not as much as hoped, this new authority did help strengthen enforcement and the effectiveness of the anti–job discrimination policy.

*Program Operations*   Many agencies are involved in the operation of loan, grant, benefit, insurance, service, or construction policies and programs that are usually not thought of as being law enforcement in nature because they are not designed *directly* to regulate or shape people's behavior. How such programs are administered helps determine policy. A couple of examples should clarify what is involved here. Since the 1930s, the Federal Housing Administration has administered a mortgage insurance program under which the risks of nonpayment and foreclosure are assumed by the government rather than by private lending agencies. Until 1967, one regulation provided that housing loans, to be FHA-insured, had to be based on the criterion of "economic soundness." Consequently, low-income people in slum or deteriorating areas usually could not secure loans because of the "excessive risk" involved. Interest costs were also high relative to the income of the poor. Because of these operating requirements, the mortgage insurance policy was much more beneficial to middle- and upper-income persons than to the poor. In 1964, only 2.4 percent of FHA loans on homes went to families with incomes below $4,800 annually. Not surprisingly, FHA gained a reputation of being unfriendly to the poor. Legislation enacted in 1968 was designed to reorder FHA priorities and make public policy in this area more helpful to low-income people. In recent years FHA has become less important because of the development of private loan guarantee companies that offer more flexible rates to borrowers.[29]

To take another case, the Elementary and Secondary Education Act of 1965, under its Title I, provided financial aid for the education of disadvantaged children in urban and rural poor areas.[30] For fiscal year 1977, these funds, which are handled by the Office of Education, amounted to about $4.7 billion. In the view of social-reform elements among its supporters, this policy was designed to help eliminate poverty by improving the educational facilities and opportunities of poor children. The Office of Education, however, generally did not act with much vigor or effectiveness to see that local school districts actually use the funds as intended. Consequently, it is unclear to what extent funds were actually expended on disadvantaged children, and whether they bought services beyond the level of those provided other children in the aided districts. The program in operation took on something of the appearance of general aid to education.

Several factors contributed to this. Although the legislation clearly specified disadvantaged children as its focus, its legislative history "provided the semblance if not the reality of general aid." This ambiguity, together with the fact that the reformers supporting the legislation did not concern themselves with its implementation, meant that officials in the Office of Education were left to interpret the legislation as they saw fit. Second, the orientation of the Office of Education was to provide assistance and advice to state and local education agencies; it was not inclined to regulate and police their activities. Third, state and local agencies have traditionally dominated the field of education, and they have strong political support in this regard. This makes it very difficult for national officials to impose directives that conflict with local priorities. Because of the manner in which it has been administered, the Title I program has not achieved the results hoped for by its supporters.

## COMPLIANCE

All public policies are intended to influence or control human behavior in some way, to induce people to act in accordance with governmentally prescribed rules or goals, whether reference is to policy or such diverse matters as patents and copyrights, open housing, interest rates, night-time burglary, agricultural production, or military recruitment. If compliance with policy is not achieved, if people continue to act in undesired ways, if they do not take desired actions, or if they cease doing what is desired, to that extent policy becomes ineffective or, at the extreme, a nullity. (Foreign policy also depends for its effectiveness on compliance by the affected foreign countries and their officials.) To make consideration of this problem more manageable, we will focus primarily, but not exclusively, on compliance with domestic economic policies.

Except, perhaps, for crime policies, social scientists have not given much attention to the problem of compliance.[31] Perhaps this is partly due to our traditional legalistic approach to government, with its assumption that people have an absolute duty to obey the law. Too, those concerned with securing action on public problems often lose interest therein or shift their attention elsewhere once they secure the enactment of legislation. Such was the case with the Elementary and Secondary Education Act of 1965 referred to above. Political scientists have certainly been far more interested in the legislative and executive formation and adaptation of policy than in its administration, which is where compliance comes in. A complete study of policymaking must be concerned not only with the events leading up to a policy decision but also with what is done to implement it and, ultimately, whether people comply with it.

In this section, some of the factors affecting compliance and noncompliance with policy will be examined, along with the role of administrative agencies in securing compliance.[32] Because of a scarcity of empirical data, the discussion must be somewhat speculative.

## Causes of Compliance

Substantial respect for authority exists in our society, including authority as expressed in the decisions of governmental agencies. Statements to the effect that Americans are a lawless people appear as exaggerations and should not be permitted to obscure this fact. Respect for, and deference to, authority is built into our psychological make-up by the process of socialization. Most of us are taught from birth to respect the authority of parents, knowledge, status, the law, and government officials, especially if these forms of authority are considered to be reasonable. Consequently, we grow up generally believing it to be morally right and proper to obey the law. Disobedience of the law may produce feelings of guilt or shame. Prior conditioning and force of habit thus contribute to policy.

Compliance with policy may also be based on some form of reasoned, conscious acceptance. Even some whose immediate self-interest conflicts with a particular policy may be convinced that it is reasonable, necessary, or just. Most people undoubtedly would rather not pay taxes, and many do try to avoid or evade paying. But when people believe that tax laws are reasonable and just, or perhaps that taxation is necessary to provide needed governmental services, such beliefs will in all likelihood contribute to compliance with tax policy. Are not factors such as this and the one discussed in the preceding paragraph contributory to the high degree of compliance with the national income tax in the United States?

Another possible cause of compliance is the belief that a governmental decision or policy should be obeyed because it is legitimate, in the sense that it is constitutional, or was made by officials with proper authority to act, or that correct procedures were followed. People would probably be less inclined to accept judicial decisions as legitimate if the courts utilized decision procedures akin to those of legislatures. Courts gain legitimacy and acceptance for their decision by acting as courts are supposed to act. Some people in the South were willing to comply with the Supreme Court's 1954 school desegregation decision because they viewed it as legitimate, as within the Court's competence, even though they disagreed with its substance.

Self-interest is often an important factor in compliance. Individuals and groups may directly benefit from acceptance of policy norms and standards. Thus, farmers have complied with production limitations in the form of acreage allotments and marketing quotas in order to qualify for price supports and benefit payments. Securities regulation is accepted by responsible members of the securities business as a way of protecting themselves and the reputation of their business against unethical practices by some dealers. Businessmen engage in industrial-plant modernization in order to receive investment tax credits. Milk price–control laws have long been sought and complied with by dairy interests as a way of improving their economic well-being. Compliance thus results because private interests and policy prescriptions are harmonious, a fact sometimes ignored. Or, to put it differently, compliance may yield positive rewards. This situation, we should note, is not likely to occur outside the economic policy area.

For any given piece of legislation, such as a minimum-wage law or a Sunday closing law, there will not be simply supporters and opponents. Rather, many points of view will exist, ranging from strong support, through indifference, to intense opposition. A considerable proportion of the population will often be indifferent or neutral toward the legislation in question, if, indeed, they feel affected by it at all. This group, given the general predisposition toward obedience, would seem especially subject to the authority of the law. Here, in effect, the law becomes a "self-fulfilling prophecy"; by its very existence it operates to create a climate of opinion conducive to compliance with it.

The possibility of punishment in the form of fines, imprisonment, and other sanctions also works to secure compliance. A number of recent studies indicate that law-abiding persons, as compared to law violators, considerably overestimate the risks of detection, conviction, and punishment for criminal actions.[33] The threat or imposition of sanctions alone, however, is not always sufficient, even given overestimation of the likelihood of their use. "The strong disposition in this country to believe that any behavior can be controlled by threatening punishment has filled American statute books with hundreds of unenforced and unenforceable laws."[34] The experience with national prohibition, World War II price and rationing controls, many Sunday blue laws, and, recently, penalties for marijuana use shows that the threat of punishment is inadequate to cause compliance in the face of widespread violations.

Although many people may comply with policies because they fear punishment, the main function of sanctions is to reinforce and supplement other causes of compliance. To a great extent, policies depend for their effectiveness upon voluntary, that is, noncoerced compliance, because those concerned with enforcement cannot effectively handle, and apply sanctions in, large numbers of cases. The Internal Revenue Service would find itself at an impasse if several millions of people decided not to file returns. If those who would normally comply with policies see others benefiting from noncompliance, they, too, may become violators. Here the application of sanctions to some violators may be an effective promoter of compliance. Thus, the IRS does prosecute flagrant and prominent tax evaders to prove by example that punishment awaits the tax evader.

In many instances, sanctions are effective more because people desire to avoid being stigmatized as lawbreakers than because they fear the penalties involved. In criminal proceedings for antitrust violations, for example, the fines levied have usually been quite nominal, given the economic resources of the violators. Not until 1961 did a businessman actually spend time in jail for an antitrust violation, although this punishment had been possible since the adoption of the Sherman Act in 1890. The real deterrent in these cases is probably the adverse publicity that flows from the proceedings. In recent years, Antitrust Division officials have been advocating more severe penalties for antitrust violators, especially jail sentences, in order to encourage compliance. Legislators and judges, however, are often reluctant to create or impose jail sentences and other severe penalties on businessmen because of their social status and because of the often diffuse and complex impact of law violations such as embezzlement or the misuse of "inside information" in stock deals. In other situations, sanctions may be more severe and uncertain and have more powerful deterrent effect.

Finally, acceptance of most policies seems to increase with the length of time they are in effect. As time passes—and it always does—a once controversial policy becomes more familiar, a part of the accepted state of things, one of the conditions of doing business. Further, increasing numbers of persons come under the policy who have had no experience with the prepolicy situation. Because "freedom is (in part) a state of mind, such men feel the restrictions to rest more lightly upon them."[35] Although at one time the Wagner Act (1935) was found highly objectionable by businessmen and the Taft-Hartley Act (1947) was vigorously opposed by labor unions, today these statutes have lost much of their controversial quality. They have become a fixed part of the environment of labor-management relations, and businessmen and labor-union officials have "learned to live with them." Predictably, environmental pollution-control policies will seem less restrictive or intrusive a decade from now than they do at present.

## Causes of Noncompliance

It will be readily apparent even to the most casual observer that all persons affected by public policies do not comply with them. Statistical information on reported violations is readily obtainable, as in the Federal Bureau of Investigation's Uniform Crime Reports. In addition, a lot of violations go undetected or unreported. Why do some people, or in some situations many people, deviate from officially prescribed norms of behavior? As the obverse of compliance, noncompliance may result when laws conflict too sharply with the prevailing values, mores, and beliefs of the people generally or of particular groups. The extensive violations of national prohibition and wartime price and rationing controls can be attributed in considerable measure to this cause as may much of the noncompliance in the South with the 1954 school desegregation decision and related policy. In such instances, the general predisposition to obey the law is outweighed by strong attachment to particular values and practices.

It is not very useful, however, to ascribe noncompliance to a broad conflict between law and morality. Those who proclaim that "you can't legislate morality" not only oversimplify but also ignore the fact that morality is frequently legislated with considerable success. Failure to comply results when a particular law or set of laws conflicts with particular values or beliefs in a particular time and situation. The law-value conflict must be stated in fairly precise terms if it is to have operational value in explaining noncompliance. Thus, there was considerable noncompliance with the Supreme Court's 1948 decision that "released time" programs of religious instruction in public schools violated the constitutional requirement of separation of church and state.[36] Such released time programs were continued in many school systems where local citizens and school officials wanted them, despite their unconstitutionality. More recently, opinion surveys have indicated that tax evasion is most common among persons who do not believe that the federal tax system is fair.[37]

The concept of selective disobedience of the law is closely related to the law-value conflict.[38] Some laws are felt to be less binding than others on the individual. Those who strongly support and obey what are ordinarily designated as criminal laws sometimes have a more relaxed or permissive attitude toward economic legislation and regulations or laws regulating the behavior of public officials. (In this regard, one should consider the behavior of former Vice President Spiro T. Agnew, who resigned his office after pleading no contest to a charge of income tax evasion.) Many businessmen apparently believe that laws relating to banking operations, trade practices, taxation, and environmental pollution control are not as mandatory for individuals as laws prohibiting robbery, burglary, and embezzlement. This may be, in part, because legislation regulating economic activity developed later than criminal laws. Moreover, economic legislation often runs counter to the businessman's ideology favoring nonintervention by government in the economy, and he may consider it bad law. In addition, the same social stigma usually is not attached to violation of economic policy as it is to criminal laws. Professor Marshall Clinard comments: "This selection of obedience to law rests upon the principle that what the person may be doing is illegal, perhaps even unethical, but certainly not criminal."

One's associates and group memberships may contribute to noncompliance (or, under other conditions, we should note, to compliance). Association with persons who hold ideas disrespectful of law and government, who justify or rationalize law violation, or who violate the law may cause the individual to acquire deviant norms and values that dispose him to noncompliance. In a study of labor relations policy, Lane found that the rate of law violations varied with the community in which the firms studied were located. It was "fairly conclusive" that one reason for these differential patterns was "difference in attitude toward the law, the government, and the morality of illegality. Plant managers stated they followed community patterns of behavior in their labor relations activities."[39] Attorneys for some of the defendant executives in the great price-fixing conspiracy in the electrical industry in the late 1950s attempted to explain and justify their actions, in the hope of lessening their punishment, as being in accord with the "corporate way of life."[40]

The desire to "make a fast buck," or something akin thereto, is often stated as a cause of noncompliance. This would certainly seem to be the case in many instances of fraud and misrepresentation, such as short-weighting and passing one product off for another in retail sales, the promotion of shady land sales and investment schemes, and price-fixing agreements. (Price-fixing is both the most obvious and the most common violation of the Sherman Antitrust Act.) It is really not possible, however, to determine how widespread greed is as a motive for noncompliance. By itself it often seems inadequate as an explanation. If two companies have equal opportunities to profit by violating the law, and one violates the law while the other does not, what is the explanation? One explanation may be that companies that are less profitable or in danger of failure are more likely to violate in an effort to survive than are more financially secure firms.[41] One should be careful, however, in attributing noncompliance to pecuniary motives. Many violations of labor-management relations policy stem from a desire to protect the prerogatives of management, while noncompliance with industrial health-and-safety standards may rest on the conviction that they are unnecessary or unworkable.

Noncompliance may also result from such factors as ambiguities in the law, a lack of clarity, conflicting policy standards, or failure to adequately transmit policies to those affected by them. Income-tax violations often stem from the ambiguity or complexity of provisions of the Internal Revenue Code, which someone once described as a "sustained essay in obscurity." In other instances, persons or companies may believe that a given practice is not prohibited by existing law, only to find upon prosecution that it is. Such a situation may arise because the frames of reference of businessmen and public officials are different, thus each interpreting the law differently. Violations may also result from difficulties in complying with the law, even when its meaning is understood. For example, insufficient time may be allowed for filing complicated forms or for making required changes in existing patterns of action, such as in the installation of pollution-control devices. Sheer ignorance of the existence of laws or rules regulating conduct cannot be discounted as a cause of noncompliance. While ignorance of the law may be no excuse, it often does account for violations. In sum, noncompliance may stem from structural defects in the law and its administration, and from ignorance and lack of understanding of the law, as well as from behavior that is more consciously or deliberately deviant.

## Administration and Compliance

The burden of securing compliance with public policies rests primarily with administrative agencies; the courts play a lesser role. The broad purpose of administrative enforcement activities, such as conferences, persuasion, inspection, and prosecution, is to obtain compliance with policies rather than merely to punish violators.

Conscious human behavior involves making choices among alternatives—deciding to do some things and not to do others. For purposes of discussion, we can assume that there are essentially three ways in which administrative agencies, or other governmental bodies, concerned with implementing public policy can influence people to act in the desired ways—to select behavioral alternatives that result in policy compliance. First, to achieve a desired result agencies can strive to shape, alter, or utilize the values people employ in making choices. Educational and persuasional activities are illustrative of this type of activity. Second, agencies can seek to limit the acceptable choices available to people, as by attaching penalties to undesired alternatives and rewards or benefits to desired alternatives. Third, agencies can try to interpret and administer policies in ways designed to facilitate compliance with their requirements. More than one of these alternatives are normally used in seeking compliance with a given policy.

Administrative agencies engage in a wide range of educational and persuasional activities intended to convince those directly affected, and the public generally, that given public policies are reasonable, necessary, socially beneficial, or legitimate, in addition to informing them of the existence and meaning of those policies. The effectiveness of public policies depends considerably on the ability of agencies to promote understanding and consent, thereby reducing violations and minimizing the actual use of sanctions. This is in keeping with our earlier comment on the importance of voluntary compliance. When changes are made in the coverage and level of the federal minimum-wage law, for example, the Department of Labor seeks to acquaint the public, and especially affected employers and employees, of their nature and implications by the distribution of explanatory bulletins, reference guides, and posters, announcements through the news media, meetings with affected groups, appearances at conventions, direct mailings, telephone calls, and the like. After the changes become effective, press releases and mailed materials are used to provide information on enforcement activities and legal interpretations of the law. The Federal Deposit Insurance Corporation relies heavily on advice and warnings to banks, based on inspections, to get them to bring their operations into accord with banking regulations. Formal proceedings are initiated only when persuasion appears ineffective.

Agencies may also use propaganda appeals in support of compliance. (Propaganda is used here not in a pejorative sense but rather to denote efforts to gain acceptance of policies by identifying them with widely held values and beliefs.) Appeals to patriotism were used to win support and acceptance of the military draft. Agricultural programs have been depicted as necessary to ensure equality for agriculture and to help preserve the family farm as a way of life. Antitrust programs have been described as necessary to maintain our system of free competitive enterprise. The Forest Service utilizes Smokey the Bear to tell us that "only you can prevent forest fires." Propaganda appeals are more emotional than rational in thrust. They can be viewed as attempts either to reduce the moral costs of adapting to a policy or to make compliance desirable by attaching positive values to policies.[42]

In the course of administering policies, agencies may make modifications or adopt practices that will contribute to compliance. Revealed inequities in the law may be reduced or eliminated, or conflicts in policy standards may be resolved, or simplified procedures for compliance may be developed, such as simplified federal income-tax forms for lower-income earners. Administrative personnel may develop knowledge and skill in enforcing policy that enables them to reduce misunderstanding and antagonism. Consultation and advice may be used to help those affected by laws come into compliance without the issuance of citations. Laws may be interpreted or applied to make them more compatible with the interests of those affected. For instance, until 1970 the administration of oil-import controls policy by the Oil Import Administration "was almost wholly in the interests of the petroleum industry."[43] They had little cause for complaint. Many of the health-and-safety "consensus" standards initially issued by the Occupational Safety and Health Administration (OSHA) were later rescinded because of widespread complaints that they were outdated, trivial, or had little usefulness in protecting against health and safety hazards. OSHA hoped to reduce the antagonism of the business community toward itself by their elimination.

Sanctions will be resorted to by agencies when the various sociological and psychological factors supporting obedience and the other methods available to agencies fail to produce compliance. Sanctions are penalties or deprivations imposed on those who violate policy norms and are intended to make undesired behavior patterns unattractive. They directly punish violators and serve to deter others who might not comply if they saw violations go unpunished.

Sanctions may be imposed by either administrative agencies or the courts. Common forms of judicial sanctions are fines, jail sentences, award of damages, and injunctions. However, in most areas of public policy (crime policy is a major exception) administrative sanctions are used much more frequently because of their greater immediacy, variety, and flexibility. Among the sanctions that agencies may impose are: threat of prosecution; imposition of fines or pecuniary penalties that have the effect of fines, as by OSHA; unfavorable publicity; revocation, annulment, modification, suspension, or refusal to renew licenses; summary seizure and destruction of goods; award of damages; issuance of cease-and-desist orders; and denial of services or benefits. To be most effective, the severity of sanctions must be geared to the violations against which they are directed. If they are too severe, the agency may be reluctant to use them; if they are too mild, they may have inadequate deterrent effects, as seems the case with most fines for antitrust violations. The Office of Education was handicapped in its administration of Title I of the Elementary and Secondary Education Act because the only sanction it had for state and local violations of the law was the cutting off of funds. Because of the reaction this would cause, it was politically reluctant to do so and, indeed, did not. Agencies clearly need appropriate and effective sanctions to help ensure policy compliance.

Agencies may also seek to induce compliance by conferring positive benefits on compliers, thereby bring self-interest into support for compliance. This method can be referred to as the "purchase of consent." Benefits may take such forms as favorable publicity and recognition for nondiscrimination in hiring, price-support payments for compliance with agricultural production limitations, tax credits for industrial plant modernization, and federal grants-in-aid for the support of state programs of medical aid to the indigent that meet federal standards. It is often difficult, however, to distinguish rewards from sanctions. Does an individual comply with a policy provision to secure a benefit or to avoid losing it? Whatever the motives of persons seeking benefits, the government does use rewards extensively to gain compliance with policy. They are undoubtedly much more acceptable politically in many situations than would be a clear-cut prohibition or requirement of some action with penalties for noncompliance. Imagine the reaction if, rather than using tax credits, businessmen were required to modernize their plants or else be subject to fines and other penalties. Subsidy payments clearly have made compliance with production controls more palatable to farmers.

Clearly, then, compliance—or noncompliance—with public policy may stem from a variety of factors. It is a complex topic that needs greater attention by policy analysts because of its importance for the actual content and impact of public policy.

## NOTES

1. John W. Ellwood and James A. Thurber, "The Politics of the Congressional Budget Process Re-examined," in Lawrence C. Dodd and Bruce I. Oppenheimer, eds., *Congress Reconsidered,* 2d ed. (Washington, D.C.: Congressional Quarterly Press, 1981), pp. 247–251.

2. For fuller discussions, see Louis Fisher, *Presidential Spending Power* (Princeton, N.J.: Princeton University Press, 1975), chaps. 7–8; and James P. Pfiffner, *The President, the Budget, and Congress: Impoundment and the 1974 Budget Act* (Boulder, CO: Westview Press, 1979).

3. Frank J. Goodnow, *Politics and Administration* (New York: Russell and Russell, 1900).

4. Martha Derthick, *Policymaking for Social Security* (Washington, D.C.: Brookings Institution, 1979), chap. 15.

5. This story is well told in Joseph P. Harris, *The Advice and Consent of the Senate* (Berkeley: University of California Press, 1953), chap. II.

6. David T. Stanley and Marjorie Girth, *Bankruptcy: Problems Process Reform* (Washington, D.C.: Brookings Institution, 1971), p. 172.

7. See Samuel P. Huntington, "The Marasmus of the ICC," *Yale Law Journal* LXI (1952), pp. 470–509.

8. Henry J. Steck, "Power and the Policy Process: Advisory Committee in the Federal Government." Unpublished paper presented at the annual meeting of the American Political Science Association (September, 1972), p. 4.

9. James W. Davis, Jr., and Kenneth M. Dolbeare, *Little Groups of Neighbors: The Selective Service System* (Chicago: Markham, 1968).

10. See generally, Aaron Wildavsky, *The Politics of the Budgetary Process,* 3d ed. (Boston: Little, Brown, 1979); Lance T. LeLoup, *Budgetary Politics,* 2d ed. (Brunswick, Ohio: King's Court Communications, Inc., 1980); and Dennis S. Ippolito, *Congressional Spending* (Ithaca: Cornell University Press, 1981).

11. Rowland Evans and Robert Novak, *Lyndon B. Johnson: The Exercise of Power* (New York: New American Library, 1966), p. 430.

12. See Emmette S. Redford and Marlan Blisset, *Organizing the Executive Branch: The Johnson Presidency* (Chicago: University of Chicago Press, 1981).

13. V. O. Key, Jr., "Legislative Control," in Fritz Morstein Marx, Jr., *Elements of Public Administration,* 2d ed. (Englewood Cliffs, N.J.: Prentice-Hall, 1959), p. 321.

14. See, for example, Louis J. Kohlmeier, Jr., *The Regulators* (New York: Harper & Row, 1969).

15. Quoted in V. O. Key, Jr., *Politics, Parties, and Pressure Groups,* 4th ed. (New York: Crowell, 1958), p. 743.

16. This discussion is based on my *Politics and the Economy* (Boston: Little, Brown, 1966), pp. 86–90.

17. *Phillips Petroleum Company* v. *State of Wisconsin,* 347 U.S. 672 (1954).

18. Cf. Matthew Holden, Jr., " 'Imperialism' in Bureaucracy," *American Political Science Review,* LX (December, 1966), pp. 943–51.

19. Holden, *ibid,* p. 944.

20. This discussion, and that in the first part of the next section, draws on Francis E. Rourke, *Bureaucracy, Politics and Public Policy,* 2d ed. (Boston: Little, Brown, 1976), chaps. 4 and 5.

21. *Ibid,* p. 75.

22. *New York Times,* May 30, 1972, p. 53; *Houston Chronicle,* December 17, 1972, p. 5, Sect. 1.

23. On the separation of the ability to decide from the authority to decide in organization, see Victor Thompson, *Modern Organizations* (New York: Knopf, 1961).

24. Rourke, *op. cit.,* p. 108.

25. Theodore C. Sorensen, *Kennedy* (New York: Harper & Row, 1965), chap. 25. On secrecy in administration generally, see Harold L. Wilensky, *Organizational Intelligence* (New York: Basic Books, 1967), chaps. 3 and 7; and Francis E. Rourke, *Secrecy and Publicity* (Baltimore: Johns Hopkins Press, 1961).

26. *Wall Street Journal* (February 5, 1973), p. 1.

27. Kenneth Culp Davis, *Administrative Law Treatise* (St. Paul, Minn.: West, 1958), vol. I, pp. 263–65.

28. A "cease-and-desist order" is a civil directive by an agency to someone to stop engaging in a practice held to be in violation of the law. Agencies such as the Federal Trade Commission and the National Labor Relations Board are authorized to issue such orders.

29. Harold Wolman, *Politics of Federal Housing* (New York: Dodd, Mead, 1971), pp. 26–28.

30. This discussion is based on Jerome T. Murphy, "The Education Bureaucracies Implement Novel Policy: The Politics of Title I of ESEA, 1965–72," in Allen P. Sindler (ed.), *Policy and Politics in America,* 2d ed. (Boston: Little, Brown, 1973), pp. 161–98. Also see Daniel A. Mazmanian and Paul A. Sabatier, *Implementation and Public Policy* (Chicago: Scott, Foresman, 1983), ch. 6.

31. A notable recent exception is Kenneth J. Meier and David R. Morgan, "Citizen Compliance with Public Policy: The National Maximum Speed Law," *Western Political Quarterly,* XXXV (June 1982), pp. 258–273.

32. This discussion draws heavily on my "Public Economic Policy and the Problem of Compliance: Notes for Research," *Houston Law Review* IV (Spring–Summer, 1966), pp. 62–72.

33. For example, Gary F. Jensen, "Crime Doesn't Pay: Correlates of a Shared Misunderstanding," *Social Problems,* XVII (Fall, 1968), pp. 189–201.

34. Herbert A. Simon, Donald Smithburg, and Victor Thompson, *Public Administration* (New York: Knopf, 1950), p. 479.

35. Robert Lane, *The Regulation of Businessmen* (New Haven: Yale University Press, 1954), pp. 69–70.

36. *McCullom* v. *Board of Education,* 333 U.S. 208 (1948). The impact of this case, and a related one, is discussed in Frank J. Sorouf, *"Zorach* v. *Clausen:* The Impact of a Supreme Court Decision," *American Political Science Review,* LIII (September, 1959), pp. 777–91.

37. Timothy B. Clark, "Honesty May Become the Best Tax Policy if Tax Compliance Bill Becomes Law," *The National Journal,* Vol. 14 (July 24, 1982), pp. 1292–1296.

38. Marshall B. Clinard, *Sociology of Deviant Behavior* (New York: Holt, Rinehart and Winston, 1957), pp. 168–71.

39. Robert E. Lane, "Why Business Men Violate the Law," *Journal of Criminal Law, Criminology, and Police Science,* XLIV (1953), pp. 151, 154–60.

40. John G. Fuller, *The Gentlemen Conspirators: The Story of the Price-Fixers in the Electrical Industry* (New York: Grove Press, 1962), pp. 88, 109–10.

41. Lane, *The Regulation of Businessmen, op cit.,* chap. 5.

42. Simon, Smithburg, and Thompson, *op. cit.,* p. 457.

43. Roger G. Noll, *Reforming Regulation* (Washington, D.C.: Brookings Institution, 1971), p. 65.

# 5

# Public Policies

In this chapter our focus shifts from the processes of policy formation and implementation to the substance or content of public policies. Given the scope, complexity, diversity, and vast numbers of public policies in the United States, we obviously cannot summarize or even mention all of them in a short chapter. Therefore our focus will be both selective and limited to domestic public policies.

Governments at all levels—national, state, and local—in the United States have been increasingly active in policy development. Every year a large volume of laws and ordinances flows from the nation's legislative bodies; their output is greatly exceeded by the myriad rules and regulations generated by administrative agencies. The expansion of public policies has occurred in such traditional areas of concern as foreign policy, international trade, education, transportation, business and labor regulation, welfare, and law enforcement. In addition, there has been growing activity in such relatively new areas of action as environmental protection, economic stability, equality of opportunity, nuclear energy, medical care, and consumer protection.

In 1980, the United States Congress adopted more than two hundred public laws. In Table 5.1 are listed some of the "major" statutes enacted (as measured by such loose criteria as number of persons affected, or likely impact on economy or society). Some represent additions to or changes in existing policies, as in the case of those including the word "amendments" in their titles. Others represent new additions to the collection of public policies. All of them contain biases which favor some groups and disadvantage

**Table 5.1   Major Congressional Legislation, 1980**

Depository Institutions, Deregulation and Monetary Control Act

Crude Oil Windfall Profit Tax Act

Federal Trade Commissions Improvement Act

Adoption Assistance and Child Welfare Act

Soft Drink Interbrand Competition Act

Energy Security Act

Regulatory Flexibility Act

Housing and Community Development Act

Automobile Fuel Efficiency Act

Privacy Protection Act

Staggers Rail Act

Veterans Rehabilitation and Education Amendments

Solid Waste Disposal Act Amendments

Agricultural Act

Paperwork Reduction Act

International Security and Development Cooperation Act

State and Local Fiscal Assistance Act Amendments

Motor Carrier Act

Multiemployer Pension Plan Amendments Act

Coastal Zone Management Improvement Act

Foreign Service Act

Small Business Investment Incentive Act

Juvenile Justice Amendments

others in varying degrees. This, indeed, is an intrinsic feature of public policies.

Students of policy analysis are confronted with the task of trying to make some sense out of all this policy activity. To assist them in this endeavor we will discuss some general aspects of public policies; namely, some ways of categorizing public policies and the control feature of public policies. A case study of natural gas rate regulation will conclude the chapter.

## CATEGORIES OF PUBLIC POLICIES

Political scientists and others have developed a number of general typologies for categorizing public policies. These help us to understand some of the differences among policies and to generalize about policies. Some traditional and widely used sets of categories include *substantive* (labor, welfare, civil rights, foreign affairs), *institutional* (legislative policies, judicial policies, departmental policies) and *time period* (New Deal era, post World War II, later part of the nineteenth century). These are convenient for designating various policies and organizing discussions about them but they are not useful for purposes of generalization as they do not get at the basic characteristics of policies. Three other typologies which seem more useful are presented and illustrated here.

First, policies may be classified as *substantive* or *procedural*. Substantive policies involve what government is going to do, such as the construction of highways or the payment of welfare benefits. Procedural policies, in contrast, involve who is going to take action or how it is going to be done. (So defined, procedural policies include organizational matters.)

A good illustration of a procedural policy of much importance is the Administrative Procedure Act of 1946. This statute, which represents a response to the expansion of administrative discretion in the twentieth century, prescribes procedures to be used by agencies in rule-making; for example, the act requires notice of the proposed rule-making, opportunity for interested persons to participate in the proceeding through oral or written submissions, publication of a proposed rule at least thirty days before it becomes effective, and opportunity for interested persons to petition for issuance, amendment, or repeal of a rule. The act's requirements for adjudication are much more detailed. Another example of a procedural policy is the environmental impact statement requirement imposed on agencies proposing major actions affecting the environment by the National Environmental Policy Act. It is intended to cause agencies to give consideration to environmental effects before making their decisions. In itself it adds nothing to the substance of policy.

Procedural policies may have important substantive *effects*. That is, *how* something is done, or *who* takes the action, may help determine what is actually done. A number of propositions concerning the possible impact of organizational decisions on substantive policy were presented in Chapter 4. Frequently, efforts are made to use procedural issues to delay or prevent the adoption of substantive decisions and policies. An agency action may be challenged on the ground that improper procedures were followed, when it is really the substance of the action that is being resisted. Some Washington lawyers have become highly skilled in manipulating procedural rules to delay agency action. Thus, because of procedural delays and complications (most of which were produced by the maneuverings of the defendant company), it took the Federal Trade Commission thirteen years to complete a case compelling the manufacturer to remove the word "liver" from a product named "Carter's Little Liver Pills." (The product has no impact on one's liver.)

Second, policies may be categorized as *distributive, regulatory, self-regulatory,* or *redistributive*.[1] This typology differentiates policies on the basis of the nature of their impact on society and the relationships among those involved in policy formation.

Distributive policies involve the distribution of services or benefits to particular segments of the population—individuals, groups, corporations, and communities. Some distributive policies may provide benefits to only one or a few beneficiaries, as in the cases of the Chrysler loan guarantee of the late 1970s and the subsidies for the construction and operation of merchant ships. Others may provide benefits for vast numbers of persons, as is true for agricultural price support programs, tax deductions for home mortgage payments, and provisions for free public school education.

Distributive programs typically involve the use of public funds to assist particular groups. Those who seek benefits do not compete directly with one another. Nor do their benefits represent a direct cost to any specific group; rather, the costs are assessed to the public treasury, which is to say all taxpayers. Given this, distributive policies appear to create only winners and no specific losers, although obviously someone does pay for them.

A superb example of a distributive policy involves the rivers and harbors improvement and flood control project legislation, which is often referred to as "pork-barrel" legislation, carried out by the Army Corps of Engineers. For fiscal year 1978, the Congress appropriated $1,727,466,000 for several hundred different projects scattered all over the country, most of which have little relationship to one another. Here there is support for Lowi's contention that distributive policies "are virtually not policies at all but are highly individualized decisions that only by accumulation can be called a policy."[2] Each locality and its supporters seek authorization and funding for their own project without questioning the right of others to do likewise. Most projects, consequently, have friends and no enemies in Congress. Presidents usually leave them alone. President Carter tried to eliminate some water projects in 1979, but with little success. He did antagonize many members of Congress.

Regulatory policies involve the imposition of restrictions or limitations on the behavior of individuals and groups. Or, to put it differently, they reduce the freedom or discretion to act of those who are regulated whether bankers, utility companies, meat packers, or whomever. In this sense they clearly differ from distributive policies, which operate to increase the freedom of discretion of the affected persons or groups.

When we think of regulatory policies our attention usually focuses on business regulatory policies, such as those pertaining to pollution control or the regulation of transportation industries. These, among other things, have been the focus of the movement for de-regulation. The most extensive variety of regulatory policies, however, is that which deals with criminal behavior against persons and property. Many civil rights policies are also regulatory in nature.

The formation of regulatory policy usually involves conflict between two groups or coalitions of groups, with one side seeking to impose some sort of control on the other side, which customarily resists, arguing either that control is unnecessary or that the wrong kind of control is being proposed. Given this situation, regulatory decisions involve clear winners and losers, although the winners usually get less than they initially sought. This is not to deny, however, that it is often difficult to identify all of the purposes and consequences of regulatory policies. It is worthwhile at this point to indicate some of the variety in regulatory policies.

Some regulatory policies set forth general rules of behavior, directing that some actions be taken or commanding that others not be taken. The Sherman Antitrust Act in effect states to businesses, "Thou shalt not monopolize or attempt to monopolize or restrain trade." These prohibitions are enforced by actions brought against particular violators. In contrast, public utility type regulation, such as the Interstate Commerce Commission handles for the railroads, involved detailed control of the railroad companies. This includes regulation of entry into the business, standards of service, financial practices, accounting procedures, and rates of charge. Comparatively, antitrust regulation entails much less restriction of business discretion than does public utility type regulation.

Consumer protection legislation can be used to illustrate some other differences in regulatory policies. Some legislation, such as the Pure Food and Drug Act of 1906 and the Drug Amendments of 1962, set standards which must be met. Thus, before new drugs can be put on the market, they must be shown to meet the standards of *safety* in use and *efficacy* for the purposes intended. Other consumer legislation—for example, the Consumer Credit Protection Act of 1964—requires creditors to provide borrowers with accurate information on interest and other financing costs for credit purchases. The first sort of policy is intended to prevent products not meeting designated standards from entering the marketplace; the second sort seeks to provide consumers with adequate information to make informed decisions.

Some regulatory policies, for instance those that restrict entry into a business such as television broadcasting or commercial air service, are implemented by decisions which confer benefits on some and deny them to others. There may be several applicants for a television broadcast license for a particular city before the Federal Communication Commission. Only one applicant can be propitiated. Here, as Lowi states, "Regulatory policies are distinguishable from distributive in that in the short run the regulatory decision involves a direct choice as to who will be indulged and who deprived."[3] Decisions are also made by the application of some kind of general rule to particular institutions.

Self-regulatory policies, like regulatory policies, involve restriction or control of some matter or group. They differ, however, in that self-regulatory policies are usually sought and supported by the regulated group as a means of protecting or promoting their own interests. The classic illustration of self-regulation is occupational and professional licensing. In 1977 it was reported that there were 2,800 state laws requiring the licensing of approximately 10 million people in 150 nonprofessional occupations.[4] In the state of Illinois alone, there were thirty-two boards regulating about one hundred professions and occupations with approximately 500,000 practitioners.[5] The usual pattern here is for a professional or occupational group to seek licensing legislation from the state legislature. Outside the ranks of the interested group there is little interest in the matter. The result is enactment of a licensing law, with delegation of its enforcement to a board dominated by the licensed group. Over time, it becomes more difficult to enter the licensed occupation and prices for its specialized services increase.

Agricultural price support programs, at the local level, have contained an element of self-regulation as a consequence of the farmer-elected committee system. These committees, elected on a county basis, have often had substantial impact on the implementation of such matters as the production control aspects of the programs in their localities. The local committee system was initially established to help make production control programs more acceptable to farmers, although official statements often stressed the virtues and desirability of "participatory democracy."

Redistributive policies involve deliberate efforts by the government to shift the allocation of wealth, income, property, or rights among broad classes or groups of the population, for example, haves and havenots, proletariat and bourgeoisie. "The aim involved is not use of property but property itself, not equal treatment but equal possession, not behavior but being."[6] In American societies redistributive policies ultimately involve disagreements between liberals (pro) and conservatives (con) and tend to be highly productive of conflict.

Redistributive policies are difficult to secure because they involve reallocation of money or power (including rights). Those who possess money or power rarely yield them willingly (regardless of how much some may discourse upon the "burdens" of their possession), and since money and power are good coinage in the political realms, those who possess them have the means for resistance.

Policies which have (or had) some redistributive impact include the graduated income tax, the war on poverty, Medicare, the Voting Rights Act of 1965, and legislative reapportionment. The graduated income tax is based on the principle of ability to pay and now has rates ranging from 14 to 50 percent. On its face it appears redistributive. However, its redistributive impact has been substantially lessened by a variety of credits, exemptions, exclusions, deductions, and other "loopholes." As a consequence, it is only mildly redistributive. The Johnson Administration's "war on poverty" represented an effort to shift wealth and resources to blacks and poor people. Encountering much resistance from conservatives, and lacking presidential support, it was gradually dispersed and dismantled. Although most of the individual poverty programs remain in existence, they have lost much of their redistributive quality. The Voting Rights Act, which has been enforced with considerable strength by the Department of Justice, has helped produce a substantial increase in black voter registration and, in turn, the election of many black officeholders in the south. Redistributive policies are not only difficult to secure, they are also hard to retain, as this discussion suggests.

Third, public policies may be described as either *material* or *symbolic,* depending upon the kind of benefits they allocate.[7] Material policies, then, actually provide tangible resources or substantive power to their beneficiaries or impose real disadvantages on those who are adversely affected. Legislation requiring employers to pay a prescribed minimum wage or appropriating money for a public housing program is in point. Symbolic policies, in contrast, distribute advantages or disadvantages which have little real impact on people. They do not deliver what they appear to promise. Many "Blue Laws" prohibiting various activities on Sundays are mostly symbolic as, because of nonenforcement, they have little effect on people's behavior. Another prime example of a symbolic policy is the Kellogg-Briand Pact of 1928, by which the United States and fourteen other countries agreed to outlaw war.

Most policies are neither entirely symbolic nor wholly material. Rather, the symbolic and material categories should be viewed as the poles of a continuum, with most policies being ranged along the continuum depending upon the extent to which they are more or less symbolic or material. Thus, it is argued that "The federal income tax law offers a rather neat illustration of the divergence between a widely publicized symbol (progressive taxation on the basis of the "ability to pay") and actual resource allocation patterns."[8] Although as was noted earlier, a variety of "loopholes" have altered the impact of the income tax, this should not blind us to the fact that it still retains some progressivity. Certainly it is more progressive than sales taxes or flat rate income taxes. Those, however, who regard the present federal income tax as a "real equalizer" have been taken in by its symbolic aspect.

Policies which are ostensibly material in nature, on the basis of legislative language, may be rendered essentially symbolic by administrative action or the failure of the legislature to provide adequate funds for their implementation. The public housing goals of the Housing Act of 1949, for example, were made substantially symbolic by the subsequent failure of Congress to provide funds needed for housing construction.[9] On the other hand, policies may move from the more symbolic to the more material category. Oppenheimer argues that oil pollution control policy was largely symbolic during the 1947–1966 period. Legislation existed but it had little enforcement impact. After 1966 oil pollution control became more material as a consequence of growing public concern about pollution, increased enforcement activity, and additional congressional action.[10]

The material–symbolic typology is especially useful to keep in mind when analyzing policy impacts as it directs our attention beyond formal policy statements. It also alerts us to the important role that symbols play in political behavior.

Fourth, public policies may involve the provision of either collective (indivisible) goods or private (divisible) goods.[11] The nature of collective goods is such that if they are provided for one person they must be provided for all. A standard example is national defense—there is no effective way to provide it for some citizens and to deny it to others, nor to calculate that some citizens benefit more from it than others. Given this, an economically rational person would never voluntarily pay for national defense. Hence it must be provided, if we want it, by government and financed through taxation. Other examples of collective goods include clean air, public safety, traffic control, and mosquito abatement.

Private goods, in contrast, may be broken into units and charged for on an individual user or beneficiary basis and are available in the marketplace. Various social goods provided by government (garbage collection, postal service, medical care, museums, public housing, and national parks) have some of the characteristics of private goods. Charges are sometimes but not always levied on users. Whether such goods—which conceivably could be provided by the market economy—are provided by the government as a function of political decisions influenced by tradition, notions of the proper functions of government, or the desire of users or beneficiaries to shift their costs to others, and the like, is dependent upon public policy.

Some might still argue that only collective goods should be the subjects of public policies. The tendency has been, however, to more and more convert private goods into social goods through government action. Ill health, unemployment, environmental pollution, industrial accidents and disease, and misrepresentation in the marketplace are viewed by many as collective rather than individual problems, as matters affecting the entire population, and hence as involving public goods for which the entire society should pay. Generally speaking, the more something is viewed as having the qualities of a public good the more likely will its provision by government be accepted. If it seems clear that some benefit more directly than others, there may also be a desire to levy charges, fees, or taxes on the direct beneficiaries to cover part of the costs. Thus we encounter user fees at national parks, tuition at public colleges, rent in public housing projects, and tolls for some bridges and highways.

Finally, debate and discussions of public policies are frequently conducted in terms of liberals versus conservatives. These terms, however, are rather slippery and difficult to define. Just what is it that distinguishes "liberal" from "conservative"? Theodore Lowi argues that in the latter part of the nineteenth century and the early years of the twentieth century, it was possible to make a fairly precise distinction between them.[12] Generally, liberals favored the use of government to bring about social change, usually in the direction of greater equality. Conservatives, in turn, were opposed to the use of government for such purposes, if not always to the purposes themselves. Liberals spoke of the need for public policies to correct injustices and shortcomings in the existing social order. Conservatives either found the existing order satisfactory or contended that change should occur slowly and gradually through "natural" social processes. By and large, those who advocated economic regulatory programs were liberals. Conservatives supplied the opposition. Later when welfare programs became an issue, support for them came from liberals, resistance from conservatives.

It is Lowi's contention, however, that the old distinction between liberals and conservatives has broken down. "The old dialogue has passed into the graveyard of consensus. Yet it persists. Old habits die hard. Its persistence despite its irrelevance means that the liberal–conservative debate has become almost purely ritualistic."[13] The nineteenth-century notion of a minimal government, of a government which would "do only those things people could not do better for themselves" (and not many things were put in this category) has been replaced by positive government, by government with extensive responsibilities for meeting human needs and problems. The old criteria no longer distinguish liberals and conservatives.

Table 5.2 illustrates the breakdown, according to Lowi. Liberal (public) policies are above the line, conservative (private) policies are below the line. Policies are ranged along the line from left to right depending upon the amount of change they are thought likely to produce. If the old criteria (attitudes toward use of government and change) were still consistently used, then liberal policies would be concentrated in the upper left-hand corner of the table while conservative policies would nest in the lower right-hand corner. However, each category ranges across the continuum. Thus, concludes Lowi, the old distinction between liberals and conservatives no longer makes sense.

Admittedly, Table 5.2 is somewhat impressionistic in nature. However, a couple of conclusions about public policies can be derived from it. Public policies can either be productive of change or designed to help maintain the existing order of things. Vigorous equal employment opportunity programs are designed to do the former, protective tariffs the latter. Public policies can derive their support from either liberal or conservative officials and groups. For example, even in the nineteenth century conservatives were not opposed to all uses of government for economic purposes. Protective tariffs and government action to restrain labor unions drew their support mostly from conservatives who in other instances might claim laissez-faire as the best policy. There has always been an element of pragmatism in the actions of both

**Table 5.2  Selected Public and Private Policies Arranged According to Probable Effect on Society**

*Public ("Liberal") Policies*

| | | | | | | |
|---|---|---|---|---|---|---|
| Social security programs based on graduated income tax | Luxury taxes | Growth of fiscal policies | Countercyclical fiscal policies | Social security programs based on insurance principles (as in U.S.) | Farm price support programs | High tariffs |
| Civil rights laws with sanctions | Real antitrust | Graduated income tax (as in U.S.) | Sales taxes | Direct regulation (FCC, ICC, CAB) | Restraint of competition (NRA, fair trade, anti-price discrimination) | Import quotas |
| Low tariffs | "Yardstick" regulation (TVA) | Civil rights laws without sanctions | Aids to small business | Antitrust by consent decree | Tax on colored margarine | Utilities (licensed monopolies) |
| | | | 1970 wage-price controls | | Revenue sharing | Very high bond reserve requirements |
| | | | Mortgage insurance | | | |

*Private ("Conservative") Policies or Practices*

| | | | | | | |
|---|---|---|---|---|---|---|
| Competition in agriculture | Competitive business | Oligopoly with research competition | Oligopoly without competition (steel, cigarettes) | Trade associations | Monopoly | |
| New interest groups | Competition by closely matched political parties | Corporate philanthropy | Brand names | Market controls through: Pools Basing points Price leadership | Old interest groups (NAM, AFL-CIO, TWU) | |
| | Merit hiring and promotion | | Ethnic appeals of political campaigns | Union policies against automation | | |

From Theodore J. Lowi, *The End of Liberalism* (New York: Norton, 1969). Policies likely to produce change ("liberal") are to the left in the table. Policies likely to maintain existing practices ("conservatives") are to the right in the table. Thus, the liberal policies should appear in the upper left-hand corner, and the conservative policies should appear in the lower right-hand corner.

conservatives and liberals when it comes to advancing the interests of groups whom they favor.

This leads us to another of Lowi's contentions, namely, *"The most important difference between liberals and conservatives, Republicans and Democrats—however they define themselves—is to be found in the interest groups they identify with."*[14] Whether one identifies with interests of business or labor, well-to-do or poor, the "establishment" or ethnic minorities, is what really matters. Support for one or another of them can be based on principle, whether this involves a desire to greater equality, the need to ameliorate social conflict, or a wish to maintain the status quo. Principles, to be legitimate, do not need to be accepted as proper or appropriate by all. Nor must they be adhered to in any and every case. Relatively few of us are constant, consistent ideologues, whether our ideology is described as conservative, neo-conservative, liberal, radical, or socialist. In short, if we can say something like conservatives tend to support policies, public or private, which advance the interests of business, while liberals tend to favor policies which protect the interests of consumers and minorities, we have said something meaningful.

Given the great changes which have occurred in our society and economy during the past century, and especially since the 1930s, it is not surprising that the liberal–conservative conflict has shifted away from the issue of whether there should be government intervention and toward the issues of when intervention should occur, in what form, and on whose behalf. As Robert McIver states:

> Wherever technology advances, wherever private business extends its range, wherever the cultural life becomes more complex, new tasks are imposed upon government. This happens apart from, or in spite of, the particular philosophies that governments cherish.... In the longer run the tasks undertaken by the governments are dictated by changing conditions, and governments on the whole are more responsive than creative in fulfilling them.[15]

The Reagan Administration took office in 1981 with the goal of substantially reducing the role of the national government in the domestic life of the nation. While the administration had some initial success in slowing the growth in domestic spending and in cutting taxes, it has produced no revolution in public policy. Or, to put it another way, it has not turned the clock back on federal policy very far. Once the "honeymoon" of the Reagan Administration was over, and it became obvious that it could not simultaneously increase defense spending, cut taxes, and balance the budget, resistance to the administration increased. In the 1982 Congressional elections the Republican Party lost 26 seats in the House of Representatives while breaking even in the Senate. Thus it appeared that in the remainder of its term the Reagan Administration would be able at best to make limited or marginal changes in domestic policies. (There was more support for increased spending on national defense.) Sweeping changes in public policy, such as occurred during the New Deal years, require major changes in the distribution of political power in society. Such did not occur in the early 1980s. As a consequence, McIver's viewpoint still seems valid.

## TECHNIQUES OF CONTROL

All public policies, whether labelled promotional, regulatory, prohibitive, re-distributive, or whatever, contain an element of control. That is, by one means or another, they are designed to cause people to do things, refrain from doing things, or continue doing things that they otherwise would not do. This is true whether reference is to a tax credit to encourage industrial plant modernization, the provision of information and other assistance to encourage international trade, or a prohibition of some activity such as restraint of trade with penalties for violators.

An important component of public policies is the control techniques by which they are to be implemented. Decisions on these matters, like those on the substance of policy itself, can be highly controversial. The control techniques authorized may have much importance for the substance and impact of policy, for policy as an "operational reality." Those who oppose a policy, for example, may attempt to lessen or even nullify its impact by restricting the administering agency's powers of enforcement or implementation. Two examples will illustrate this point. The first state minimum wage law was enacted in 1912 in Massachusetts over strong opposition from manufacturers. The only means of enforcement provided was publication in newspapers of the names of employees who did not meet the standard. The law, as one might guess, was not overly effective. In 1976, after much controversy, including a Senate filibuster by opponents, legislation was passed requiring that the Antitrust Division of the Department of Justice be notified in advance of proposed large corporate mergers. Proponents believed that this would increase the effectiveness of antitrust enforcement activity. The opponents, drawn mostly from conservative and business ranks apparently did also. If not, why the controversy?

In short, for a policy to be effective, more is needed than substantive authority and the appropriation of funds to pay the financial costs of implementation. Adequate techniques of control, and policy implementation must also be provided. In this section a variety of techniques will be examined. Our list is not exhaustive, however.

*Noncoercive Forms of Action*   Many of the methods used to implement policies, to bring about compliance, are noncoercive in nature. By "noncoercive" is meant that they do not involve the use of legal sanctions or penalties, rewards or deprivations. The effectiveness of these forms depends largely upon the voluntary collaboration or acceptance by the affected parties, although social and economic pressures arising out of society may lend an element of compulsion to them. Examples of noncoercive forms of action include the following:

Declarations of policy by themselves may cause people to comply, "to go along." This would seem to be the case especially if the declarations are made by respected or high-status officials. Presidential appeals to labor and management to avoid making inflationary wage contracts or price increases may have a restraining effect in and of themselves.

Voluntary standards may be established by official action. The National Bureau of Standards has developed commercial standards, such as uniform weights, measures, and grades of products and materials, which are not mandatory in nature. They are widely adhered to because their use facilitates or promotes business and economic activity. While the use of most of the standard grades, such as prime, choice, good, etc., for beef established by the United States Department of Agriculture for agricultural commodities is permissive (some are mandatory for interstate commerce), they are widely followed in practice.

Mediation and conciliation are often used in an effort to settle labor–management disputes, as by the Federal Mediation and Conciliation Service. The mediator works to bring the parties together, to clarify the facts of the disputes and the points at issue, and to offer advice and suggestions to promote settlement. He has, however, no formal powers of decision or sanction. Many labor–management disputes are successfully ended by these procedures.

The use of publicity to bring the social and economic effects of adverse public opinion to bear on violators may induce compliance with policy. Much stress was placed on "pitiless publicity" during the Progressive Era as a means of preventing monopoly. Although labor and business organizations today exhibit much concern about their "public image," it is impossible to measure the effectiveness of publicity as a control device. Still, the revelation of "poor" working conditions or "undesirable" business practices by congressional or agency investigations may produce some correction or improvement.

Educational and demonstration programs are widely used by agencies in securing compliance with policy. Much effort is expended to inform people of their rights under social security and veterans' benefits programs. Employers are informed through publications and conferences of the meaning and requirements of wage and hours legislation. The demonstration technique is especially used in the field of agriculture. Preferred practices in soil conservation and crop production are shown and explained to farmers with the hope that their demonstrated superiority will lead to their acceptance and use.

*Inspection*  Inspection is the examination of some matter (premises, products, records) to determine whether it conforms to officially prescribed standards. It may be either continuous, as in the inspection of meat, or periodic, as in the inspection of banks. Whichever form it takes, inspection is intended to reveal compliance or noncompliance by all those involved in a particular matter, with the objective of preventing or correcting undesirable or dangerous conditions. Typically an effort is first made to persuade violators to conform with the law, with the imposition of sanctions or penalties as a last recourse. Indeed, the ultimate purpose of inspection is to aid in obtaining the cooperation of the regulated.

Inspection is the most commonly used form of regulatory action. Examples of its use at the national level include the inspection of locomotives and railroad safety devices by the Federal Railroad Administration, sanitary conditions in food and drug manufacturing establishments by the Food and Drug Administration, income tax return by the Internal Revenue Service, and national banks by the Comptroller of the Currency.

*Licensing*  Licensing, or enabling action as it is sometimes called, involves government authorization to engage in a particular business or profession or to do something otherwise forbidden. Licensing is an extensively used form of action which goes by a variety of names. "Licenses" are required to engage in many professions and occupations and to do such things as operate motor vehicles and radio stations. The term "certificate of public convenience and necessity" is used in the public utility field. "Permits" may be necessary to drill oil wells; the "corporate charter" constitutes authorization to use a particular form of business organization; "franchises" are granted to utilities to use city streets, and so on.

Licensing is a form of advance check in which a person who wishes to engage in a particular activity must demonstrate the possession of certain qualifications or the meeting of certain standards. The burden of proof in securing a license rests with the applicant rather than the granting official. The use of licensing ordinarily goes beyond the initial authorization or denial to do something. It may also include: "(1) imposition of conditions as part of the authorization; (2) modification of the terms or conditions at the discretion of the granting authority; (3) renewal or denial of the authorization at periodic intervals; (4) revocation of the authorization."[16] When these are involved licensing becomes a form of continuing control. Radio and television broadcasters, for example, must periodically renew their broadcasting licenses with the FCC and may have them revoked under certain circumstances.

*Loans, Subsidies, and Benefits*   Loans, subsidies, and benefits are means by which public economic policies are advanced through aid, in the form of money or other resources, to private economic units. Cash operating subsidies are granted to some airlines to maintain an adequate system of air transport. Construction and operating subsidies are used to promote the domestic shipbuilding industry and the American merchant marine. Commodity loans and payments are made to farmers to support farm prices and income. Small businesses are assisted by loans from the Small Business Administration. Also related here is the guarantee of loans by the government for the purpose of expanding the volume of private lending, as in the case of the guarantee of home mortgages by the Federal Housing Administration.

In addition to their broad control, loans, subsidies, and benefit programs may include an explicit regulatory feature. For example, under the agricultural price support programs, commodity loans and payments are available only to those who comply with production and marketing controls. Farmers Home Administration loans for the purchase of farms are made under conditions intended to ensure good farm management. In effect, the government is using loan and benefit operations to purchase consent to particular policies. The effectiveness of such operations depends considerably upon the need or desire for the assistance offered.

*Contracts*   Many government programs are carried out through contracts with private companies. The defense, atomic energy, and space programs are well-known examples. Many private companies want to do business with the government and some, such as in the aerospace industry, depend heavily upon government contracts for their very existence. The power to grant or deny contracts contains an obvious element of control.

Contracts are sometimes used as the basis for specific economic controls. Under the Walsh-Healey Act, for example, companies wishing to supply goods or services to the national government must comply with statutory standards on wages, hours, and conditions of work. Presidential executive orders prohibit discrimination in employment by federal contractors. Some companies have been denied contracts because they violated such requirements.

*General Expenditures*    Apart from their use in connection with the device and loan and benefit operations, government expenditures for the purchase of goods and services can be used to attain policy goals. Administrative agencies often have considerable discretion in spending funds appropriated by Congress. The expenditures of funds for goods and services can be used to foster domestic or local industries, or to increase the level of economic activity in depressed areas. Competition may be promoted by purchasing from smaller rather than larger businesses so as to strengthen the economic position of the former. The rate and timing of expenditures may be geared to counteract inflationary or deflationary trends in the economy.

*Market and Proprietary Operations*    When government enters the market to buy, sell, or provide goods and services, its actions often have control effects. Thus the purchase and sale of government securities in the market (that is, open market operations) is a potent tool used by the Federal Reserve Board to expand or contract the money supply in the economy. The prices of some agricultural commodities, such as milk, have been supported by direct purchases in the market by the Department of Agriculture. The Johnson Administration sold some of the government's previously acquired stockpiles of aluminum and copper in its efforts to prevent price increases in those industries in the mid-1960s.

Government enterprises also may have a control effect, as when they compete with private enterprises. Thus the sale of electric power at "reasonable" rates by the Tennessee Valley Authority led to rate reductions by private companies operating in the region. This is sometimes referred to as "yardstick regulation" in that the reasonableness of private utility rates can be measured by the public rates. Government competition has not been used extensively as a control device, although it remains as a possibility.

*Taxation*    The power to tax has occasionally been used for regulatory purposes. A 10 percent annual tax on state bank notes levied by Congress in 1865 drove them out of existence. For several decades high taxes on colored oleomargarines were levied to discourage its use in preference to butter. The Carter Administration proposed increasing the federal tax on gasoline as a means of discouraging its consumption and promoting energy conservation. Congress refused to act on the recommendation because of strong public opposition.

In recent years, some have advocated the use of taxation in more positive fashion. Thus it has been contended that environmental pollution could be better reduced through use of a tax on effluents rather than the present system of standards-setting and enforcement.[17] The tax would provide an economic incentive to reduce discharges while permitting firms to determine the most efficient manner to do this. Resistance to the use of taxation in this fashion has been based on various premises: taxes should be used only to raise revenue; the present pattern of regulation is adequate; the tax device would be difficult in practice to administer. As a consequence, no use has been made of taxation as a more positive regulatory technique.

Exemptions from existing taxes have now become a widely used promotional device and are often referred to as "tax expenditures." A variety of deductions, exclusions from income, preferential rates, and the like permit individuals and corporations who engage in favored activities, such as capital investment or charitable giving, to retain funds that would otherwise be paid in taxes. The effect is the same as if the government had made a direct payment to the favored party, but it is a little less open and obvious. The use of tax expenditures has become widespread and, in 1978, it was estimated that on a combined basis they amounted to 31.8 billion for corporations and 93.1 billion for individuals. This technique capitalizes on the general aversion to paying taxes which seems characteristic of Americans. It also makes the subsidization of private activity less obvious.

*Directive Power* Many agencies have authority, on the basis of adjudicatory proceedings, to issue orders or directives applicable to private parties. (In the preceding chapter, the general nature of administrative adjudication and its use in policy development were discussed.) Agencies may issue orders to settle disputes between private parties, as when a shipper claims to have been charged an unreasonable rate by a railroad; to resolve complaints, as when a company is charged with false or misleading advertising; and to approve or deny applications, as for a license for a nuclear power project or a social security benefit. Congressional standards governing administrative adjudication are usually more specific for benefit programs, such as social security and veteran's benefits, than for regulatory programs. This may result from the fact that political conflict is often less intense over benefit legislation than regulatory legislation.[18] Congress is consequently less inclined to pass the buck to agencies through general legislation.

*Informal Procedures* Much of the work of agencies in settling questions involving private rights, privileges, and interests is accomplished through the use of informal procedures, that is, without the use of formal action and adversary hearings. For example, most disputes arising out of income tax returns are settled by consultation and correspondence between the Internal Revenue Service and the private parties involved. Claims for benefits under the social security program are mostly settled by administrative officials on the basis of work records, personal interviews, and eligibility rules. A large portion of the unfair labor practice complaint cases initiated with the National Labor Relations Board are informally disposed of as a result of conferences between agency field examiners and the parties in dispute.

Informal procedures have been referred to as "the lifeblood of the administrative process." Certainly they are an important facet of policy implementation. Many decisions affecting private rights and interests are reached through such means as negotiations, bargaining and compromise, consultation, conference, correspondence, reference to technical data, and examination of material. Extensive use is made of such methods because of such factors as the large number of cases coming before agencies, the need or desire for quick action, the wish of agencies to avoid becoming embroiled in formal proceedings, and the desire of private parties to avoid the courthouse and unfavorable publicity.

*Sanctions* These are the means—penalties and rewards—which agencies have to encourage or compel compliance with their decisions.[19] Sanctions put some "sting" into administrative action. In some instances, sanctions are built into control techniques. Thus, when an agency decides to grant or deny a conditional benefit, the sanction rests in this action. Other external sanctions which may be applied by agencies include the threat of prosecution, monetary penalties, favorable or unfavorable publicity, modification or revocation of licenses, seizure or destruction of goods, the award of damages, and the issuance of injunctions. Agencies may also seek to impose criminal penalties (fines and jail sentences), but this requires action through the courts. Further, those who deal with agencies often seek to maintain their goodwill and hence are often reluctant to challenge agency actions.

There appears to be general agreement that policies should be implemented in such manner as to cause the least necessary material and psychological disturbance to the affected persons. This being so, the most technically or economically efficient method of enforcement may not be the most acceptable politically. The consideration will affect both the legislature in authorizing control techniques for an agency and the agency in the use of the techniques and sanctions which it possesses. Another consideration in the choice of control techniques stems from the fact that the general objective of public policy is to control behavior (or secure compliance) and not to punish violators except as a last resort. Consequently, there will usually be a preference for less harsh or coercive techniques. Some sanctions may be viewed as so harsh that they are rarely used, as has been the case with jail sentences for businessmen who violate the antitrust laws. Government tends to follow a rule of parsimony in the employment of legal restraint and compulsion in policy implementation.

In seeking to determine whether a public policy is likely to be effective, the policy analyst should be concerned not only with the substantive purposes of the policy and whether these are likely of attainment but also with the techniques of implementation available and whether these are appropriate to its effectuation.

## THE DYNAMICS OF POLICY FORMATION: THE CASE OF NATURAL GAS

The regulation of the natural gas industry, especially as it involves the exemption of independent producers or, later, all producers from price regulation, presents an instructive example of the policy-making process. It illustrates many of the aspects of policy-making discussed in previous chapters, demonstrates the continuous nature of the policy process, and indicates how the different levels and branches of government can become involved with a given policy problem. Public policy in this area is a topic of much current concern so it is an apt matter for discussion.

Initially, natural gas had little commercial value. Usually discovered in the search for oil, gas was regarded as a nuisance and most of it was either vented (released into the air) or flared (burned) to dispose of it. In the late 1920s, however, the development of seamless pipe made it possible to move gas over long distances, as from producing areas in the southwest to cities in the northeast.

The natural gas industry encompasses three basic economic functions: the production and gathering of gas in the field, transportation to the market area, and distribution to the ultimate consumers.[20] A series of Supreme Court decisions has placed the first and third functions within the scope of state regulatory power. Most of the transportation of gas, however, takes place in interstate commerce (that is, across state lines) and therefore falls under the jurisdiction of the national government. State utility commissions could regulate the prices charged to local consumers, but not the wholesale prices at which gas was sold to local distributing companies by interstate pipeline companies. As large quantities of natural gas began to move across state lines, the problem of regulating this traffic gained in importance. It was argued that the states could not effectively regulate gas prices for local consumers so long as wholesale prices were uncontrolled.

The jurisdictional gap which existed was filled without much controversy when Congress enacted the Natural Gas Act of 1938. Gas pipeline companies were directed to file rate schedules with the Federal Power Commission and could not alter their rates without its approval. The FPC was empowered to set "just and reasonable" rates and to exercise broad control over pipeline companies, including control of entry into the business. Production and gathering of gas, direct sales to industrial users, and the local distribution of gas were exempted from control by the commission. A problem soon arose, however, because the act was not clear as to whether field prices of gas—the prices charged by processors and gatherers to pipeline companies—were sales in interstate commerce and thus subject to regulation by the Federal Power Commission. Gas producers, it should be noted, had not opposed the enactment of the Natural Gas Act as they assumed they were exempt from its control.

At first the FPC held that it did not have jurisdiction over the field prices of gas. Then, in 1943, the commission reversed itself and held that it did have such jurisdiction. The Supreme Court upheld the commission, and ruled, in effect, that all sales to interstate pipeline companies were sales in interstate commerce and within the jurisdiction of the FPC. The Court declined to accept the contention that such sales were part of the processing and gathering function and thus exempt from national regulation. To say the least, the Court's interpretation of the Natural Gas Act differed considerably from that of the gas interests and their supporters.

Even before the Supreme Court issued its 1947 decision, a move started in Congress, led by members from the south and southwest and supported by oil and gas interests, to amend the Natural Gas Act. One bill, introduced by Representative Ross Rizley of Oklahoma, would have exempted sales by both integrated and independent producers from FPC regulation. (An integrated producer is one having its own pipelines or affiliated with a pipeline company. An "independent" is the value-laden title given to a company, regardless of size, which does not control its own pipelines.) The FPC opposed the Rizley Bill but gave its support to another bill designed to exempt only independent producers. Further by a 4–1 decision in 1947, the FPC issued its Order No. 139, by which it interpreted the Natural Gas Act as denying it power to regulate prices charged by independent producers. This, however, did not abate the Congressional effort to amend the act. Moreover, by 1949 the position of the commission had shifted and three members now opposed exemption of independents. Leland Olds, the FPC chairman, was especially strong in his opposition.

Activity now began to pick up in Congress and natural gas legislation became an important item on its policy agenda. In 1949, Senator Robert Kerr of Oklahoma introduced a bill to exempt sales by independent producers. The House had earlier passed a similar bill by a 183–131 vote. At first the Senate Committee on Interstate and Foreign Commerce refused to report out the Kerr Bill, partly because of the strong opposition of Chairman Olds. About this time Olds' term on the commission expired and his name came before the Senate for renomination. A bitter attack against his renomination was launched by oil and gas interests and Senators from gas-consuming states and consumer interests. Olds' renomination was rejected by a 51–15 vote.[21] With Olds out of the way, the Senate turned its attention to the Kerr Bill and passed it by a vote of 44–38. Most of the opposition to it came from the gas-consuming states in the North and East. Former Senator Mon Wallgren, who had been appointed to take Olds' place on the FPC, now joined with two "consumer-minded" incumbent commissioners to recommend a presidential veto. Following President Harry Truman's veto of the Kerr Bill, the commission repealed its Order No. 139.

The FPC now became the primary location of the policy struggle. While the Court upheld that the commission possessed power to regulate independent producers, it had not said the commission was *required* to do so. In 1951, in the Phillips Petroleum Company case, the commission again changed its mind, deciding by a 4–1 decision that the Natural Gas Act's exemption of production and gathering from regulation included the sale of gas by independents to pipeline companies. This was, of course, unsatisfactory to proponents of regulation and the commission's action was challenged judicially. In 1954 the case reached the Supreme Court. Allied in support of the commission's position were the FPC itself, the Phillips Petroleum Company, and the State of Texas. In opposition were the State of Wisconsin and several cities, acting in support of consumers' interests. The Court reversed the FPC decision and held that the commission was required to regulate independent producers' prices.[22] The Court said this was consistent with the legislative history of the 1938 Act, even though the FPC had relied heavily on the same history in reaching the opposite conclusion. The effect of the Court's action was to increase the responsibility of a reluctant commission for the balancing of consumer and producer interests through regulation.

Following the Court's 1954 decision the struggle over exemption of independents shifted back to Congress. Much pressure was exerted on Congress by oil and gas interests to amend the 1938 Act to exempt independents. An intensive public relations campaign was started to convince the public that exemption was necessary to free independents from regulation and to insure adequate supplies of gas at reasonable prices for consumers. Thousands of gas producers gave their support to the exemption campaign. Further support came from President Dwight Eisenhower who favored exemption of independents from national regulation as a means of reducing excessive centralization in government. Strong opposition to exemption came from cities in the North and East, labor groups, gas consumers, and local utility companies (who feared exemption would increase the prices they paid for gas). Coal interests also opposed exemption in an attempt to protect their competitive position vis-à-vis the gas industry in the sale of fuel.

Identical bills to exempt all independents from national regulation were introduced in the House and Senate by two Arkansas Democrats, Representative Oren Harris and Senator William Fulbright. The House passed the bill toward the end of 1955 by a 209–203 vote, which is indicative of the closeness and intensity of the struggle over the bill. The next February the bill came before the Senate for floor consideration. During the Senate debate, Senator Francis Case (Rep., S.D.) announced that he would vote against the bill, although he previously had favored it. In explanation he stated that an oil company lawyer had offered him a $2500 campaign contribution on condition that he vote for the measure. The Senate was undeterred by the publicity and controversy which this disclosure touched off and subsequently passed the bill by a 53–38 vote. Voting in both houses on the bill was based on regional and economic conditions rather than party lines. In the House, for example, representatives from gas-producing states tended to favor it while representatives from northern, gas-consuming areas tended to oppose it, regardless of their party affiliation.

This legislative effort came to naught when President Eisenhower, who had favored the bill, vetoed it because of the "Case incident." In his veto message the President stated:

> Since the passage of this bill a body of evidence has accumulated indicating that private persons, representing only a very small segment of a great and vital industry, have been seeking to further their own interests by highly questionable activities. These include efforts I deem to be so arrogant and so in defiance of acceptable standards of propriety as to risk creating doubt among the American people concerning the integrity of governmental process.[23]

In other words, those involved in the "Case incident" had violated the basic "rules of the game" governing the political struggle. The exertion of pressure is one thing, bribery quite another.

To add another dimension to our study, we should mention that the gas interests also attempted to overcome the 1954 decision by action in the state policy-making arena. In the fall of that year, the Oklahoma Corporation Commission acted to set minimum field prices for natural gas. This move, had it been constitutional, would have prevented the FPC from setting lower prices. A somewhat similar ploy was attempted in Texas, where it was presented as necessary for conservation of natural gas. This stratagem failed when the United States Supreme Court declared that it was unconstitutional for Oklahoma to regulate the field prices of natural gas moving in interstate commerce. The Court thus invoked the constitution on the consumer side of the conflict. Its decision meant that policy on natural gas prices would continue to be developed in the national policy arena.

In 1958, another effort was made in Congress to amend the Natural Gas Act. A bill to exempt several thousand *small* independent gas producers from price regulation was introduced. Although it was sponsored by senators from both gas-producing and gas-consuming states it never really got off the ground. This bill was unappealing to the large gas companies, who produce most of the supply of natural gas, as exemption of the "little fellow" did not really help them. After 1958, natural gas disappeared from the legislative agenda for a decade.

After 1954, the task of reconciling producer and consumer interests through the medium of rate regulation rested directly with the Federal Power Commission. At first, the commission sought to handle the problem by setting rates through adjudication based on the traditional individual company cost of service methods used in public utility regulation. This alternative proved unsatisfactory because of the complexity of the problem, the large number of gas producers involved (over 18,000), and the commission's own lethargy. In 1960, the FPC ceased its efforts to set gas rates on a case-by-case basis and moved to a system of area pricing, under which the country was divided into twenty-three gas-producing regions for rate-making purposes.

In August 1965, the FPC completed action in its first area rate case, involving the Permian Basin area of western Texas and eastern New Mexico. The commission's decision was regarded as a victory for consumer interests. Ceilings of 16½ and 15½ cents per thousand cubic feet (mcf) were set for gas produced in Texas and New Mexico respectively. Higher rates were permitted for "old" gas (from wells in production for 1961) than for "new" gas (from wells starting production after January 1961 or from wells also producing oil). The higher price for new gas was intended to stimulate production and move more gas into the interstate market. Gas producers had argued for a 20-cent ceiling, while the going market price was 17 to 18 cents per mcf. The area pricing action was unsuccessfully challenged in the federal courts by the gas industry. Subsequently, rate proceedings were completed for other areas. Intense struggles occurred over whether gas prices should be a penny or two higher or lower per mcf than proposed by the FPC.

The consumption of natural gas increased at a rapid rate during the 1960s, stimulated by such factors as low prices; convenience in the use of gas; its cleanliness, which helped industrial users meet air quality standards; and the absence of any regulation of the end-uses of gas.[24] By the early 1970s a shortage in the supply of natural gas had emerged. Existing users were not always able to get all the gas they wanted while prospective new users were sometimes denied access to gas by gas companies. What had produced this situation? Generally, two conflicting explanations have been advanced for the gas shortage. The critics of rate regulation, including the gas producers, contend that the low gas rates set by the FPC are the problem, having operated to discourage exploration and production and to divert gas into the intrastate (and unregulated) market where prices are higher. De-regulation of the price of natural gas is necessary in their view to call forth adequate supplies. Those who support gas regulation contend that the gas shortage is a product of two factors: first, greatly increased demand for natural gas and, second, the possibility of de-regulation and higher prices for gas, which is said to have caused gas companies both to produce less gas and to sell less gas in the interstate market. They contend that eliminating uncertainty over the continuation of regulation will help to eliminate the shortage of gas. Notice how policy evaluation and policy advocacy become blended in this situation.

In 1975, natural gas de-regulation again became a major item on the national policy agenda. With the support of the Ford Administration, a strong effort was made in 1975 and 1976 to enact legislation repealing the FPC's authority to regulate the field price of interstate gas. The repeal legislation was passed by the Senate fairly readily. It ran into difficulty in the House, however, where supporters of continued regulation were able to amend the bill to retain regulation of large gas producers and to extend federal regulation to intrastate sales while removing most small producers from control. This, of course, was not acceptable to the gas industry and its supporters as they insisted on total de-regulation. No conference committee action was taken on the bill and it died.

Now let us return to the Federal Power Commission and, to begin, backtrack a bit. Under the Nixon Administration the FPC had become pro-industry in orientation, in contrast to its consumer orientation through most of the 1960s. In 1974 the commission abandoned its area pricing scheme and, through a rule-making proceeding, adopting a single *national* price of 52 cents for all "new" natural gas (that is, all gas sold after 1972). When it became apparent in the summer of 1976 that Congress was not going to end natural gas regulation, the commission made a drastic change in gas rates, setting a nationwide price of $1.42 per mcf with annual escalation.[25] According to the commission majority, this higher rate was added in order to get producers to increase exploration, production, and sale of gas, although they did not guarantee that production would actually increase. In effect, the commission had substantially done what Congress refused to do, de-regulate the price of natural gas. The new price for gas was seven times higher than what it had been in 1968 at the end of the Johnson Administration. Where previously rates had been kept low for consumer protection, now they were set in the interest of gas production (and producers).

This shift in policy did not do much to lessen the demand of the gas industry for total deregulation. In the winter of 1976–1977 the price of gas in the intrastate market was higher than the new FPC rate, running over two dollars per mcf in Texas, for example. The industry and its supporters continued to proclaim the virtues of an unregulated market and to present it as a solution for the gas problem. They were disappointed in the spring of 1977, however, when President Jimmy Carter, who along with Gerald Ford favored deregulation during the 1976 presidential campaign, unveiled his comprehensive energy policy proposal. In apparent contradiction of a campaign pledge, he recommended continued regulation of natural gas prices, albeit with an increase to $1.75 per mcf. An energy bill was passed by the House in September which included provisions for both this price and for its extension to intrastate sales as well. The gas industry still wanted total de-regulation, while consumer spokespersons protested that the $1.75 per mcf price was too high. A few weeks later, however, the Senate passed a bill by a 50–46 vote which provided for an end to federal regulation of natural gas sales. Contributing to the Senate action was the fact that the Senate leadership was much less supportive of President Carter than was the House leadership.

The House–Senate conference, set up to resolve the differences between the two bills, was soon able to reach agreement on most matters. However, the conference deadlocked on natural gas deregulation. Negotiations dragged through the remainder of 1977 and on into the spring of 1978. Finally, in late

May, they were able to come into accord. Rate regulation of all "new gas" was to be ended by 1985. The price of new gas, which was initially set at $1.85 per mcf, was permitted to rise about 10 percent annually until controls were lifted. Industrial users were initially to bear a greater portion of the burden of higher price than consumers. The pricing system for "old gas" was quite complicated, containing numerous price categories depending upon such factors as when the gas war committed to the interstate market, whether it was produced onshore or offshore, by large or small producers, and so on. Federal regulation was extended for the first time to intrastate gas (that produced and sold in the same state). Even the supporters of this compromise were not happy with it. Opposition to it was strong and not until the Carter Administration mounted an intensive lobbying campaign in support of it was it enacted into law in October, 1978 as the Natural Gas Policy Act.[26] Given the complexity of the act, it imposes a large burden on the administering agency—the Federal Energy Regulatory Commission (FERC).

The FPC was abolished in 1977 by the legislation creating the new Department of Energy, which was one facet of the Carter Administration's response to the energy crisis. Created to take its place was FERC which, while formally located in the Department of Energy, operates independently departmental controls. President Carter had wanted natural gas rate-making authority to be vested in the Secretary of Energy, but Congress refused to go along and set up a new regulatory commission to replace the FPC.

Natural gas rate regulation has continued to be a matter of controversy. The Reagan Administration, which advocated deregulation of natural gas, did not actively push the issue during its first two years in office. In 1981 the energies of the administration were focused on its economic program. Moreover, a "windfall" profits tax seemed to be a condition for deregulation, and the President had promised to veto a windfall tax on decontrolled gas in his efforts to win votes for his economic program. The 1982 congressional elections made that year unpropitious for launching a deregulation effort. Other priorities thus kept natural gas deregulation off the administration's immediate policy agenda. In 1983 the administration did recommend deregulation.

If changes are not made in the Natural Gas Policy Act to accelerate or delay deregulation, rate controls on new gas will cease in 1985. Estimates are that this will involve from one-half to two-thirds of total gas supplies.[27] The remainder (old gas) will be federally regulated until its production ceases. The volatility of the natural gas issue makes this scenario seem problematic.

## NOTES

1. The basic typology is from Theodore J. Lowi, "American Business, Public Policy, Case Studies, and Political Theory," *World Politics,* XVI (July, 1964), pp. 677–715. The self-regulatory category is from Robert H. Salisbury, "The Analysis of Public Policy: A Search for Theories and Roles," in Austin Ranney, ed., *Political Science and Public Policy* (Chicago: Markham, 1968), pp. 151–175.

2. Lowi, *op. cit.,* p. 690.

3. *Ibid.,* pp. 690–691.

4. *New York Times,* June 8, 1977, p. 60.

5. *Wall Street Journal,* June 14, 1977, p. 40.

6. Lowi, *op. cit.,* p. 691. On redistributive policies, see Randall B. Ripley and Grace A. Franklin, *Congress, the Bureaucracy, and Public Policy* (Homewood, Ill.: Dorsey, 1976), chap. 6.

7. On the symbolic aspects of policies see Murray Edelman, *The Symbolic Uses of Politics* (Urbana: University of Illinois Press, 1964), chap. 2.

8. *Ibid.,* p. 28.

9. Richard O. Davis, *Housing Reform During the Truman Administration* (Columbia: University of Missouri Press, 1966), chap. 10.

10. Bruce I. Oppenheimer, *Oil and the Congressional Process* (Lexington, Mass.: Heath, 1974), pp. 130–145.

11. Cf. L. L. Wade and R. L. Curry, Jr., *A Logic of Public Policy* (Belmont, Calif.: Wadsworth Publishing Company, 1970), chap. 5.

12. This discussion draws on Theodore J. Lowi, *The End of Liberalism* (New York: Norton, 1969), chap. 3.

13. *Ibid.,* p. 57.

14. *Ibid.,* p. 72. His emphasis.

15. Robert McIver, *The Web of Government* (New York: Macmillan, 1947), pp. 314–315.

16. Emmette S. Redford, *The Administration of National Economic Control* (New York: Macmillan, 1952), p. 104.

17. Charles Schultze, *Public Use of Private Interest* (Washington: Brookings Institution, 1977).

18. Peter Woll, *American Bureaucracy,* 2d ed. (New York: Norton, 1977), p. 95.

19. Redford, *op. cit,* pp. 164–177.

20. See Ralph K. Huitt, "National Regulation of the Natural-Gas Industry," in Emmette S. Redford, ed., *Public Administration and Policy Formation* (Austin: University of Texas Press, 1958), pp. 53–116, for further discussion and background on gas regulation.

21. Joseph P. Harris, "The Senatorial Rejection of Leland Olds," *American Political Science Review,* XXV (September, 1951), pp. 674–693.

22. *Phillips Petroleum Company* v. *State of Wisconsin,* 347 U.S. 672 (1954).

23. *Congressional Record,* CII (1956), p. 2793.

24. Carl Solberg, *Oil Power* (New York: New American Library, 1976), chap. 8.

25. Richard Corrigan, "FPC's Gas Price Ruling Leaves Consumers Out in the Cold," *National Journal,* VIII (November 13, 1976), pp. 1626–1631.

26. For a good study on the topic, see M. Elizabeth Sanders, *The Regulation of Natural Gas: Policy and Politics, 1938–1978* (Philadelphia: Temple University Press, 1981).

27. Richard Corrigan, "Soaring Prices from Deep Wells May Force Early Rewriting of 1978 Law," *The National Journal,* XIII (November 21, 1981), pp. 2063–67.

# 6

# Policy Impact, Evaluation, and Change

The final stage of the policy process, viewed as a sequential pattern of activities, is the evaluation of policy. Generally speaking, policy evaluation is concerned with the estimation, assessment, or appraisal of policy, including its content, implementation, and effects. As a functional activity, policy evaluation can and does occur throughout the policy process and not simply as its last stage. For instance, an attempt is usually made to determine, that is, estimate, the consequences of various policy alternatives for dealing with a problem prior to the adoption of one of them. In this chapter, the focus will be primarily but not exclusively on policy evaluation connected with efforts to implement or carry out policies. As we will see, evaluational activity may restart the policy process (problem, formulation, and so on) in order to continue, modify, or terminate existing policy.

Policy evaluation, as a functional activity, is as old as policy itself. Policymakers and administrators have always made judgments concerning the worth or effects of particular policies, programs, and projects, Many of these judgments have been of the impressionistic, or "seat of the pants," variety, based often on anecdotal or fragmentary evidence, at best, and strongly influenced by ideological, partisan self-interest and other valuational criteria. Thus, a welfare program may be regarded as "socialistic" and hence undesirable by some, regardless of its actual impact. Or a tax cut may be considered necessary and desirable because it enhances the electoral chances of the evaluators' political party. Unemployment compensation may be deemed "bad" because the evaluator "knows a lot of people" who improperly receive benefits. Most of us are quite familiar with this kind of policy evaluation and have undoubtedly done, and enjoyed doing, a bit of it ourselves. Much conflict may result from this sort of evaluation, because different evaluators, employing different value criteria, reach different conclusions concerning the merits of the same policy.

Another common variety of policy evaluation has centered on the operation of particular policies or programs. Questions asked may include: Is the program honestly run? What are its financial costs? Who receives benefits (payments or services) and in what amounts? Is there unnecessary overlap or duplication with other programs? Were legal standards and procedures followed? This kind of evaluation may tell us something about the honesty or efficiency in the conduct of a program, but, like the first kind of evaluation, it will probably yield little, if anything, in the way of hard information on the societal effects of a program. A welfare program, for example, may be ideologically and politically satisfying to a given evaluator, as well as being honestly and prudently conducted. Assuming we are in agreement with this evaluation, it will in all likelihood tell us little about the impact of the program on the poor or its *social* cost-benefit ratio, or whether it is achieving its officially stated objectives.

A third type of policy evaluation, which is comparatively new in usage, and which has been receiving increasing attention within the national government in recent years, is the systematic, objective evaluation of programs to measure their societal impact and the extent to which they are achieving their stated objectives. We shall refer to this as systematic evaluation, for want of a better term. The Departments of Labor, and of Health and Human Services have assistant secretaries whose responsibilities include program evaluation. Bureaus within these and other departments often include policy and program evaluation staffs. More attention appears to be given to the evaluation of social welfare programs than most other areas of government activity. This probably arises from their proliferation in recent decades, their substantial costs, and the controversies which surround them.

Systematic evaluation directs attention to the effects a policy has on the public need or problem to which it is directed. It permits at least tentative, informed responses to such questions as: Is this policy achieving its objectives? What are its costs and benefits? Who are its beneficiaries? What happened as a consequence of the policy that would not have happened in its absence? Consequently, systematic evaluation gives policy-makers and the general public, if they are interested, some notion of the actual impact of policy and provides policy discussions with some grounding in reality. Evaluation findings can be used to modify current policies and programs and to help design others for the future.

Of course, evaluation can also be used for less laudable purposes. As Carol Weiss has noted: "Program decision-makers may turn to evaluation to delay a decision; to justify and legitimate a decision already made; to extricate themselves from controversy about future directions by passing the buck; to vindicate the program in the eyes of its constituents, its funders, or the public; to satisfy conditions of a government or foundation grant through the ritual of evaluation."[1] In short, evaluators may be motivated by self-service as well as public service, by a desire to use analysis as ammunition for partisan political purposes. Thus, the various analytical studies used by members of Congress in the 1977–1978 debate over natural gas pricing were based on assumptions that predetermined their conclusions. Members tended to rely on the studies which were supportive of their particular preferences.[2]

## POLICY IMPACT

In discussing impact and evaluation, it is important to have in mind the distinction between policy outputs and policy outcomes. Policy outputs are the things governments do—highway construction, payment of welfare benefits, arrests for burglary, or operation of public schools. These activities may be measured by such standards as per capita highway expenditures, per capita welfare expenditures, arrests for burglary per 100,000 population, per pupil school expenditures, and the like. Such figures tell us little about the outcomes, or impacts, of public policies because, in trying to determine policy outcomes, our concern is with the changes in the environment or political system caused by policy action. Knowing how much is spent on pupils in a school system on a per capita, or some other, basis will tell us nothing concerning the effect schooling has on the cognitive and other abilities of students, let alone the consequences of education for society generally.

Policy evaluation is concerned, then, with trying to determine the impact of policy on real-life conditions. The phrase "trying to determine" is used here because, as will become apparent, determining the actual effects, or consequences, of policies is often a very complex and difficult task. At a minimum, policy evaluation requires that we know what we want to accomplish with a given policy (policy objectives), how we are trying to do it (programs), and what, if anything, we have accomplished toward attainment of the objectives (impact or outcomes, and the relation of policy thereto). And, in measuring accomplishment, we need to determine not only that some change in real-life conditions has occurred, such as a reduction in the unemployment rate, but also that it was due to policy actions and not to other factors, such as private economic decisions.

The impact of a policy has several dimensions, all of which must be taken into account in the course of evaluation.[3] These include:

**1.** The impact on the public problem at which it is directed and on the people involved. Those whom the policy is intended to affect must be defined, whether the poor, small businessmen, disadvantaged school children, petroleum producers, or whatever. The intended effect of the policy must then be determined. If, for example, it is an antipoverty program, is its purpose to raise the income of the poor, to increase their opportunities for employment, or to change their attitudes and behavior? If some combination of such purposes is intended, analysis becomes more complicated because priorities must be assigned to the various intended effects.

Further, it must be noted that a policy may have either intended or unintended consequences, or even both. A welfare program may improve the income situation of the benefited groups, as intended. But what impact does it also have on their initiative to seek employment? Does it decrease this, as some have contended? A public-housing program may improve the housing situation of urban blacks, but it may also contribute to racial segregation in housing. An agricultural price-support program, intended to improve farmers' incomes, may lead to overproduction of the supported commodities, or to higher food prices for consumers, or to increased land values.

A good illustration of a policy with unintended consequences is the 1970 legislation prohibiting the broadcasting of cigarette advertising on radio and television.[4] This ad ban represented a legislative victory for the antismoking forces. However, the ban also eliminated the need for broadcasters, under the Federal Communications Commission's fairness doctrine, to donate air time to antismoking groups on the controversial issue of smoking. Research has indicated that the antismoking messages prepared by these groups had a substantial deterrent effect upon cigarette consumption. The antismoking ad campaign, however, was substantially dependent upon donated time. As a consequence, after the cigarette ad ban went into effect, most of the antismoking ads were also eliminated. The short-term effect was clearly a significant increase in smoking, which was obviously not what the proponents of the ad ban intended. Although the long-run effects are less clear, "the weight of the evidence seems to favor the conclusion that the ad ban was myopic policy."

**2.** Policies may have effects on situations or groups other than those at which they are directed. These can be called either externalities or spillover effects.[5] The testing of nuclear explosives in the atmosphere may provide needed data for weapons development, but it also generates hazards for the current and future population of the world. This is a negative externality, but externalities may also be positive. When tariffs are lowered at the behest of American exporters to increase their sales abroad, American consumers may benefit from lower prices caused by increased imports that lower tariffs stimulate. Many of the outcomes of public policies can be most meaningfully understood in terms of externalities.

**3.** Polices may have impacts on future as well as current conditions. Is a policy designed to improve some immediate, short-term situation, or are its consequences to be long-term, stretched over many years or decades? Is the Head Start program supposed to improve the cognitive abilities of disadvantaged (i.e., poor) children in the short run, or is it to affect their long-range development and earning capacity? Is a price-control program intended only to check incipient price increases, or is it to have a long-term impact on economic behavior, as by helping eliminate the existence of "inflationary psychology"? Did regulation of the price of natural gas at the wellhead, a policy begun in the 1950s, really contribute to the current energy shortage as some now contend (notably, those in the petroleum industry who long opposed the policy)? If so, this would be a long-term effect of the policy and a negative externality (or cost).

**4.** The direct costs of policies are another element for evaluation. It is usually fairly easy to calculate the direct dollar costs of a particular policy or program, when it is stated as the actual number of dollars spent on a program, its share of total government expenditures, or the percentage of the gross national product devoted to it. Other direct costs of policies may be more difficult to discover or calculate, such as expenditures for pollution-control devices by the private sector necessitated by an air-pollution control policy. A direct cost of the selective service system (the "draft") was the loss of freedom of choice by those conscripted. The measurement of such costs is no easy matter.

**5.** Policies may have indirect costs or effects that are experienced by the community or some of its members. Such costs often have not been considered in making policy evaluations, at least partly because they defy quantification. How does one measure the costs of inconvenience, dislocation, and social disruption resulting from an urban-renewal project? Or the aesthetic costs of building a highway through a scenic park? Or the cost of the Vietnam war in internal strife and loss of credibility by public officials?

**6.** Of course, it is also difficult to measure the indirect benefits of public policies for the community. Assuming that patent and copyright policies do indeed stimulate inventive and creative activity, and that these contribute to economic growth and social development, how may we assess their benefits quantitatively? The social security program may contribute to social stability and political contentment as well as the retirement incomes of recipients. The problem of measurement is again apparent.

The evaluation of policy becomes even more complex when we give explicit consideration to the fact that the effects of policy may be symbolic (or intangible) as well as material (or tangible). Symbolic outputs, in the view of Gabriel Almond and G. Bingham Powell, "include affirmations of values by elites; displays of flags, troops, and military ceremony; visits by royalty or high officials; and statements of policy or intent by political leaders" and "are highly dependent on tapping popular beliefs, attitudes, and aspirations for their effectiveness."[6] Symbolic policy outputs produce no real changes in societal conditions. No one eats better, for example, because of a Memorial Day parade or a speech by a high public official on the virtues of free enterprise, however ideologically or emotionally satisfying such actions may be for many people. More to the point of our discussion, however, is the fact that policy actions ostensibly directed toward meeting material wants or needs may turn out, in practice, to be more symbolic than material in their impact.

This is well illustrated by the graduated income tax levied by the national government. Based on the principle of ability to pay, which is widely, if not universally, regarded as a standard of fairness in taxation, rates range from 14 percent to 50 percent, depending upon the taxpayer's taxable income. Taken at face value, the graduated income tax is a symbol of equality and progressivity in taxation and draws wide support on that basis. In actuality, the impact of the income tax on many people, particularly the wealthy, is greatly reduced by provisions such as those for income splitting, family partnerships, depletion allowances, and capital gains. The result is that the effective tax rates for the rich are substantially lower than imagined. What is symbolically promised is quite different from what materially results. This was brought home to many people in 1973, when it became known that President Nixon had paid, for the years 1970 and 1971, only $1,671 in taxes on an income of more than $400,000. This is a very token payment indeed, or about what was then paid by the average family of four with an annual income of $9,500. (He subsequently agreed to make a much larger tax payment, but as of 1978 he apparently has never done so.)

Other public policies that appear to promise more symbolically than their implementation actually yields in material benefits include antitrust activity, public utility rate regulation, and equal-employment opportunity. Even though the actual impact of a policy may be considerably less than is intended or desired, it nonetheless may have significant consequences for society. An antipoverty program that falls short of the mark may nonetheless assure people that the government is concerned about poverty. Equal employment–opportunity legislation assures people that their government, officially at least, does not condone discrimination in hiring on the basis of race, sex, and nationality. Apart from whatever effects such policies have on societal conditions, they may contribute to social order, support for government, and personal self-esteem, which are not inconsequential considerations.

The analysis of public policy is usually focused upon what governments actually do, why, and with what material effects. We should not, however, neglect the symbolic aspects of government, despite their intangible and nebulous nature. The rhetoric of government—what governments say, or appear to say—is clearly a necessary and proper concern for the policy analyst.

## PROBLEMS IN POLICY EVALUATION

The most useful policy evaluation for policy-makers and administrators, and policy critics who wish to have a factual basis for their positions, is the systematic evaluation that tries to determine cause-and-effect relationships and rigorously measure the impact of policy. It is, of course, often impossible to measure quantitatively the impact of public policies, especially social policies, with any real precision. In this context, then, to "measure rigorously" is to seek to assess as carefully and objectively as possible the impact of policy.

The burden of the discussion in this section will be to indicate a number of barriers, or obstacles, that may create problems for the evaluation of policy. This is not intended to be a discourse on futility, but policy evaluation is typically neither easy nor simple, and one should be aware of this. Determining whether a policy is doing what it is supposed to is not an easy, straightforward task, as one might assume. Anyone, of course, can express a judgment on policies without really examining them, and many do. The value of such judgments is often directly proportional to their factual basis—almost nothing.

*Uncertainty over Policy Goals* When the goals of a policy are unclear, diffuse, or diverse, as they frequently are, determining the extent to which they have been attained becomes a difficult and frustrating task.[7] This situation often is a product of the policy adoption process. Because support of a majority coalition is needed to secure adoption of a policy, it is often necessary to appeal to persons and groups possessing differing interests and diverse values. Commitments to the preferred policy goals of various groups may be included in legislation in order to secure their votes. The Model Cities Act of 1966 reflects this process. Its goals included, among others, the rebuilding of slum and blighted areas, the improvement of housing, income and cultural opportunities, the reduction of crime and delinquency, lessening dependency on welfare, and the maintenance of historic landmarks. No priorities were assigned to the various goals. Model-cities evaluation research had to try to come to grips with these diverse goals. It may thus be no easy task to determine what the real goals of a program are. Officials in different positions in the policy system, such as legislators and administrators, or national and state officials, may define them differently, act accordingly, and reach differing conclusions concerning the accomplishments of the program.

*Causality* Systematic evaluation requires that changes in real-life conditions must demonstrably be caused by policy actions. But the mere fact that action A is taken and condition B develops does not necessarily mean that a cause-and-effect relationship exists. Some things may happen with or without policy action. An anecdote reported by Robert Levine is in point.[8] A few months after the Office of Economic Opportunity began operating, the Census Bureau reported a substantial drop in poverty from 1963 to 1964. Sargent Shriver received a note from a White House staff official that said "Nice going Sarge." But, since the data for both 1963 and 1964 antedated the existence of OEO, it is unlikely the agency had any effect on the poverty reduction. The staff official had carelessly implied a causal relationship where none existed.

To illustrate further the problem of determining causality, let us take the case of crime-control policies. The purpose, or at least one of the purposes, of these policies is the deterrence of crime. Deterrence may be defined as the prevention of an action that can be said to have had a "realistic potential of actualization,"[9] that is, that really could have happened. (This assumption is required in order to avoid the kind of analysis that holds, for example, that consumption of alcoholic beverages prevents stomach worms, since no one has ever been afflicted with them after starting to drink.) The problem here is that "not doing something" is a sort of nonevent, or intangible act. Does the fact that a person does not commit burglary mean that he has been effectively deterred by policy from so acting? The answer, of course, first depends upon whether he was inclined to engage in burglary. If he was so inclined, then was he deterred by the possibility of detection and punishment, by other factors such as family influence, or by the lack of opportunity? As this should indicate, the determination of causality between actions, especially in complex social and economic matters, is a difficult task.

*Diffuse Policy Impacts* Policy actions may affect groups other than those at whom they are specifically directed. A welfare program may affect not only the poor but also others, such as taxpayers, public officials, and low-income people who are not receiving welfare benefits. The effects on these groups may be either symbolic or material. Taxpayers may grumble that their "hard-earned dollars are going to support those too lazy to work." Some low-income working people may decide to "go on welfare" rather than continue working at unpleasant jobs for low wages. So far as even the poor who do receive material benefits are concerned, what effects do benefits have on their initiative and self-reliance, on family solidarity, and on the maintenance of social order? We should bear in mind that policies may have unstated goals: Thus, an antipoverty program may be covertly intended to help defuse the demands of black activists; or, to take another case, a beef control program may be intended to appease cattlemen politically, while not really doing much to limit imports.

The effects of some programs may be very broad and long-range in nature. Antitrust is an example. Originally intended to help maintain competition and prevent monopoly in the economy, how does one now evaluate its effectiveness? We can look at on-going enforcement activity and find that particular mergers have been prevented and price-fixing conspiracies broken up, but this will not tell us much about competition and monopoly in the economy generally. It would be nice to be able to determine that the economy is *n* percent more competitive than it would have been in the absence of antitrust policy. Given the generality of its goals and the difficulties of measuring competition and monopoly, this just is not possible. Interestingly enough, after more than eighty years of antitrust action, there are still no agreed upon definitions of monopoly and competition to guide policy action and evaluation. No wonder those assessing the effectiveness of antitrust sometimes come to sharply different conclusions.

*Difficulties in Data Acquisition*   As some previous comments have implied, a shortage of accurate and relevant statistical data and other information may handicap the policy evaluator. Thus, econometric models may predict the effect of a tax cut on economic activity, but suitable data to indicate its actual impact on the economy are hard to come by. Again, think of the problems involved in securing the data needed to determine the effect on criminal law enforcement of a Supreme Court decision such as that in *Miranda* v. *Arizona,*[10] which held that a confession obtained when a suspect had not been informed of his rights when taken into custody was inherently invalid. The members of the President's Crime Commission in 1967 disagreed about its effect. The majority said it was too early to determine its impact. A minority, however, held that, if fully implemented, "it could mean the virtual elimination of pretrial interrogation of suspects. . . . Few can doubt the adverse effect of *Miranda* upon the law enforcement process."[11] An absence of data does not necessarily hinder all evaluators. The use of "Miranda cards" has now become standard police practice and law enforcement appears not to have suffered.

For many social and economic programs, a question that typically arises is: "Did those who participated in programs subsequently fare better than comparable persons who did not?" Providing an answer preferably involves an evaluation design utilizing a control group. The task of devising a control (or comparison) group for a manpower program is summed up in the following passage:

> A strict comparison group in the laboratory sense of the physical sciences is virtually impossible, primarily because the behavior patterns of people are affected by so many external social, economic, and political factors. In fact, sometimes the legislation itself prevents a proper comparison group from being established. For example, the Work Incentive Program legislation of 1967 required that *all* fathers must be enrolled in the WIN program within 30 days after receipt of aid for their children. Therefore, a comparison group of fathers with comparable attributes to those fathers enrolled in the program could not be established. Even if all the external factors of the economy could be controlled, it would still be impossible to replicate the social and political environment affecting any experimental or demonstration program. Thus, it is easy for a decision-maker to discount the results of almost any evaluation study on the basis that it lacks the precision control group.[12]

Because of difficulties such as those noted in the quotation, experimental designs often cannot be used. (This is apart from their often high dollar costs.) Second best alternatives must then be utilized, such as a quasi-experimental design using a nonequivalent control group.[13] They will provide useful but less than conclusive data on program accomplishments.

Another kind of data problem can be illustrated by reference to cost-benefit analysis, which has been widely proposed and sometimes used in recent years to evaluate economic regulatory policies.[14] Cost-benefit analysis is a formal, quantitative evaluation technique which requires enumeration of the various costs and benefits of a regulatory policy (actual or proposed) and their translation into dollars. Supposedly a regulation should be adopted or retained only if the dollar value of its benefits exceed its costs. To make this determination, one must first identify the various costs and benefits of a policy. Some of the problems involved in doing this are discussed in the previous section. Assuming that can be done, then dollar values must be assigned to them. It is relatively easy to do for some matters, such as the direct administrative costs of a policy. However, it is very difficult, if not impossible, for other matters, especially some policy benefits for which there is no market value (e.g., prolongation of human life, clean air, redistribution of income, or equity [fairness]). Some of the problems in appraising policy benefits are pointed up in the following statement by an Environmental Protection Administration official:

> Take one of our water pollution effluent guidelines.... It will be set at, say, 10 micrograms per gram of water. So you have an immediate measurement possible—the number of tons of pollution you will avoid putting in the water and a percentage reduction from the previous level.
>
> But that's not very meaningful, in terms of measuring benefits. So you try to convert that into the standard's effect on water quality. Using models of a stream's rate of flow, you can tell when you have done enough to make the ambient water quality good, but, of course, the quality will vary from the Mississippi to some small river. It costs a bundle to develop models, and often we just don't have data on individual streams.
>
> But if you can reach the judgment that a stream's water quality now will be improved enough to sustain fish life and to permit industrial use of the water without further treatment, so that a brewery might possibly locate there, you have now characterized the uses of the water and you have started to characterize the actual benefits.
>
> If you want to quantify the benefits, you must assign a dollar value to swimming or fishing. You must estimate the number of recreational visits there will be and how much they are worth. You must calculate the number of adverse health effects avoided and assign a dollar value to them.
>
> Each step is very uncertain. The water quality models are uncertain. The projections of how many fishing trips and illnesses there will be are uncertain. The range of error is larger and larger. Is it really worth the large expense entailed going to the end of the chain?...[15]

Clearly cost–benefit analysis is not the precise evaluation instrument that some of its more enthusiastic proponents consider it to be. Nonetheless, it can still be a useful source of information for policy evaluators.

*Official Resistance*  The evaluation of policy, whether it be called policy analysis, the measurement of policy impact, or something else, involves the making of judgments on the merits of policy. This is true even if the evaluator is a university researcher who thinks of himself as objectively in the pursuit of knowledge. Agency and program officials are going to be concerned about the possible political consequences of evaluation. If the results do not come out "right" from their perspective and if the results come to the attention of decision-makers, their program, influence, or careers may be in jeopardy. Consequently, program officials may discourage or disparage evaluation studies, refuse access to data, or keep records that are incomplete. Within agencies, evaluation studies are likely to be most strongly supported by higher-level officials, who must make decisions concerning the allocation of resources among programs and whether to continue given programs. They may, however, be reluctant to require evaluations, especially if their results may have a divisive effect within the agencies. Finally, we should note that organizations tend to resist change, while evaluation implies change. Organizational inertia may thus be an obstacle to evaluation, along with more overt forms of resistance.

*A Limited Time Perspective*   Public officials and others often expect quick results from government programs, even social and educational programs whose effects may take time to appear. As a consequence, short-run evaluations of programs may be unfavorable. Take as an illustration the New Deal's resettlement program, which provided land ownership opportunities for thousands of black sharecroppers in the South during the late 1930s and early 1940s. It was judged as a failure, as just another New Deal boondoggle, by contemporary critics. However, a recent evaluation of the program by Lester Salamon concluded that it had significant, positive long-term effects, although not as an agricultural policy.[16] It did, however, at modest cost transform "a group of landless black tenants into a permanent landed middle class that ultimately emerged in the 1960s as the backbone of the civil-rights movement in the rural South." If the time dimension is ignored in evaluation studies, the results may be flawed and neglect important impacts. The pressure for rapid feedback concerning a policy can then create a dilemma for the evaluator.

*Evaluation Lacks Impact*   Once completed, an evaluation of a program may be ignored or attacked as inconclusive or unsound on various grounds. Thus it may be alleged that the evaluation was poorly designed, the data used was inadequate, or the findings are inconclusive. Those who have an interest in a program, whether as administrators or beneficiaries, are unlikely to lose their affection for it merely because an evaluation study concluded that its costs are greater than its benefits. Moreover, there is also the possibility that the evaluation may be wrong. I am unable to think of a government program that has been terminated solely as a consequence of an unfavorable systematic evaluation effort. Of course, evaluation may lead to changes or improvements in a program, which may be all that should be asked of most evaluations.

## POLICY EVALUATION PROCESSES

Within the national government, policy evaluation is carried on in a variety of ways by a variety of actors. Sometimes it is highly systematic, other times rather haphazard or sporadic. In some instances policy evaluation has become institutionalized; in others it is quite informal and unstructured. A few forms of official policy evaluation, including congressional oversight, the General Accounting Office, Presidential commissions, and agency action, will be examined briefly.

There is, of course, a lot of policy evaluation carried on outside government. The communications media, university scholars, private research organizations such as the Brookings Institution, the Urban Institute and the American Enterprise Institute, pressure groups, and public-interest organizations such as Common Cause and Ralph Nader and his "raiders" all make evaluations of policies that have greater or lesser effects on public officials. They also provide the larger public with information, publicize policy action or inaction, sometimes serve as advocates of unpopular causes, and often effectively represent the unrepresented—for example, the aged confined to negligently run nursing homes, or exploited migrant workers. Limitations of space do not permit discussion of the activities of such groups here, but this should not be taken to mean that they are not important in the policy process. Consider, for example, the impact of television journalism on American policy in Southeast Asia or of Ralph Nader and his associates upon consumer protection policies.

*Congressional Oversight*   One of the primary functions of Congress, although it is not specified in the Constitution, is the scrutiny and evaluation of the application, administration, and execution of laws or policy. Some, agreeing with John Stuart Mill, think that this is the most important function performed by a legislature. Oversight, however, is not a separable, distinct activity; rather, it is a part of almost everything that congressmen do—for example, gathering information, legislating, authorizing appropriations, helping constituents. It may be intended either to control the actions of agencies, as when they sometimes are required to clear actions in advance with particular committees, or to evaluate agency actions, as when individual congressmen or committees seek to determine whether administrators are complying with program objectives established by Congress. It is the evaluative aspect of oversight that is pertinent here.

Oversight may be exercised through a number of techniques, including: (1) casework, that is, intercession with agencies as a consequence of constituent demands and requests; (2) committee hearings and investigations; (3) the appropriations process; (4) approval of presidential appointments; and (5) committee staff studies. In the course of these activities, and others, congressmen reach conclusions regarding the efficiency, effectiveness, and impact of particular policies and programs—conclusions that can have profound consequences for the policy process. Congressional oversight is, in essence, more fragmented and disjointed than continuous and systematic. Bits and pieces of information, impressionistic judgments, and the congressmen's intuition and values are blended to yield evaluation of policies and those who administer them. On the whole, however, members of Congress are more likely to be concerned with policy initiation and adoption, rather than with the evaluation of policy.

*General Accounting Office*   This agency, generally regarded as an "arm of Congress," has broad statutory authority to audit the operations and financial activities of federal agencies, evaluate their programs, and report its find-ings to Congress.[17] In recent years, the GAO has become increasingly con-cerned with evaluating programs as well as auditing program operations. The Legislative Reorganization Act of 1970 increased the authority of the agency in this area by directing it to "review and analyze the results of government programs and activities carried on under existing law, including the making of cost-benefit studies," and to make personnel available to congressional committees to assist them in similar activities. A 1974 statute authorized the GAO to establish an Office of Program Review and Evaluation.

Evaluation studies may be undertaken by the GAO on its own initiative, on the basis of directives in legislation, at the request of congressional com-mittees, or sometimes at the request of individual members of Congress. The Comprehensive Health Manpower Training Act directed GAO to make a study of health-facilities construction costs. The completed report "dealt in great depth with the objective of reducing the high cost of constructing health facilities and also identifying and evaluating ways for reducing the de-mand for such facilities."[18] Another study, requested by the Joint Economic Committee, sought to measure the extent to which poor people, living in six selected geographical areas, benefited from various federal welfare programs. A third study found that the testing program of the National Highway Traffic Safety Administration was inadequate to ensure compliance by manufacturers with national motor-vehicle safety regulation. The results of such studies are delivered to Congress for use in its oversight and decision-making activities.

*Presidential Commissions*   Earlier we dealt with the role of presidential commissions in policy formulation. Now we will see that they can also be used as a means of policy evaluation. Whether set up specifically to evaluate policy in some area or for other purposes such as fact-finding, making policy recommendations, or simply creating the appearance of concern, most com-missions do involve themselves in policy evaluation.

The President's Commission on Income Maintenance Programs was established by President Johnson with a mandate to evaluate existing and proposed income-maintenance programs and to recommend a new income-maintenance program that would better serve the nation's needs. The com-mission reported twenty-two months later, in November, 1969. On the basis of such criteria as whether existing programs had favorable cost-benefit ra-tios, clearly defined the rights and duties of potential participants, provided adequate levels of support, were perceived as equitable, had adverse incen-tive effects, and minimized administrative costs, the commission concluded that existing income-maintenance programs were "simply inadequate for al-leviating existing poverty and protecting the non-poor against risks that they are incapable of dealing with themselves."[19] The commission's main recom-mendation (there were numerous others) was for the creation of a universal federal income-support program making cash payments to all needy persons at a level providing a base income of $2,400 for a family of four. One can only speculate about what impact the commission's report and its recom-mendations had on the controversy, during 1969 and 1970, surrounding the Nixon Administration's proposed Family Assistance Plan, which, as initially proposed, in August, 1969, provided for a guaranteed income of $2,400 for a family of four.[20]

Generally, it appears that the policy evaluations made by presidential commissions do not have much immediate effect on policy-making. The impact they have is probably due primarily to factors other than the quality and soundness of their findings. Charles Jones concludes that an evaluation commission is likely to have the largest effect when its report coincides with other supporting events and is in accord with the President's policy preferences, when it includes some members who hold important government positions and are committed to its recommendations, and when commission staff personnel return to government positions from where they can influence the acceptance of its recommendations.[21]

*Administrative Agencies*  Much program and policy evaluation is engaged in by the administering agencies, either on their own initiative or at the direction or behest of Congress or the executive. In this section we will look first at efforts to build program evaluation into the budgetary process, then at examples of specific agency action, and finally at the effort during the past decade to incorporate cost-benefit analysis into the economic regulatory process.

Much attention in the 1960s was given to the Planning-Programming-Budgeting System (PPBS), which was first introduced in the Department of Defense by Secretary Robert McNamara. Essentially, it was intended to facilitate rational choice among policy and program alternatives on the basis of explicit criteria and firm cost and performance data. On August 25, 1965, President Johnson signed an executive order requiring the use of PPBS throughout the national government. In his view, it would enable decision-makers to:

1. Identify our national goals with precision and on a continuing basis
2. Choose among those goals the ones that are most urgent
3. Search for alternative means of reaching those goals most effectively and at the least cost
4. Inform ourselves not merely on next year's costs, but on the second, and third, and subsequent years' costs of our programs
5. Measure the performance of our programs to insure a dollar's worth of service for each dollar spent.

But things did not go well for PPBS within the bureaucracy, and in June, 1971, the rather turgid prose of an Office of Management and Budget memorandum announced its passing: "Agencies are no longer required to submit with their budget submissions the multi-year program and financing plans, program memoranda and special analytic studies ..."[22]

Many factors contributed to the death of PPBS. Many agency heads and congressmen were not interested in, or were opposed to, program analysis. Legislation often did not clearly specify program goals or provide funds needed to perform needed data collection and analyses. Moreover, there was often a lack of adequate data to develop measures of the costs and benefits of many programs and a scarcity of personnel skilled in policy analysis. Also, many employees were basically resistant to economic analysis and the difficult task of program evaluation.[23]

In 1973, the Office of Management and Budget announced the official birth of another planning and evaluatory technique—Management by Objective (MBO).[24] More modest in its scope than PPBS, MBO required agencies to determine, subject to Office of Management and Budget and presidential approval, the most important objectives they intended to accomplish during the next year or so. Office of Management and Budget officials periodically met with agency officials to review progress toward the objectives. (An example of an objective is the Department of Health, Education, and Welfare's intention to implement the 1971 amendments to the Work Incentive Program. This is broken down into component parts, such as registration of 1.5 million people for the program.) MBO, like PPBS, sought to determine whether agencies were meeting their objectives (goals); unlike PPBS, however, it did not attempt to evaluate alternative programs for meeting agency objectives.

Management by Objective was not viewed with enthusiasm by many agency officials, who saw it as a technique for centralizing power in upper administrative levels and for reducing their own power. It also encountered resistance simply because it was new and different. While PPBS died, MBO appears to have simply disappeared. As a recent study puts it: "MBO has evaporated, becoming a part of the climate of management, albeit a part whose specific influence is limited and incapable of precise measurement."[25]

In 1977 zero-base budgeting (ZBB), brought to Washington by the Carter Administration, made its national government debut. The Office of Management and Budget was in charge of implementation. Under zero-base budgeting, an agency would define the objectives of each of its programs (e.g., the school lunch programs or prevention of credit card fraud) and then determine whether the existing program or some other program would be the best way to achieve the objectives. Then the agency would establish a minimum budget level for the program, below which it would have no value. Beyond that, the agency would develop "add-ons" for the program that would increase its performance and effectiveness. These programs and "add-ons" would then be ranked in order of their importance. An OMB official says that zero-base budgeting will cause agencies to define what they are trying to accomplish, provide a means for assessing the worth of existing programs, and show the government where to spend money so as to do the most good. Fears of agency officials include that zero-base budgeting will be used mostly to cut their budgets and that it will require excessive amounts of time and paperwork. One official described as "crazy" the requirement that agencies rank all their programs. ZBB demonstrated no greater lasting power than PPBS and MBO and it too has passed from the budgetary scene.

It has now become more common for agencies to be specifically directed by Congress to undertake program evaluations. An illustrative case involves the Department of Energy, created by Congress in 1977 by the Department of Energy Organization Act. Title X of the statute directs the Department to submit a comprehensive review of each of its programs to Congress by January 1982. The information to be provided for each program is spelled out in detail, including but not limited to the following requirements:

An identification of the objectives intended for the program and the problem or need which the program was intended to address. . . .

An assessment of alternative methods of achieving the purposes of the program. . . .

An assessment of the degree to which the original objectives of the program have been achieved, expressed in terms of the performance, impact, or accomplishments of the program and of the problem or need which it was intended to address, and employing the procedures or methods of analysis appropriate to the type or character of the program. . . .

A statement of the number and types of beneficiaries or persons served by the program. . . .

An assessment of the effect of the program on the national economy, including but not limited to, the effects on competition, economic stability, employment, unemployment, productivity, and price inflation, including costs to consumers and to businesses. . . .

An assessment of the degree to which the overall administration of the program, as expressed in the rules, regulations, orders, standards, criteria, and decisions of the officers executing the program, are believed to meet the objectives of Congress in establishing the program. . . .

The availability of such information will facilitate evaluation of the effectiveness of the Department's programs.

Cost-benefit analysis has been used by the national government since the 1902 Rivers and Harbors Act required that a water project's costs be less than the benefits it conferred. In the 1960s cost-benefit analysis was extended first to defense programs and then to domestic programs (PPBS). In the 1970s Presidents Ford and Carter directed regulatory agencies to prepare "inflation impact statements" and "regulatory analyses," respectively, to accompany proposed regulations. The Carter Administration made it clear that its requirement did not mean that regulations should be subjected to a cost-benefit test.

A marked change occurred with the advent of the Reagan Administration in 1981, one of whose major goals was a substantial reduction in economic regulatory activity. In February the President issued Executive Order 12291, which required that any proposed major rule be accompanied by a regulatory analysis assessing the potential benefits, costs, and net benefits, including effects which could not be quantified in monetary terms, unless such calculations were prohibited by law.[26] (Some statutes ban cost-benefit analysis for the programs they involve.) Major rules were defined as those likely to have an annual effect on the economy of $100 million or more, to lead to major cost or price increases, or to have "significant adverse effects on competition, employment, investment, productivity, innovation, or the ability of U.S.-based enterprises to compete with foreign-based enterprises in domestic or export markets." The Office of Management and Budget was authorized to supervise the evaluation process and to delay the issuance of proposed or final rules when it reviewed the agency analyses. Power to block the issuance of rules rests with the Vice President's Task Force on Regulatory Relief or the President. All of this is intended to ensure, among other things, that "Regulatory action shall not be undertaken unless the potential benefits to society for the regulation outweigh the potential costs to society."

The Reagan Administration's regulatory evaluation program shifts the burden of proof to those advocating new regulatory actions. If the program is rigorously enforced it will require substantial amounts of analysis, and many more analysts, in the regulatory agencies. Administration officials obviously view cost-benefit analysis as a useful tool in reducing the volume of regulation. Whether they will convert it from an analytical tool into a decision rule which automatically determines the fate of proposed regulations is not now clear, although that seems to be their preference. What is clear is that they are more concerned with the costs than with the benefits of regulation. To the extent that this happens, cost-benefit analysis becomes an instrument of partisan political analysis.[27]

Policy evaluation, as the discussion thus far should indicate, is more than a technical or analytical process; it is also a political process. In the next section, a case study of the evaluation of the Headstart program illustrates how political factors may affect the conduct and impact of program evaluations. It also demonstrates that evaluations, even when intendedly neutral or objective, become political when they affect the allocation of resources.

## THE POLITICS OF EVALUATION: THE CASE OF HEAD START

The Economic Opportunity Act of 1964 contained no provisions specifically concerned with the educational problems of poor children. Advocates of a preschool program for poor children, however, found Sargent Shriver, Director of the Office of Economic Opportunity, sympathetic to the idea. Support for such a program as part of the antipoverty program also came from Congress. In January, 1965, President Johnson announced that a preschool program named Head Start would be created as part of the Community Action Program. Initially, $17 million in CAP funds were to be committed for the summer of 1965, to enable 100,000 children to participate. The announcement of Head Start produced a large volume of requests for funds from many localities. OEO officials decided to meet this demand, with the result that ultimately $103 million was committed to provide places for 560,000 children during the summer of 1965. To say the least, the program was highly popular, undoubtedly because it directed attention to preschool poor children who readily aroused the sympathy of the public.

Late in the summer of 1965, Head Start was made a permanent part of the antipoverty program. According to President Johnson, Head Start had been "battle-tested," and "proven worthy." It was expanded to include a full-year program. In fiscal year 1968, $330 million were allocated to provide places for 473,000 children in summer programs and another 218,000 in full-year programs, making Head Start the largest single component of the Community Action Program. Essentially, Head Start was a multifaceted program for meeting the needs of poor children. More than a traditional nursery school or kindergarten program, it was designed also to provide poor children with physical and mental health services and meals to improve their diet. Further, an effort was made to involve members of the local community in the program.

With this as a background, let us turn to evaluation of the program.[28] OEO was among the leaders in efforts to evaluate social programs. Within the agency the task of evaluating the over-all effectiveness of its programs was assigned to the Office of Research, Plans, Programs and Evaluations (RPP&E). Some early efforts had been made to evaluate the effectiveness of the Head Start program, mostly by Head Start officials and involving particular projects, but, as of the middle of 1967, no good evidence existed regarding overall program effectiveness. This was becoming a matter of concern to OEO offi-

cials, the Bureau of the Budget, and some members of Congress. Consequently, the Evaluation Division of RPP&E, as part of a series of national evaluations of OEO programs, proposed an *ex post facto* study design for Head
Start in which Head Start children currently in the first, second, and third
grades of school would be given a series of cognitive and affective tests.
Their test scores would then be compared with those of a control group. The
Evaluation Division believed such a design would yield results more quickly
than a longitudinal study that, though more desirable, would take longer to
complete. (A longitudinal study examines the impact over time of a program
on a given group.)

Within OEO, Head Start officials opposed the proposed study on various
grounds, including its design, the test instruments to be used, and the focus
on only the educational aspect of the program to the neglect of its health,
nutrition, and community involvement goals. RPP&E evaluations acknowl-
edged the multiplicity of Head Start goals but contended that cognitive improvement was its primary goal. They agreed with Head Start officials that
there were risks, such as possible misleading negative results, in making a
limited study but insisted that the need for evaluative data necessitated taking the risks. Following much internal debate, the OEO Director decided the
study should be made, and in June, 1968, a contract was entered into with
the Westinghouse Learning Corporation and Ohio University. The study was
conducted in relative quiet, but hints of its negative fundings began to surface as it neared completion.

Early in 1969, a White House staff official became aware of the Westinghouse study and requested information on it because the President was preparing an address on the Economic Opportunity Act that would include a
discussion of Head Start. OEO officials reported the preliminary negative findings of the study. In his message to Congress on Economic Opportunity on
February 19, 1969, President Nixon referred to the study, noting that "the
preliminary reports ... confirm what many have feared: the long term effect
of Head Start appears to be extremely weak." He went on to say that "this
must not discourage us" and spoke well of the program. Nonetheless, his
speech raised substantial doubts about Head Start in the public arena.

The President's speech touched off considerable pressure for the release
of the study's findings. OEO officials were reluctant to do so because what
had been delivered to them by Westinghouse was the preliminary draft of
the final report. It was to be used to decide such matters as what additional
statistical tests were needed and what data required reanalysis. From Congress, where hearings were being held on OEO legislation, claims were made
that the study was being held back to protect Head Start, and that the report
was going to be rewritten. The pressure on the White House became sufficiently great that it directed OEO to make public the study by April 14. A
major conclusion of the report was that the full-year Head Start program produced a statistically significant but absolutely slight improvement in participant children.

The release of the report set off a flood of criticism from Head Start proponents, including many academicians, concerning the methodological and
conceptual validity of the report. A sympathetic article in the *New York
Times* bore the headline "HEAD START REPORT HELD 'FULL OF HOLES.'"
Much of the ensuing controversy focused on the statistical methods of the

report and involved a considerable range of claims, charges, rebuttals, and denials. The proponents of Head Start seemed to fear that their program was being victimized by devious design. This fear had several dimensions. One was that persons within OEO who favored Community Action over Head Start wanted a study that would indicate Head Start's deficiencies. Another was that the administration was going to use the findings to justify a major cutback in Head Start. Finally, there was the fear that "enemies of the program" in Congress would use the negative results to attack the program. Although there now appears not to have been much factual basis for these fears, they were "real" to the proponents of Head Start and contributed to the intensity of their attack on the evaluation study.

The methodological issues in the controversy over the study focused on such standard items as the sample size, the validity of the control group, and the appropriateness of the tests given the children. An examination of these issues would be too lengthy and too technical to include here. However, an assessment of the study by Walter Williams can be quoted to advantage on methodological issues.

> In terms of its methodological and conceptual base, the study is a *relatively* good one. This in no way denies that many of the criticisms made of the study are valid. However, for the most part, they are the kinds of criticisms that can be made of most pieces of social science research conducted outside the laboratory, in a real-world setting, with all of the logistical and measurement problems that such studies entail. And these methodological flaws open the door to the more political issues. Thus, one needs not only to examine the methodological substance of the criticisms which have been made of the study, but also to understand the social concern which lies behind them as well. Head Start has elicited national sympathy and has had the support and involvement of the educational profession. It is understandable that so many should rush to the defense of such a popular and humane program. But how many of the concerns over the size of the sample, control-group equivalency, and the appropriateness of co-variance analysis, for example, would have been registered if the study had found positive differences in favor of Head Start? . . .
>
> We imagine that this type of positive, but qualified assessment will fit any relatively good evaluation for some time to come. We have never seen a field evaluation of a social action program that could not be faulted legitimately by good methodologists, and we may never see one.

Interestingly enough, the results of the Westinghouse study were as favorable to Head Start as were the earlier evaluations of particular projects made by Head Start officials. These, too, showed that the program had limited lasting effects on the children. What the Westinghouse study, and the controversy over it, did was to put these findings into the public arena and extend the scope of the conflict over them.

Despite the essentially negative evaluations of its impact, the Westinghouse report recommended that Head Start be preserved and improved, at least partly on the ground that "something must be tried here and now to help the many children of poverty who may never be helped again." Head Start was, and is, a politically popular program. Congress and the executive generally have been favorably disposed toward the program, and it has suffered little of the criticism directed at other aspects of the antipoverty program.

Ten years after the Westinghouse study was made public, the findings of another group of researchers on the long-term effects of Head Start were published by the Department of Health, Education and Welfare. On the basis of a series of longitudinal studies, it was concluded that Head Start had significant, long-lasting social and educational benefits for its participants. Thus children who had been in the program had much less need for remedial classes, were less likely to be retained in grade, and were half as likely to drop out of high school than were adolescents of comparable age who had not been in the program. As a consequence, Head Start was now hailed as a success by the media. Why the substantial difference in the findings of the two evaluations? The explanation rests primarily with the different methodological approaches. The Westinghouse study, using an experimental design, focused on short-run effects, especially as measured by intelligence test scores. The second study focused on long-range effects.

In 1981, Head Start was designated as part of President's Reagan's "social safety net" and thus was not marked for reduced funding as were several other programs for poor people. Indeed, Head Start emerged from the budgetary struggle with an increased level of funding. Members of Congress were influenced not only by Head Start's success as an education program but also by the belief that it would lead to reduced future spending for other programs.

## WHY POLICIES MAY NOT HAVE THEIR INTENDED IMPACT

Policy evaluation and experience often indicate that policies do not achieve their ostensible goals or have the impact on public problems they were intended to have. A variety of factors may impede the attainment of policy goals.

First, inadequate resources may be devoted to dealing with a problem. The Johnson Administration's War on Poverty was not wholly successful because, as many commentators have pointed out, only limited resources were allocated to what was supposed to be an "all-out war." Public-housing programs have never produced the amount of housing projected because Congress has failed to appropriate the required amounts of funds.

Second, policies may be administered in a fashion that lessens their impact. The Federal Power Commission, for example, has never been very enthusiastic about regulating the wellhead price of natural gas. The Texas legislature enacted a state minimum wage law in 1969 but provides no funds for its enforcement. As one might imagine, its impact is limited.

Third, public problems are often caused by a multitude of factors, while policy may be directed at only one or a few of them. Job-training programs may help those who are unemployed because they lack adequate job skills but do little for those who have chronic ailments or inadequate motivation. Price inflation may be the product of several factors, with the result that efforts to counteract it by monetary policy, which deals with the money supply, are alone inadequate.

Fourth, people may respond or adapt to public policies in such manner as to negate much of their impact. The effectiveness of agricultural production control programs in the 1950s and 1960s was reduced because the programs were based on acreage limitations, and farmers were able, through scientific and technological developments such as improved plant varieties and increased use of chemical fertilizers, to produce higher yields on fewer acres. Consequently, there was little reduction in production, and "surpluses" persisted.

Fifth, policies may have incompatible goals that bring them into conflict with one another. Thus, within the Department of Agriculture, the Agricultural Conservation and Stabilization Service was concerned with limiting the production of some commodities, while the Agricultural Research Service was concerned with trying to increase agricultural productivity. The ASCS's price support program for tobacco, which encourages production, does not seem consistent with the quest of the National Cancer Institute, given the link between smoking and cancer. The use of tax benefits and exemptions to encourage various forms of economic activity has lessened the attainment of income equality through the graduated income tax.

Sixth, the solutions for some problems may involve costs that are greater than the problems. "Crime in the streets" could probably be eradicated entirely if we were willing to pay the costs in greatly enhanced police surveillance, individual repression, curfews, and the like. The effect of this on individual freedom would be vast and disastrous, and the lack of individual freedom would then become a problem. The *total* elimination of environmental pollution might be another example. An estimate in the early 1970s put the cost of eliminating 85 to 90 percent of water pollution at $61 billion. Elimination of 100 percent of water pollution in the United States would cost another $258 billion.[29] These estimates would have to be increased substantially because of inflation.

Seventh, many public problems may not be soluble, or at least completely so. Given human nature and national interests, tension and strife to some degree will undoubtedly continue to exist in the world. Some children simply may not be able to learn much in the public schools, regardless of how many times the curriculum is revised and other changes are made.

Eighth, the nature of the problem at which policy is directed may change while policy is being developed or applied. The farm problem may shift from one of too much to one of too little production, and then return to one of excess production. An oversupply of petroleum may give way to a shortage thereof. Petroleum industry spokespersons, who like to blame the energy crisis on the government, conveniently ignore or forget that past policies to restrict domestic production and foreign imports were in accord with the industry's interest in higher prices.

Finally, new problems may arise that distract attention and action from a given problem. The "energy problem" may draw attention from the "environmental pollution problem" just as the war in Vietnam did from the War on Poverty. As this happens governmental action tends to be diverted from the older to the newer problems. It is difficult in the American political system to secure the sustained, substantial effort required to deal effectively with many public problems.

If few public problems are entirely resolved by policy action, many are partly solved or ameliorated. Employment problems may still exist, but not to the extent they would have, had there been no job training, area development, unemployment compensation, and other programs. Usually, indeed, policy goals are stated, implicitly or explicitly, in relative rather than absolute terms. The intent is to reduce the prevalence of heart disease, not entirely eliminate it, to lessen movements in price levels, not entirely prevent them.

## THE RESPONSE TO POLICY

In this chapter, quite a bit has been said about the systematic evaluation of policy. It has clearly become a more widespread and potentially significant part of the policy process. Up to the present time, however, as various observers have remarked, systematic evaluation does not appear to have had really significant effects upon policy decision-making. As was seen in the case of Head Start, an essentially unfavorable early evaluation of its impact did not lead to its abandonment nor, we might add, to major change in its substantive form. This should not be taken to mean that systematic evaluation is either useless or unlikely ever to have much impact on policy-making. It is a relatively new activity, and it encounters many problems, as we have noted. As time goes on, and as evaluation techniques and designs become more effective, its impact will undoubtedly increase. After all, few would contend that intelligence does not provide a more sound basis than intuition in determining public policy.

People and groups, citizens and officials alike, do, of course, make many judgments concerning the impact and desirability of existing policies and, on this basis, react to them with support, opposition, or indifference. There is much evaluatory activity of the first two kinds discussed at the beginning of this chapter. Political decision-makers may frequently temper their evaluations of the substantive content or impact of policies with responsiveness to political factors—for example, partisan pressures, emotional appeals, or re-election considerations. Ralph Huitt notes that "political feasibility" is a concern entering into the selection of policy priorities and programs designed to meet them by decision-makers. "Will it 'go' on the Hill? Will the public buy it? Does it have political 'sex appeal'? What 'can't be done' is likely to get low priority."[30]

At this point the concept of feedback can be injected usefully into the discussion. This concept, which was briefly touched upon in the treatment of systems theory in Chapter 1, tells us that past policy decisions and impacts can generate demands for change or support for them. Thus, the enactment and administration of the National Environmental Policy Act of 1969 has given rise to various demands for its repeal, modification, and continuation.[31] Its use by opponents of the Alaskan oil pipeline to prevent its construction finally resulted in legislation exempting the project from NEPA requirements. The Soil Conservation Act of 1935, and the administering agency, the Soil Conservation Service, gave rise to a pressure group, the National Association of Soil Conservation Districts, that has strongly supported their continuation. As a consequence of feedback to decision-makers, a variety of actions subsequently can be taken concerning policy, including: continuation; legislative amendment to strengthen or weaken the policy; adjustments in its administration, such as strong or lax enforcement of given provisions; increasing, decreasing, or restricting funds to support its administration; challenges to its meaning or constitutionality in the courts (this is more likely to be done by private interested parties than by officials); and repeal of the statute (or permitting it to expire if it has a time limit).

So far as major policies and programs are concerned, repeal or termination of them is unlikely to occur, even when much controversy, and even bitterness, attend their adoption. They soon come to be taken for granted, as a part of the environment, and debate over their propriety, if not their details or impact, soon quiets down. This has been the case with the Social Security Act (1935), the Taft-Hartley Act (1947), the Civil Rights Act (1964), and the Elementary and Secondary Education Act (1965), to cite a few. Few statutes have stirred as much controversy as the Economic Opportunity Act, and yet, although it has been variously amended and control of the programs it created has been transferred from the now defunct Office of Economic Opportunity to other agencies, the Act remains in existence. As a general proposition, it can be suggested that the longer a policy, program, or agency remains in existence, the less likely it is to be terminated. Over time, accommodations are made and support developed that enable them to survive. Exceptions include policies, programs, or agencies established to deal with emergency problems such as relief during the Depression of the 1930s (e.g., Works Progress Administration) and price controls and rationing as well as production allocation during World War II (e.g., Office of Price Administration, War Production Board).

The revision, or demands for revision, of existing policies will depend upon such factors as the extent to which they are held to "solve" the problem at which they are directed or their perceived impact, the skill with which they are administered, defects or shortcomings that may be revealed during implementation, and the political power and awareness of concerned or affected groups. In addition, the manner in which the costs and benefits of a policy are distributed will have important consequences for its future.

The costs and benefits of public policies may be either broadly or narrowly distributed. In the case of social security, both benefits and costs are broadly distributed; a statute regulating relationships between automobile manufacturers and dealers involves a narrow distribution of costs and benefits. Narrow costs–broad benefits and broad costs–narrow benefits are other possible patterns. The costs and benefits of policies, it will be recalled, can be either material or symbolic. The proposition here advanced is that the response to *existing* policies, and demands for changes thereon, will be affected by the way their benefits and costs are distributed.[32]

*Broad Benefits and Broad Costs* Policies that involve a broad distribution of costs and benefits, such as social security, highway construction, police and fire protection, public education, and national defense, tend to become readily accepted, institutionalized, and beyond major challenge. Controversy may focus on such particular features as the location of highways, whether to provide sex education, or the acquisition of a weapons system, but the continuation of the programs as a whole is not seriously in question. It has been easy to propose and difficult to resist increases in the benefits of a program like social security because of the many specific beneficiaries. National defense provides a collective good (all benefit from it, although the amount of benefit cannot be precisely measured or defined) related to the important value of national security and survival. (Note the defensive position you tend to find yourself in when you argue that something proposed is not really necessary for national defense.) Radical changes in most policies in this category are unlikely.

Some policies, however, that fall in this category may never really gain wide and continued acceptance, as with the War on Poverty. It had many potential beneficiaries, but most of them were poor, and the poor in our society have long lacked substantial political power and, consequently, effective ability to secure and support policies benefiting them. Many changes have been made in the poverty programs since 1964 although most of them remain in existence. OEO was finally abolished, however, because it had become such a strong negative symbol and focus of controversy.

Occasionally, the costs of a program may come to be seen by many as exceeding its benefits. This has been true in recent years with the public-assistance programs that provide aid to various needy groups, such as the "working poor" and families with dependent children. Controversy has been especially intense over aid to families with dependent children. Much has been spoken and written about the "welfare mess," "welfare crisis," and so on. Many proposals for change, including elimination of the programs, have been made, and some have been adopted. A major change proposed by the Nixon Administration, the Family Assistance Plan, failed of enactment in the early 1970s. After much furor, the public-assistance programs remain much the same as they were a few years ago, except that most are now totally funded by the national government. Only Aid to Families with Dependent Children is now jointly funded by the national and state governments. The groups supporting public assistance programs are sufficiently strong to maintain them, if not to bring about basic reform. The critics are sufficiently strong to prevent major expansion while perhaps securing some restrictive changes that somewhat reduce the scope or impact of the programs. Public education is another policy area in which this kind of conflict, promising much but delivering little, may develop.

*Broad Benefits and Narrow Costs*   Some policies seem to provide benefits for large numbers of people, while their costs fall primarily upon fairly distinct, identifiable groups in society. Illustrative are environmental pollution control, automobile safety, food and meat inspection, public utility regulation, and industrial and coal mine safety policies. Coal mine companies have felt that they are being asked to bear the burden of safety regulation, and that many specific requirements are unnecessary. They have complained of the unfairness of the regulatory program and have sought both legislative and administrative amelioration of its impact upon them. Just so, many industries have protested having to meet the costs and inconveniences of pollution-control programs. Of course, they may be able to pass the financial costs of them on to consumers as part of the final price of their product. Small business groups have been especially shrill in their criticism of the National Occupational Safety and Health Act, even though a great many small businessmen have undoubtedly never seen an OSHA inspector.

The enactment of policies falling within this category is usually achieved through the actions of a loose coalition of interests, perhaps in response to a crisis of some sort. Once the legislation is enacted, the supporting coalition tends to lose interest in the matter, assuming that with the enactment of legislation the problem is adequately cared for. The groups that opposed the law and perceive themselves as bearing the brunt of it remain concerned and active, as in the cases of automobile manufacturers and safety legislation and, earlier, the railroads and rate regulation. Much more is heard from them by the enforcing agencies and the legislature concerning the undesirable effects of the legislation. The result may be administrative action and legislative changes tempering the original legislation.[33] Conversely, it may become very difficult for supporters of the original legislation to get together again to secure amendments to strengthen the law. For instance, a loophole was created in the antimerger provision for the Clayton Act in the early 1920s by judicial interpretation. Not until 1950 were the supporters of antitrust able to secure corrective legislation in the form of the Celler Antimerger Act. Again, automobile manufacturers have been unremitting in their opposition to emission control standards for cars since their adoption a few years ago and have succeeded in delaying implementation of some EPA standards.

*Narrow Benefits and Broad Costs*   Some policies and programs are of benefit to readily identifiable interest groups, while their costs do not appear to fall upon any particular groups. Veteran's benefits, agricultural subsidies, hospital construction grants, rivers and harbors projects, and special tax provisions (for example, the oil depletion allowance) fall within this category. The costs of these policies are usually in the form of higher taxes or prices that affect people generally. Those who benefit from these policies have a clear incentive to organize and act to maintain them. As Wilson notes, policies of this variety encourage the formation of pressure groups to support their continuation, often in close relationship with the administering agency. Good examples are the National Rivers and Harbors Congress and the Corps of Army Engineers, the National Rural Electrification Cooperative Association and the Rural Electrification Administration, and veterans' groups and the Veterans Administration.

Those who are critical of such policies find it difficult to mobilize sufficient interest and political support to bring about changes. Presidents Johnson and Nixon both urged Congress to reduce greatly the funds for the Rural Environmental Assistance Program, which provides financial grants to farmers for soil-conserving activities, such as the application of limestone to the soil and the construction of erosion-control terraces, on the grounds that such costs can and should properly be borne by farmers. They did not have much success, because those who benefit from the program work actively for its continuation at present levels, and Congress has been responsive to them. The cost is paid by the fabled John Q. Taxpayer, who is little aware of either the program or the way in which it affects his tax bill. Sometimes, though, policies in this category may arouse sufficient opposition, both among citizens and officials, as to lead to their alteration. One example is the oil-depletion allowance, which had become a symbol of privilege for the oil industry. In 1969 it was reduced from 27.5 percent to 22 percent. The energy crisis helped bring it under further attack and in 1975 the depletion allowance was repealed for all but small producers. The deregulation movement, which began in the middle 1970s, provided the political impetus needed to enact legislation in 1978 to eliminate economic regulation of commercial airlines by the Civil Aeronautics Board. CAB regulation had long been criticized on the ground that by restricting competition it imposed costs on many travelers in order to benefit a few airlines. The deregulation movement expanded the conflict over the program by focusing public attention on it and by increasing the forces in favor of change.

*Narrow Benefits and Narrow Costs*    Policies that provide benefits to a well-defined group but at the cost of another distinct group tend to be productive of continuing organized conflict among the groups and their partisans. In point here are the conflicts between organized labor and management over the Wagner and Taft-Hartley Acts, commercial banks and savings and loan associations over banking policies, and railroads and motor carriers over freight regulation by the Interstate Commerce Commission. Conflict repeatedly and continually develops over amendments to, and interpretations of, the original policy. Efforts may also be made to secure a repeal. Top-level appointments to the administering agency are another item of contention. The National Labor Relations Board has alternated between prolabor and promanagement treatments of the labor laws, as Democratic administrations have appointed prolabor people to the board and Republican administrations have reciprocated with promanagement people when the opportunity has arisen.[34] In situations where the costs and benefits of policy are concentrated on active, organized groups, major policy changes tend to result either from shifts in the balance of power among them, such as that leading to the Taft-Hartley Act, or from negotiated settlements, such as that which led to mandatory oil-import quotas in the late 1950s.

These four policy categories based on the allocation of costs and benefits are only approximate. All policies will not fit neatly and exclusively into one or another of them. The reader may want to refine and develop them further, which he is encouraged to do. The categories are put foward here as being useful in gaining insight into why the responses to policies vary and in estimating what the feedback responses will be to policy actions. Moreover, the categories should also be helpful in analyzing the struggles that attend the adoption of policy, as, to some extent, the kind of policy proposed will help shape the enactment process.

## NOTES

1. Carol Weiss, *Evaluating Action Programs: Readings in Social Action and Education* (Boston: Allyn and Bacon, 1972), p. 14.
2. This matter is ably discussed by Michael J. Malbin, *Unelected Representatives: Congressional Staff and the Future of Representative Government* (New York: Basic Books, 1979), chap. 9.
3. Thomas R. Dye, *Understanding Public Policy,* 2d ed. (Englewood Cliffs, N.J.: Prentice-Hall, 1975), pp. 327–330.
4. Kenneth E. Warner, "Clearing the Airwaves: The Cigarette Ad Ban Revisited," *Policy Analysis* (Fall, 1979), pp. 235–50.
5. A useful discussion of externalities in public policy can be found in Larry L. Wade, *The Elements of Public Policy* (Columbus, Ohio: Merrill, 1972), chap. 3.

6. Gabriel A. Almond and G. Bingham Powell, *Comparative Politics: A Developmental Approach* (Boston: Little, Brown, 1966), p. 199.
7. Carol H. Weiss, "The Politics of Impact Measurement," *Policy Studies Journal*, I (Spring, 1973), pp. 180–81.
8. Robert A. Levine, *The Poor Ye Need Not Have with You* (Cambridge, Mass.: MIT Press, 1970), pp. 91–92.
9. Solomon Kalirin and Steven G. Lubeck, "Problems in the Evaluation of Crime Control Policy." Paper presented at the 1973 annual meeting of the American Political Science Association, p. 29.
10. 384 U.S. 436 (1966).
11. President's Commission on Law Enforcement and the Administration of Justice, *The Challenge of Crime in a Free Society* (Washington, D.C.: Government Printing Office, 1967), p. 305.
12. Jeremy A. Lifsey, "Politics, Evaluations and Manpower Programs." Paper presented at the 1973 annual meeting of the American Political Science Association.
13. See the discussion of policy evaluation techniques in Carol H. Weiss, *Evaluation Research: Methods of Assessing Program Effectiveness* (Englewood Cliffs, N.J.: Prentice-Hall, 1972).
14. Robert H. Haveman and Julius Margolis, eds., *Public Expenditure and Policy Analysis*, 2d ed. (Chicago: Rand McNally, 1977), contains several useful essays on cost benefit analysis. On the use of cost benefit analysis for regulatory policies, see House Committee on Interstate and Foreign Commerce, *Hearings on Use of Cost-Benefit Analysis by Regulatory Agencies*, 96th Cong., 1st Sess., 1979.
15. Quoted in Timothy B. Clark, "Do the Benefits Justify the Costs? Prove It, Says the Administration," *National Journal*, Vol. 13 (August 1, 1981), p. 1385.
16. Lester M. Salamon, "The Time Dimension in Policy Evaluation: The Case of the New Deal Land-Reform Experiments," *Public Policy*, XXVII (Spring, 1979), pp. 129–184.
17. This discussion draws on Elmer B. Staats, "General Accounting Office Support of Committee Oversight," in *Committee Organization in the House*, panel discussion before the House Select Committee on Committees, 93d Cong., 1st Sess. (1973), II, pp. 692–700. Staats was the head of the General Accounting Office.
18. *Ibid.,* p. 696.
19. *Poverty Amid Plenty: The American Paradox,* report of the President's Commission on Income Maintenance Programs (Washington, D.C.: Government Printing Office, 1969). The quotation is on page 2.
20. An excellent account of this policy episode is Daniel P. Moynihan, *The Politics of a Guaranteed Income* (New York: Random House, 1973).
21. Charles O. Jones, *An Introduction to the Study of Public Policy* (Belmont, Calif.: Wadsworth, 1970), p. 118. Insight into the operation of a commission set up in 1966 to appraise legislation regulating the political activities of public employees can be gained from Charles O. Jones, "Reevaluating the Hatch Act: A Report on the Commission on Political Activity of Government Employees," *Public Administration Review*, XXIX (May–June, 1969), pp. 249–54.
22. Quoted in Allen Shick, "A Death in the Bureaucracy: The Demise of Federal PPB," *Public Administration Review*, XXXIII (March–April, 1975), p. 146.
23. Robert H. Haveman, "Public Expenditure and Policy Analysis: An Overview," in Robert H. Haveman and Julius Margolis (eds.), *Public Expenditure and Policy Analysis* (Chicago: Markham, 1970), pp. 14–15. Several selections in this volume are useful for gaining an understanding of PPBS.

24. Joel Havemann, "Administration Report: OMB Begins Major Program to Identify and Attain Presidential Goals," *National Journal,* V (June 2, 1973), pp. 783–93.

25. Richard Rose, "Implementation and Evaporation: The Record of MBO," *Public Administration Review,* XXXVII (January–February, 1977), p. 70.

26. *Federal Register,* Vol. 46 (February 19, 1981), pp. 13193–13198.

27. Charles E. Lindblom, The Policy Making Process, 2d ed. (Englewood Cliffs, N.J.: Prentice Hall, 1980), chap. 4.

28. This account draws upon Walter Williams, *Social Policy Research and Analysis* (New York: American Elsevier, 1971) and Walter Williams and John W. Evans, "The Politics of Evaluation: The Case of Head Start," *Annals of the American Academy of Political and Social Sciences,* CCCLXXXV (September, 1969), pp. 118–32.

29. Allen V. Kneese and Charles L. Schultz, *Pollution Prices, and Public Policy* (Washington: Brookings Institution, 1975), p. 21.

30. Ralph K. Huitt, "Political Feasibility," in Austin Ranney (ed.), *Political Science and Public Policy* (Chicago: Markham, 1968), p. 266.

31. Walter A. Rosenbaum, *The Politics of Environmental Concern* (New York: Praeger, 1973), pp. 265–72.

32. This discussion leans heavily upon James Q. Wilson, *Political Organizations* (New York: Basic Books, 1973), chap. 16. The student of policy formation cannot afford to ignore this book.

33. In some instances, the regulated group may succeed, at least for a time, in "capturing" the administering agency. A classic case study is Samuel P. Huntington, "The Marasmus of the ICC: The Commission, the Railroads, and the Public Interest," *Yale Law Journal* LXII (December, 1952), pp. 171–225. Agency "capture," however, is more frequently alleged that proven in the literature of political science.

34. Cf. Seymour Scher, "Regulatory Agency Control Through Appointment: The Case of the Eisenhower Administration and the NLRB," *Journal of Politics,* XXIII (November, 1961), pp. 667–88.

# 7

# Policy Study and the Public Interest

In the preceding chapters I have sought to present a general scheme for the analysis of public policy-making, along with a discussion that focuses primarily on policy-making at the national level in the United States. This scheme should not be viewed as a general theory of the policy process (obviously, it is not), but as one means for organizing and directing one's inquiry into that process.

Several general observations can be made, by way of conclusion, concerning the policy process. First, the process of policy-making on most problems—certainly those of any magnitude—is continuous. A problem is recognized and reaches governmental agendas, alternatives are presented, a policy is officially adopted and implemented, some sort of evaluation and feedback occur, changes or adjustments may be made, more implementation follows, evaluation and feedback again take place (in infrequent instances a policy may be terminated), and so on. Somewhere along the line the problem at which policy is directed may be redefined, as when the "energy problem" shifts from one of too much petroleum production to insufficient domestic production. When this happens, the result may be a substantial change in the content and thrust of policy. Again, a change in the socioeconomic environment may create a need to alter a policy, as when the aging of the population creates a crisis in the financing of social security. Public problems are often ameliorated but seldom fully resolved by public policies.

Second, in a modern, pluralistic political system, public policy-making is usually a complex process. Many participants, official and unofficial, may be involved and many factors may help shape its outcome. Those who provide easy and quick answers to why a particular policy was adopted, or rejected, often engage in gross oversimplifications. Some historians, for instance, have described the enactment of the Sherman Act simply as "a sop to public opinion." Journalists and others sometimes explain legislative enactments in idiosyncratic fashion. The contention that the United States became deeply involved in Vietnam in the 1960s because Lyndon Johnson "was not going to be the first President to lose a war" is in point here. While one should indeed try to be parsimonious in explaining political phenomena, all major relevant factors should be taken into account. As a consequence, policy analysis will often be complex in style and uncertain or tentative in its results.

Third, the analysis of public policy-making can provide much information and insight into the nature and operation of the political system and political processes generally. It helps shift our attention from a narrow concern with micropolitical phenomena (voting behavior, political attitudes, political socialization, and so on) to their role in the broad governmental process. I do not wish to argue that we should not be concerned, for example, with how individuals acquire political attitudes. This can be an interesting activity and can yield much information on learning behavior and the process of socialization, among other things. We should, however, also be concerned with the "So what?" question. What difference does it make, for example, so far as governance and public policy are concerned, how people acquire certain political values and beliefs, and when? The focus on policy-making can perform an integrating and unifying function in political inquiry, as well as providing a criterion of relevance to use in determining what political phenomena to analyze. It is a highly useful approach to the study of policy that can yield knowledge that has both social scientific and immediate practical value.

Fourth, much remains unknown or unexplained concerning how political decisions and public policies are made, although our knowledge here has expanded significantly in the last couple of decades. The field of policy study is open and challenging. It should be especially attractive to those who wish to be "relevant," to engage in research and discovery that has some immediate social utility. Policy study provides ample room for those who are more traditional or more behavioral, more quantitative or nonquantitative, more analytical or more inclined to advocacy, to exercise their talents and pursue their interests. All can contribute through careful scholarship to our knowledge and understanding of public policy and the policy process. Eclecticism in approach helps ensure that fruitful avenues of inquiry will not be closed off by narrow or particular theoretical concerns.

Fifth, as of yet we still have limited systematic knowledge concerning the actual impacts of public policies, whether on the problems at which they are directed or on their unintended or unforseen consequences. Policy evaluation, whether conceived of as an art or science, is still in a developmental stage, although interest, activity, and sophistication in this area have increased substantially during the last decade. Social scientists, however, still have a tendency to write about how to do evaluations rather than actually engage in policy evaluation. Policy evaluation is, of course, a difficult task. One must identify the goals of policies, determine and measure the results of programs for their implementation, and separate the effects of policies from the other social and economic factors which may be operative. No wonder then that some find other things to do. Nonetheless, more and better policy evaluations are needed, both for the benefit of students of the policy process and for those actively engaged in the formation of public policy.

Sixth, the policy-making process in the United States is an adversarial process, characterized by the clash of competing and conflicting viewpoints and interests rather than an impartial, disinterested, or "objective" search for "correct" solutions for policy problems. Public officials—legislators, administrators, and perhaps to a lesser extent, judges—do not stand impartially about the policy struggle. Rather, they have their own values and positions which they seek to advance and hence are often partisans in the policy struggle. Given this, policy analyses done by social scientists, for instance, may have little impact except as they provide support for the positions of particular participants in the policy process. Nor are there any generally agreed upon criteria to define what constitutes good public policy. Consequently, policies which win adoption in one arena may be challenged in other arenas in an attempt to secure their elimination or modification. It is this conflict over policy which helps make the policy process continuous, as noted at the beginning of this discussion. It also means that most policy decisions will take the form of compromises.

The remainder of this chapter will be devoted to brief treatments of two matters: some methodological problems in the study of public policy, and the concept of the public interest as an evaluative standard.

## METHODOLOGICAL PROBLEMS

Methodological problems exist for all research, and policy research is not without its share, especially given the complexity of its subject matter.[1] These problems may impede or limit policy research, they may make it frustrating at times, but they do not prevent it. An awareness of some of these problems will help prevent needless errors, wasted efforts, and unsound conclusions.

Solid evidence, facts, or data, as one prefers, on the values and motives of decision-makers, the nature of public problems, the impact of policy, and other facets of the policy process are often hard to acquire or simply not available. The urge to treat assumptions or speculations about what happened as facts must be resisted, as must the often self-serving explanations or statements of political officials and other participants in the policy process. Sometimes quantitative measures of political phenomena such as policy impact are used more because of their availability than anything else. The acquisition of hard facts regarding who did what, why, and with what effects must be the goal of research. We need to be able to say with reasonable confidence that congressmen respond to constituency interests on certain policy matters, for example.

In the explanation of behavior in the policy process empirical evidence is needed that will permit the demonstration or inference of cause-and-effect relationships. Once one gets involved in data-based analysis, it is important to resist the notion that the collection of empirical data is of prime importance, and that the more data one has, the more one can explain. One can drown in a sea of data as well as thirst for a lack thereof. To explain or account for behavior, theory is necessary to guide analysis in potentially fruitful directions. Hypotheses about cause-effect relationships need to be developed and tested on the basis of available evidence.

So, too, one must resist the notion that policy analysis must always involve the manipulation of quantitative data (what some would call "hard data") through the use of high-powered statistical techniques. At this point, some policy areas and problems have not proved amenable to rigorous quantitative measurement and analysis, although this is not to contend that such analysis will never be possible. Many aspects of social welfare economic regulatory policies currently fall into this category. How, for example, does one measure the comparative impact of pressure groups, agency values, and economic criteria on railroad rate-making? Or, how does one measure the total benefits of a public housing program? These present real puzzles.

Yet, it must be emphasized, quantitative measurement, explicit theory, and careful, rigorous analysis have not been as frequently employed in policy study as would be either possible or desirable. Thus, Bernstein's contention that regulatory commissions go through a four stage life cycle (gestation, youth, maturity, and old age), often culminating in their "capture" by the regulated groups is often cited as a fact in political science literature.[2] Bernstein, however, provided no real proof for his theory, and it still lacks meaningful empirical support. Conventional wisdom of this sort frequently rests on a rather murky, intellectual foundation. We should strive to avoid it.

Many valuable and perceptive studies of policy formation exist that employ little or no statistical analysis.[3] The quality of analysis and the use of solid evidence is more important than whether and to what extent quantitative analysis is employed when it comes to determining the value of a study. Those who use quantitative statistical techniques have been known to quarrel with enthusiasm and even a little rancor over the reliability of their techniques and the validity of their findings.[4] On the other hand, one must avoid developing a phobia for quantitative or statistical analysis, as many did during the 1950s and the 1960s in reaction to the behavioral movement in political science.

Data derived through interviews and questionnaires administered to public officials and others involved in the policy process is often invaluable and may not otherwise be available to the researcher. Care, however, is required in the use of such techniques and the data acquired. Questions must be properly framed to elicit the needed information. Questions that are "loaded" or are so general as to create strong doubt concerning their intent must be avoided. The data or information so acquired should not be blindly accepted. Officials may not always respond fully or candidly to questions. Self-serving rather than accurate responses may be made. Care must be taken to recognize these and to treat them accordingly.

In conducting research or inquiry, one should avoid a too narrow frame of reference that unduly restricts investigation or predetermines the outcome. If one fervently believed that U.S. policy in the 1960s in Southeast Asia was based on imperialism, and conducted an inquiry into this matter accordingly, it would not be surprising if the findings supported one's preconception. A more open-minded inquiry might find that racism, anticommunism, errors in judgment by public officials, presidential egoism, or yet other factors may also have been contributory. Of course, any research efforts begin with some premises or assumptions about the value of the event being studied, who was involved, and so forth. This is necessary to focus one's efforts and thus avoid a grab-bag approach. Theories or premises should not be so narrow or rigid as to bias the results.

Case studies of policy-making have come in for much criticism because, in concentrating a particular policy event, they do not permit generalization. "What is a case study a case of?" is a familiar jibe. Preferred are studies that deal either with all the cases in a given universe or with a meaningful sample thereof, such as a study of welfare policy in all the American states or a sample of Supreme Court "decisions" involving free speech. Case studies, however, have a variety of uses. They can be employed to test existing theories, to provide detailed analysis of particular events, to analyze deviant cases that run counter to our generalizations, and to help provide an "intuitive feel" for the subtleties and nuances of the policy process and the practice of politics. Both case studies and more broadly conceived studies are needed in policy analysis.

Finally, the preceding chapters should have indicated the invalidity of the assumption that all policy formation occurs within the framework of formal governmental institutions. Much, of course, does, but a lot of policy activity occurs elsewhere, and this also must receive the attention of the policy analyst. We have seen, for example, that in some instances legislatures may simply ratify agreements reached by private groups, or that enacted policies either may not be carried out or not have the intended impact because of successful counterpressures from outside sources. Research efforts should be pragmatic and flexible, shaped by what is useful to describe and explain satisfactorily the topic being studied, and not bound or limited by conformity to such categories as institutional or noninstitutional, formal or informal, traditional or behavioral.

## THE PUBLIC INTEREST

The task of government, it is often proclaimed, is to serve or promote the public interest. Statutes sometimes include the public interest as a guideline for the actions of public officials. In this section, we will briefly discuss this rather elusive normative concept.

Most readers, I am certain, if asked whether public policy should be in accord with the public interest or with private interests (the latter could further be described as narrow, selfish, greedy, and the like, but I see no need to overload the argument), would opt for the public interest. Difficulty arises, however, when one is asked to define the public interest. Is it the interest of the majority? If so, how do we determine what the majority really wants in policy? Is it the interest of consumers, who are a rather large group? Is it what people would want if they "thought clearly and acted rationally"? How do you, the reader, define the public interest?

Many people, including most political scientists, would say that it is not possible to provide a universally accepted or objective definition of the concept, especially in substantive terms.[5] Some would contend that whatever results from the political struggle over policy issues is the public interest. If all groups and persons had an equal chance to engage in that struggle, which in fact they do not, that notion of the public interest might be more appealing.

I, for one, do not care to define a multitude of tax loopholes or inaction that permits the wanton destruction of natural resources as in the public interest. (By making that statement I indicate a normative bias, which will be especially disturbing to those who hold that "one person's opinion is as good as another's.") Sometimes the public interest is depicted as a myth by which policy, however particularistic, can be rationalized as being in the general interest and hence made more publicly acceptable. This, of course, is attempted or done with regularity (just as scoundrels sometimes wrap themselves in the flag or cite scripture to justify their predations). Beyond that, however, I think that the concept can be given enough content to render it a useful general standard for the evaluation of public policy. When evaluating policy, we need to be able to state not only whether the policy is accomplishing its asserted objectives but also whether the objectives are worthy of accomplishment. In this latter regard, a standard of more noble quality than "it is (or is not) in *my* interest" seems needed.

The question now arises of how one can seek to determine the nature of the public interest. Emmette Redford has suggested three approaches to this task.[6] One is to look at policy areas where there is much conflict among group interests, as in agriculture, labor relations, energy, and transportation. In some instances, the direct interests of one or another group may prevail and become accepted as the public interest. There is no reason to assume that private interests and the public interest must always be antithetical. If it is in the private interest of medical doctors to prevent the practice of medicine by various "quacks," so it is in the public interest not to have unqualified people practicing medicine. (It would seem difficult to argue the contrary position reasonably.) However, in the struggle among private group interests, it may become apparent that others are indirectly involved and have interests that should be considered in policy-making. These "public interests," while not represented by organized groups, may be responded to by decision-makers and thus influence the outcome. In the conflict between labor and management over the terms and conditions of employment, it becomes apparent that the public has an interest in maintaining industrial peace, preventing oversevere disruptions of the flow of goods and services, and the like. The result has been the development of various procedures for the settlement of labor disputes. In a particular dispute, such as in the railroad interest, a public interest may clearly emerge along with those of the railroad companies and brotherhoods.

A second approach is to search for widely and continuously shared interests that, because of this characteristic, can be called public interests. Illustrative are the interests of people in such matters as world peace, education, clean air, the avoidance of severe inflation, and an adequate traffic control system. Here the public interest appears as public needs. Clearly, especially in large cities, there is a public interest in having a traffic control system to facilitate the safe, orderly, convenient movement of pedestrians and vehicles. The fact that there are various alternatives for meeting this need can be taken to mean that more than one way exists to meet the public interest; it does not negate its existence. Nor does the concept, to be meaningful, need to be so precise as to indicate whether the traffic flow on a given street should be one-way or two-way. Must a concept, to be useful, always yield an answer to the most minute questions?

There is nothing very mystical in talking about the public interest as a widely shared interest. We speak of the shared-interest of wheat farmers in higher wheat prices or of sport fishermen in an adequate fish-stocking program and attribute much reality to such interests. The public interest differs only in its wider scope. There is no way to determine precisely at what point an interest is sufficiently widely shared as to become a public interest. Few interests, indeed, would be shared by everyone. The survival of the nation-state may be opposed by the advocate of world government; even at old-time western rustler lynchings there was at least one dissenter. Qualitative judgments are obviously called for in determining the existence of a public interest, as in many areas of political life and academic activity. They should be made with as much care and rigor as possible.

A third approach to the public interest is to look at the need for organization and procedure to represent and balance interests, to resolve issues, to effect compromise in policy formation, and to carry public policy into effect. There is, in short, a public interest in fair, orderly, and effective government. The focus here is on process rather than policy content. As Walter Lippmann once wrote:

> The public is interested in law, not in the laws; in the method of law, not in the substance; in the sanctity of contract, not in a particular contract; in understanding based on custom, not in this custom or that. It is concerned in these things to the end that men in their active affairs shall find a *modus vivendi*; its interest is in the workable rule which will define and predict the behavior of men so that they can make their adjustments.[7]

Although the public is obviously interested in particular laws as well as *the* law, Lippmann's statement well points up the concern with adequate process. How things are done, moreover, often affects the attitudes of the public concerning their acceptability.

The public interest is thus diverse in nature and must be searched for in various ways. While it probably cannot be converted into a precise set of guidelines to inform the action of decision-makers, neither can it fairly be described as merely a myth. It directs our attention beyond the more immediate toward broader, more universal interests. It directs our attention toward unorganized and unarticulated interests that otherwise may be ignored in both the development and evaluation of policy. As policy analysts and citizens we cannot afford to ignore the concept, especially in the evaluation of policy content and impact.

## NOTES

1. The lead volume of this series presents an able introductory statement of methodological concerns. See William A. Welsh, *Studying Politics* (New York: Praeger, 1973).
2. Marver H. Bernstein, *Regulatory Business by Independent Commission* (Princeton, N.J.: Princeton University Press, 1955), pp. 74–95.
3. E.g., Raymond A. Bauer, Ithiel de Sola Pool, and Lewis Anthony Dexter, *American Business and Public Policy* (New York: Atherton Press, 1963); Mark V. Nadel,

*The Politics of Consumer Protection* (Indianapolis, Ind.: Bobbs-Merrill, 1971); and Graham T. Allison, *Essence of Decision: Explaining the Cuban Missile Crisis* (Boston: Little, Brown, 1971).

4. Various controversies of this sort are manifested in recent issues of the *American Political Science Review.* Also see Glendon Schubert, *The Public Interest* (New York: Free Press, 1960).

5. *Ibid.*

6. Emmette S. Redford, *Ideal and Practice in Public Administration* (Tuscaloosa: University of Alabama Press, 1958), chap. 5.

7. Walter Lippmann, *The Phantom Public* (New York: Harcourt, Brace, 1925), p. 105, Cf. Frank J. Sorauf, "The Public Interest Reconsidered," *Journal of Politics,* XIX (November, 1957), pp. 616–39.

# Annotated
# Bibliography

ACKERMAN, BRUCE A., AND WILLIAM T. HASSLER, *Clean Coal Dirty Air* (New Haven: Yale University Press, 1981). A case study of the Environmental Protection Agency's requirement that new plants use smokestack scrubbers. Good on the decision-making process.

ALLISON, GRAHAM T., *Essence of Decision: Explaining the Cuban Missile Crisis* (Boston: Little, Brown, 1971). Examines decision-making on the Cuban missile crisis from the rational actor, organizational process, and governmental politics perspectives.

ART, ROBERT J., *The TFX Decision: McNamara and the Military* (Boston: Little, Brown, 1968). A case study of the controversy over the decision to select a multipurpose aircraft for the military, contrary to its wishes. Insightful on the decision process in the bureaucracy.

BAILEY, STEPHEN K., *Congress Makes a Law* (New York: Columbia University Press, 1950). A classic case study of the legislative process, showing how ideas, interests, individuals, and institutions contributed to the adoption of the Employment Act of 1946.

BAUER, RAYMOND A., AND KENNETH J. GERGEN (eds.), *The Study of Policy Formation* (New York: Free Press, 1968). A series of original essays dealing with theoretical and methodological concerns in the study of public policy.

BERMAN, LARRY, *Planning a Tragedy: The Americanization of the War in Vietnam* (New York: Norton, 1982). Outstanding case study of the Johnson Administration's decision in mid-1965 to escalate U.S. involvement in Vietnam.

BERNSTEIN, MARVER H., *Regulating Business by Independent Commission* (Princeton, N.J.: Princeton University Press, 1955). A dated but still useful treatment of independent regulatory commissions as policy formulators and implementors.

BOCK, EDWIN A. (ed.), *Government Regulation of Business: A Casebook* (Englewood Cliffs, N.J.: Prentice-Hall, 1965). Case studies of administrative agencies in regulatory policy formation and implementation.

COBB, ROGER W., AND CHARLES D. ELDER, *Participation in American Politics: The Dynamics of Agenda-Building* (Boston: Allyn and Bacon, 1972). Highly useful treatment of how problems get on the systemic and policy agendas in American society.

DAHL, ROBERT A., AND CHARLES E. LINDBLOM, *Politics, Economics, and Welfare* (New York: Harper & Row, 1953). Comparison of policy-making by polyarchy, hierarchy, bargaining, and the market system. A classic work.

DAVIES, J. CLARENCE, *The Politics of Pollution*, 2d ed. (Indianapolis: Bobbs-Merrill, 1975). On the formation and implementation of pollution control legislation. Especially good on the administrative aspects thereof.

DERTHICK, MARTHA, *Policymaking for Social Security* (Washington: Brookings Institution, 1979). Superb analysis of the social security program and policy-making process. Views the current program as the product of an incremental, vertical process.

DONOVAN, JOHN C., *The Policy Makers* (New York: Pegasus, 1970). Discusses policy formation at the national level in the United States.

DROR, YEHEZKEL, *Public Policymaking Reexamined* (Scranton, Pa.: Chandler, 1968). A comparative treatment of policy-making procedures with suggestions for reform. Tough reading and general in approach but useful.

DYE, THOMAS R., *Politics, Economics, and the Public: Policy Outcomes in the American States* (Chicago: Rand-McNally, 1966). A leading study that compares the effects of political and socioeconomic variables on state policies. Conclusion: Socioeconomic variables are more important.

———, *Policy Analysis* (University, Ala.: University of Alabama Press, 1976). A series of lectures setting forth Dye's ideas on public policy research.

———, *Understanding Public Policy*, 4th ed. (Englewood Cliffs, N.J.: Prentice-Hall, 1981). Discusses a number of models of policy analysis, illustrates them with case studies, and compares their utility for policy analysis.

EDWARDS, GEORGE C., III, *Implementing Public Policy* (Washington: Congressional Quarterly Press, 1980). Discusses communication, dispositions or attitudes, resources, and bureaucratic structure as major future shaping policy implementation. Draws on a wide variety of illustrative materials.

———, and IRA SHARKANSKY, *The Policy Predicament* (San Francisco: Freeman, 1978). Another introduction to the study of public policy formation. Covers such matters as problems in rational decision-making and economic and political constraints on decisions.

ELDER, CHARLES D., AND ROGER W. COBB, *The Political Uses of Symbols* (New York: Longman, 1983). A solid perceptive study of this topic, which has much utility for the study of policy formation as well as politics generally.

ENGLER, ROBERT, *The Politics of Oil* (New York: Macmillan, 1961). An analysis of the impact of the petroleum industry on pertinent public policies. Good background reading for the current "energy crisis."

———, *The Brotherhood of Oil* (Chicago: University of Chicago Press, 1977). A sequel to *The Politics of Oil* in which Engler remains critical of the industry.

FREEMAN, J. LEIPER, *The Political Process*, 2d ed. (New York: Random House, 1965). A brief analysis of the role of executive bureau–congressional committee–interest group subsystems in policy formation.

FROHOCK, FRED M., *Public Policy: Scope and Logic* (Englewood Cliffs, N.J.: Prentice-Hall,

1979). A political philosopher combines theory and practice in treating both normative and empirical policy issues and the policy process.

FROMAN, LEWIS A., JR., *The Congressional Process* (Boston: Little, Brown, 1967). How congressional procedures can shape policy outputs is one of the concerns of this volume.

HALPERIN, MORTON H., *Bureaucratic Politics and Foreign Policy* (Washington, D.C.: Brookings Institution, 1974). Analysis of bureaucratic participation and decision-making in American foreign policy in the post-World War II era.

HARDIN, CHARLES M., *Food and Fiber in the Nation's Politics* (Washington, D.C.: Government Printing Office, 1967). An insightful survey of the politics of agricultural policy formation and administration.

HEIDENHEIMER, ARNOLD, HUGH HECLO, AND CAROLYN TEICH ADAMS, *Comparative Public Policy*, 2d ed. (New York: St. Martin's Press, 1983). Comparative treatment of public policies on health care, housing, education, taxation, and other topics in the United States and Western Europe. Well done.

JACOB, HERBERT, AND KENNETH N. VINES (eds.), *Politics in the American States*, 2d ed. (Boston: Little, Brown, 1971). Comparative treatment of policy-making and public policies in the American states.

JONES, CHARLES O., *An Introduction to the Study of Public Policy*, 2d ed. (North Scituate, Mass.: Duxbury, 1977). Jones presents a sequential approach to policy formation in clear, straightforward fashion. Case studies and other materials illustrate this very useful work.

KINGDON, JOHN W., *Congressmen's Voting Decisions*, 2d ed. (New York: Harper & Row, 1981). A very valuable empirical study of how members of the House of Representatives make decisions and the factors influencing them.

KOHLMEIER, LOUIS J., *The Regulators* (New York: Harper & Row, 1969). A journalist's account of the policy actions of federal administrative agencies.

KRASNOW, ERWIN G., AND LAWRENCE D. LANGLEY, *The Politics of Broadcast Regulation*, 2d ed. (New York: St. Martin's, 1978). An analysis, with case studies, of the development of broadcast regulation policy by the Federal Communication Commission.

LINDBLOM, CHARLES E., *The Intelligence of Democracy* (New York: Free Press, 1965). An examination of bargaining and other forms of mutual adjustment in policy formation.

LINEBERRY, ROBERT L., *American Public Policy: What Government Does and What Difference It Makes* (New York: Harper & Row, 1977). Equally divided between a discussion of how to analyze policy formation and consideration of four domestic policy problems (e.g., inequality). Readable and chatty.

LOWI, THEODORE J., "American Business, Public Policy, Case Studies, and Political Theory," *World Politics*, XVI (July, 1964), 667–715. An influential essay that seeks to develop a new framework for policy study. He suggests that the kind of policy (distributive, regulatory, or redistributive) involved in a situation shapes the nature of the policy-making process.

———, *The End of Liberalism: The Second Republic of the United States*, 2d ed. (New York: Norton, 1979). Argues that American public policies no longer are responsive to public needs because of impact of interest-group liberalism. Legislation delegates too much discretion. Juridical democracy is needed.

MC CONNELL, GRANT, *Private Power and American Democracy* (New York: Knopf, 1966). An examination of the role of private groups in policy formation and how pluralism and decentralization have often made them the dominant force. A highly insightful study.

MOYNIHAN, DANIEL P., *The Politics of a Guaranteed Income* (New York: Random House, 1973). A rambling account by an "insider" of the development of a proposal by the Nixon Administration for a guaranteed annual income and its rejection by Congress.

NACHMIAS, DAVID, *Public Policy Evaluation: Approaches and Methods* (New York: St. Martin's, 1979). Analyzes and compares various conceptual models for evaluatory policies and statistical techniques useful in evaluation research.

NADEL, MARK V., *The Politics of Consumer Protection* (Indianapolis: Bobbs-Merrill, 1971). Good analysis of the formation and adoption of consumer protection legislation.

NEUSTADT, RICHARD E., *Presidential Power: The Politics of Leadership from FDR to Carter* (New York: Wiley, 1980). A study of presidential power and leadership in the policy process. Finds the President limited in effective influence. A classic study.

PERTSCHUK, MICHAEL, *Revolt Against Regulation: The Rise and Pause of the Consumer Movement* (Berkeley: University of California Press, 1982). A Federal Trade Commissioner provides a spirited analysis of consumer policy and politics.

PETERS, B. GUY, *American Public Policy: Process and Performance* (New York: Franklin Watts, 1982). General introduction to the policy process, plus coverage of some substantive areas. Good section on policy analysis.

PIERCE, LAWRENCE C., *The Politics of Fiscal Policy Formation* (Pacific Palisades, Calif.: Goodyear, 1971). A political scientist analyzes the process and politics of fiscal policy formation. Especially strong in its treatment of the development of policy proposals by fiscal agencies.

PIVEN, FRANCES FOX, AND RICHARD A. CLOWARD, *Regulating the Poor* (New York: Pantheon Books, 1971). A normative evaluation of welfare policies that finds them to be more a means for controlling the poor than for meeting their substantive needs.

PRESSMAN, JEFFREY L., AND AARON B. WILDAVSKY, *Implementation* (Berkeley: University of California Press, 1973). An account of the problems of implementing the Economic Development Act public works program in the Oakland area.

QUIRK, PAUL J., *Industry Influence in Federal Regulatory Agencies* (Princeton, N.J.: Princeton University Press, 1981). An empirical examination of some theories on the influence of industry on regulatory agencies' policy incentives. A very valuable study.

RANNEY, AUSTIN (ed.), *Political Science and Public Policy* (Chicago: Markham, 1968). An uneven collection of essays on issues, problems, and theoretical concerns in the analysis of policy and policy outcomes.

REDFORD, EMMETTE S., *Democracy in the Administrative State* (New York: Oxford University Press, 1969). An insightful examination of the role of administration in the policy process, together with concern for democratic control of administration.

———, *The Regulatory Process* (Austin: University of Texas Press, 1969). An analysis of the economic regulatory process, with emphasis on administrative agencies and commercial aviation regulation.

RIPLEY, RANDALL B., AND GRACE A. FRANKLIN, *Bureaucracy and Policy Implementation* (Homewood, Ill.: Dorsey Press, 1982). Discussion is organized around the categories of distributive, competitive regulatory, protective regulatory, and redistributive programs. The focus is empirical.

ROGERS, HARRELL R., JR., AND CHARLES S. BULLOCK III, *Law and Social Change* (New York: McGraw-Hill, 1972). An evaluation of the impact of the civil rights legislation of the 1960s.

ROSENBAUM, WALTER A., *The Politics of Environmental Concern* (New York: Praeger,

1973). Concerned with the formation and implementation of national policies affecting the environment.

ROURKE, FRANCIS E., *Bureaucracy, Politics, and Public Policy* (Boston: Little, Brown, 1969). Focused on the role of administrative agencies in the formation of public policy.

SCHATTSCHNEIDER, E. E., *The Semi-Sovereign People* (New York: Holt, Rinehart and Winston, 1960). A critique of group theory and a discussion of the impact of conflict on political decision-making.

SCHNEIER, EDWARD V. (ed.), *Policy-Making in American Government* (New York: Basic Books, 1969). An anthology organized under the headings of policy formulation, articulation, mobilization, codification, application, and redefinition.

SCHULTZE, CHARLES L., *The Public Use of Private Interest* (Washington: Brookings Institution, 1977). An essay concerned with how market incentives can be used to improve government intervention in the economy.

SHAPIRO, MARTIN, *Law and Politics in the Supreme Court* (New York: Free Press, 1964). Discusses the impact of the Supreme Court on such areas of public policy as labor relations, antitrust, and taxation.

SHERMAN, HOWARD J., *Stagflation* (New York: Harper & Row, 1976). An insightful discussion of action on inflation and unemployment in the United States by a leading radical economist.

SMITH, T. ALEXANDER, *The Comparative Policy Process* (Santa Barbara, Calif.: Clio Books, 1975). A distinctly comparative treatment of policy formation employing case studies from western democracies and organized around the categories of distribution, sectoral fragmentation, emotive symbolism, and redistribution.

SORENSEN, THEODORE C., *Decision-Making in the White House* (New York: Columbia University Press, 1963). Short analysis of presidential decision-making by the former counsel to President John Kennedy.

SPANIER, JOHN, AND ERIC M. USLANER, *How American Foreign Policy Is Made*, 2d ed. (New York: Holt, Rinehart and Winston, 1978). Introductory treatment of foreign policy formation which deals with the interaction of President and Congress, and foreign and domestic policy.

STEINER, GILBERT Y., *Social Insecurity: The Politics of Welfare* (Washington, D.C.: Brookings Institution, 1966). An analysis of welfare policy-making that illustrates the relationship between the nature of the policy process and the substance of policy.

STEVENSON, GORDON MC KAY, JR., *The Politics of Airport Noise* (North Scituate, Mass.: Duxbury, 1972). Systematic analysis of the participants in, and process of, the development of noise abatement policies. Good on the details of policy action.

STOKEY, EDITH, AND RICHARD ZECKHAUSER, *A Primer for Policy Analysis* (New York: Norton, 1978). A useful and comprehensive treatment of quantitative approaches to policy analysis and decision-making.

STONE, ALAN, *Economic Regulation and the Public Interest* (Ithaca: Cornell University Press, 1977). A thorough, insightful, and critical examination of the Federal Trade Commission and trade regulation policies.

———, *Regulation and Its Alternatives* (Washington: Congressional Quarterly Press, 1982). A good analysis of the nature, justifications, and politics of economic regulation. A wide-ranging, insightful study.

———, AND EDWARD J. HARPHAM, *The Political Economy of Public Policy* (Beverly Hills: Sage, 1982). A collection of essays dealing with various big issues in policy formation and public policy. Critical, challenging.

STRAAYER, JOHN A., AND ROBERT D. WRINKLE, *American Government, Policy, and Non-Deci-*

*sion* (Columbus, Ohio: Merrill, 1972). Short analysis of the policy process and a number of areas of public policy.

SUNDQUIST, JAMES L., *Politics and Policy: The Eisenhower, Kennedy and Johnson Years* (Washington, D.C.: Brookings Institution, 1968). Highly informative case studies of several major areas of domestic policy are combined with a general explanatory analysis.

TRUMAN, DAVID B., *The Governmental Process* (New York: Knopf, 1951). A classic treatment of the role of interest groups in the American political process. Indispensable for an understanding of group theory.

TUFTE, EDWARD R., *Political Control of the Economy* (Princeton, N.J.: Princeton University Press, 1978). A carefully prepared study which contends that economic policy is substantially shaped by the quest for partisan political advantages (has a comparative perspective).

WADE, LARRY L., *The Elements of Public Policy* (Columbus, Ohio: Merrill, 1972). An introduction to policy analysis, focusing especially on decision-making and policy costs and benefits.

————, AND R. L. CURRY, JR., *A Logic of Public Policy* (Belmont, Calif.: Wadsworth, 1970). An examination of American public policy from the "new political economy," or public choice, perspective.

WASBY, STEPHEN L., *The Impact of the United States Supreme Court* (Homewood, Ill.: Dorsey, 1970). Nonquantitative analysis of the Court's impact on public policy. Attempts to develop a theory of impact.

WELBORN, DAVID M., *Governance of Federal Regulatory Agencies* (Knoxville: University of Tennessee Press, 1977). A valuable and perceptive study of the organization, operation, and decision-making of the "big seven" independent regulatory commissions.

WHOLEY, JOSEPH S., *et al., Federal Evaluation Policy* (Washington, D.C.: Urban Institute, 1970). Survey and assessment of the extent and quality of social policy evaluation by federal administrative agencies.

WILLIAM, WALTER L., *Social Policy Analysis and Research* (New York: American Elsevier, 1971). Solid introduction to the systematic evaluation of social policies.

WOLMAN, HAROLD, *Politics of Federal Housing* (New York: Dodd, Mead, 1971). Succinct analysis of the formation and implementation of public housing policies.

# INDEX